When Hope Is Gone

The Story of Papo Salsa

by

Pedro E. Acevedo

Order this book online at www.trafford.com
or email orders@trafford.com

Most Trafford titles are also available at major online book retailers.

Cover design by Heidi L. Acevedo.

Printed in the United States of America.

ISBN: 978-1-4269-6330-8 (sc)
ISBN: 978-1-4269-6331-5 (hc)
ISBN: 978-1-4269-6332-2 (e)

Library of Congress Control Number: 2011904843

Trafford rev. 04/06/2011

 www.trafford.com
North America & international
toll-free: 1 888 232 4444 (USA & Canada)
phone: 250 383 6864 ♦ fax: 812 355 4082

"I could still remember that time
When I thought the world was mine,
And as I sang this same tune
Which we called the boogaloo blues.
The crowd burst out with cheers....."

Johnny Colon, "Boogaloo Blues"

skip. Dad hated to hear Tito Rodriquez get the hiccups right in the middle of his mambo solo. Back in those days if you had one of those old-fashion phonographs you'd know that the best way to keep the records from skipping was by taping a penny to the top of the needle. That kept the weight of the needle down on the record and made it plow right through the scratches and dirt. The older the record, the more weight it needed. I once got up to 87 cents on top of that damn needle.

Growing up in the South Bronx was a wild experience. There was always something going on. The Bronx always had the bad rap that in order to survive you had to know how to fight. That wasn't always true. You had to be able to run fast too. But really, I lived my whole life there and never had a problem. Not because I was a good fighter, but because the block I grew up in was very close-knit. It was filled with Hispanic families, mostly Puerto Rican. Some of these families lived in the same apartments for years, so even neighbors who were of no relation were close enough to be thought of as family. That created a support and protection group that came in very handy in tough times.

You'd see all kinds of characters in my neighborhood, some good, some bad. I remember this one cat, his name was Papo. Everybody called him Papo Salsa. See, on every block there were at least 10 guys named Papo, just like in every Italian neighborhood there were a dozen kids named Anthony. Everywhere you turned there was some kid named Papo. It's like their brilliant parents couldn't come up with a different nickname when their sons were small. They called them all 'Papo'. When it was time to eat dinner, somebody's mom would yell out the window "P- A - P - O ! ! *Vén a comer*, come up and eat!!" Six hungry 'Papos' would show up at her door.

So in order for us to tell them apart we'd give them a second nickname, usually for something they were known for. There was "Papo DJ", who was the first on the block to have a big stereo system. He always provided the music for the hooky parties. There was "Papo Cocólo". He was a kid who had a darker complexion than the rest of us, so he was a "cocólo", which was a slang word for the blacks in the neighborhood. Papo Cocólo was the fastest runner on the block. He could even beat the older kids.

Then there was "Papo Salsa". This guy loved his Latin music so much he refused to listen to anything else. He was one of the older guys, too cool for us to hang out with. He was the best Salsa dancer you'd ever seen, they called him the "Fred Astaire of Soundview". He had a full head of dark, shiny hair that looked like it was always wet. He wore sharkskin pants and knit shirts, suede shoes with thick rubber soles. They called them shoes "Playboys".

All the older girls were crazy about Papo Salsa. Not only was he handsome, he was also very smooth and gentle with the ladies. He was one of the few guys at that time who would be willing to dance with anybody. For most of the so-called "tough" guys in the neighborhood, it wasn't a real hip thing to dance in the first place. But if you had to dance, or at least be seen with a girl, you always wanted to make sure the chick was fairly decent looking. If you hooked up with an ugly girl you'd never hear the end of it from your boys. Papo Salsa wasn't like that, though. He'd take anybody out to dance. It didn't matter if she was fat or tall or ugly or old. He'd be the one at family functions who would be seen dancing with everybody's moms. *Tias* too! He just loved to dance. Being with him would give these ladies the biggest thrill of their night. Of course, he was always surrounded by the fine mamas too. They all would form a line for a chance to be his partner, even if it was just for one song. I'm sure each one of them - young or old, pretty or ugly - thought that she was the one who would win his heart. That's just how he was. He made them all feel special, if only for just a brief moment. The girls loved him.

But then Papo met this young chick whose family moved to New York from Puerto Rico, and that was it. He fell in love and the other girls no longer had a chance. She was the perfect combination of beauty and innocence. The fact that she was new in the neighborhood meant that none of the other guys on the block had been with her. That was a big deal for him, as it is for all Latin men. Check it out: women are put into two categories. There are those who you can bring home to meet your mother, and there are those you bring home when your mother is not around. From the first group, you choose a girl you can fall in love with and hopefully get married to someday. You defend her honor when your boys are talking bad about women. You actually spend money on her and care how you smell when you're around her. We used to call those "the main squeeze" (not to their faces, of course).

In the second group are the girls you fool around with and learn the things you'll need to know when you finally get a chance with your main squeeze. These are the girls you take to the hooky parties to make out with. She could be with you one day and be with your *pana* the next day and you wouldn't give a shit. These poor souls usually are the ones that end up with two or three babies from different guys before they're eighteen. Try bringing one of these girls home to meet your mother and you can kiss the next plate of your mom's rice and beans good-bye.

Papo's girl was definitely one from the first group. He treated her like a queen and she could never say three sentences without mentioning his name. Stuff like "Do you think Papo will like this new dress?" Or "I have to hurry home because Papo said he was going to call me after he comes home from school."

Everybody was sure that this was a couple that God had selected to be together forever. He got a job and started saving up to get married. Her father wasn't too crazy about that idea. He was one of those old-fashion Puerto Rican men who was very protective of his daughter. It's like he didn't want her to even have a boyfriend until she was thirty. But even Dón Ramón liked Papo Salsa, that's how charming this kid was.

Like a lot of other guys in the neighborhood at that time, Papo was drafted into the Army and sent to Vietnam. I was young, so I don't remember when he came back. Years later, when I'd be home listening to some of my old records, I'd close my eyes and think about those times back in the days and I'd think about Papo Salsa, wondering whatever happened to him. Then one day, not too long ago, I was coming home from work.......

*　*　*　*　*　*　*　*　*　*　*　*　*

"Hey, *Compy*. Hey, man can you spare a quarter, man? (Sniff) I need to get on the subway. Aw, shit, man(sniff). Hey, m'MAN, can you spare a quarter? Damn, ain't nobody givin' up NUTTIN' today. Shit, I need to get me some money (sniff). HEY! You in the suit, can you spare a quarter, man? Aw c'mon, *pana*, you got money, look at you, all dressed up like you somebody (sniff). Yeah, man I only need a dollar, I gotta get on the subway, man ....huh?....I know the subway cost more than a dollar, but....hey! Where ya goin', HEY! *Cabrón*!! (sniff).

"Damn, it's gettin' cold out here (sniff). Hey, my brother, can I get a dollar, man? I'm hungry. I ain't eaten in so long I forgot when was the last time I took a shit. Even when I fart nothing but fresh air comes out (sniff). All I need is a dollar... No, I don't want you to buy me no sandwhich. I buy my own food, man, that shit in there is poison. (Sniff)........... Anyways (sniff), as I was sayin', I only need a couple of dollars, man. You see, I got a job interview (sniff) and I gotta get on the subway and...what?... My nose?! Man, I got a cold! Whatchu THINK is wrong with my nose...(sniff).....can't you see it's cold out here, man?....I know you wanna help a brother out, or else you wouldn't be standing here talkin' to my ass....Huh? *Hell* no, I ain't gonna use the money to buy no drugs! What? I look like a junkie to you?.....So what you gonna do, man? (sniff) You gonna give me the money? I ain't got all day. You got a job, man? Shit yeah, you do. I used to have a job once. I sold peanuts at Yankee Stadium. That was a great gig, man (sniff). I'd get to watch all the games, meet all kinds o'ladies. Reggie Jackson, that was my man. You know his middle name is Martinez? People don't know that, he's one of us, a 'Rican'. That's right. Business was jumpin' that summer, man (sniff). My Yankees were winning and the place was always packed. I sold a lotta peanuts. Never missed a day either 'cause I remember what my Pops used to tell me, he said '*Hijo*, always work hard, even when you don't feel well and the weather is bad you still gotta go out and work'. Then one day I got into a fight with this *hijo puta* who didn't want to pay for the peanuts and that was it. They fired me, man. I missed the World Series and everything.

"Hey, *Compy*, that's a nice coat you have on (sniff). *Puñeta*, it's cold, man. C'mon, bro', all I need is twenty dollars, maybe I can get me a coat like that one. Let me see how it feels...... What? What's the matter with my ARMS? Man, ain't nothin', man (sniff). What, you never seen a man with measles before? The scars just bunched around my forearm, man. I don't know why. They just came out like that. Ey, man, it's not what you think (sniff). I told you, I'm not a junkie, I'm just sick, that's all. If I had some money maybe I could go to a doctor and get checked up. I didn't used to be like this, you know. Back then I had it all...(sniff)...."

CHAPTER TWO

Papo's Story

It was a long time ago, man, when I was young. I used to live up by Randall Avenue. It was like the sun was always shinin' back then, you know what I'm sayin'? The neighborhood wasn't that great, but it was our whole world and it was home. Even though Pops worked hard we didn't have much. It was rough sometimes, but I was good, man. I didn't go around robbin' and stealin' like some of these other motherfuckers. My thing was dancing, man. *Salsa* dancing. And none of that *merengue* or boogaloo bullshit, either, man. It was Salsa *caliente*, HOT Salsa. Willie Colon, Larry Harlow, Eddie Palmieri. The Corso, the Cheetah, I snuck into all those places. Had to 'cause I was only sixteen. But it was all right 'cause I was *good!* They called me the "Fred Astairs of Soundview". I wanted to be the first salsa dancer on American Bandstand, with that *gringo* Dick Clark, you heard of him, right? ALL the *mami's* wanted to hang with me. Little kids used to look up to me, wanting me to teach them how to dance like me. They all wanted to be like Papo Salsa, an' get all the girls.

I remember one day I was hanging out on the stoop with my homies, makin' time, listening to Joe Bataan on "Radio WADO".

"Hey, Papo," said my boy, Chico. He lived next door to me. "Show Johnny that new turn you been practicin' with my sister. She said she was with you last night at the Corso and all the people was checking the two of you out, cheering and whistling. She said you were so good you did shit she never even saw before. Go ahead, show 'im."

"Man, that was nothin', *'mano*. I was just playin' around, that's all, just having some fun. Besides, I been dancing with your sister since she was nine, she's seen it all already."

"Oh yeah? She said that on one song you even had TWO girls dancing with you at the same time. You know ain't NOBODY seen that shit before."

"*Two* girls?", said my other friend, Johnny. "Man, how do you DO that? I can't even dance with one girl without messin' up. If I don't look down at my feet I get all confused and I miss my steps."

"*Pues, ese es el problema,* man, that's the problem," I told him. "You shouldn't look down. That makes you think too much. Dancing Salsa is all about rhythm, you dig? You hear the beat and just go with it. Let it flow. To be good it's gotta come from the inside, man, *del corazón.*"

"Hey, I got *corazón*," challenged Chico. "But that don't get me all the girls wanting to dance with me like they do with you, Papo."

"Yeah, Papo," said Louie. Louie Jimenez, he was the older of the Jimenez brothers who lived up the block. "I know how to listen to the beat and stay in step. I don't trip over my own feet and fall all over the place like Chico here."

"Ey, fuck you, Louie!"

"I'm just makin' a point, *panín*, don't take it personal. So, tell us, Papo, what do you got that we don't got that makes all the women want to dance only with you?"

"You want to know what it is, fellas?"

"Yeah, tell us, Mr. Fred Astaire of Latin Music", said Johnny, real sarcastic-like. "What's the secret?"

I began to explain: "Two things. First thing is *style*. You gotta have your own style. You can't be afraid to put on a show, no matter where you are, no matter what kind of party it is. You know how some *pendejos* won't get up to dance unless there's a hundred other motherfuckers already on the dance floor? They don't want to be out there all alone with everybody checkin' them out. They think that if they mess up everybody will see and start laughing at them. You can't think like that, especially since most women don't care about that shit. Somebody's gotta break the ice and get the party goin'. Girls admire a man when he's got the *cojones* to take a chance, even if he ends up makin' a fool outta himself. Do you really think people are there lookin' at you, waiting for you to fuck up so they can goof on you? The real deal is that THEY wish they were the ones out there gettin' all the attention.

"Once you get past being shy then you can start doing different things and gettin' your own style. It may feel stupid at first, but after a while trying the same moves you start getting it right. Even if you mess up, you do it with style and nobody will notice the difference. They'll think it's all part of the show. That's square business."

All my boys' eyes were fixed on me, hangin' on my every word. The floor was mine once more.

"And what's the second thing?" asked Chico impatiently.

"*Calma, hijo*, I'm getting to it. The second thing is the way you treat the ladies themselves. All women love to dance and they love it when a man spends some time with them, even if it's just for a five minute dance. In those five minutes you have to make that *mami* feel like the most important person in your world. You have to know when to grab her tight and hold her close to you as you glide around the floor, looking deep into her eyes so she can practically see what you are thinking. Then you have to know when to let her go so she can shake and show off *her* style. You still gotta keep your eyes on her, watching every move of her body *con gusto* and *deseo*. You should never let your eyes roam around the room no matter how cool you want to look, because then she'll think you're bored with her and are already checkin' out the scene for the next dance. Women are *orgullosa*, my friends, very proud. If they feel like you're not interested they'll just leave you out on the dance floor. THAT is embarrassing, much more than just falling out of step. For those five minutes you and her have to be the most romantic, sexy, and passionate couple on earth. You do that and they'll always come back for more."

My wiseguy buddy Johnny piped in, "Papo, man, I saw you dancing with my Titi Marta last Christmas. You bein' romantic and sexy with *her*?" The other guys cracked up laughing.

"Man, that's the thing with you *idiotas*. You guys are so hung up with what a chick looks like. If she ain't a fox you guys won't give her the time o'day. So *what* if a girl is a little fat or ugly." The guys cracked up again. "I'm serious, man. They deserve to have a good time too. Besides, if some fine *mamis* see you dancing real good with someone that ain't so good lookin', they'll think you're sweet and sensitive and they'll want to be with you even more." The guys weren't laughing much no more.

"When I go to a club and I see a table full of women, the first one I ask to dance is the ugliest one. Because you know that no matter how fine they all might be, there's always one that came up a bit short in the looks and body department. She's usually the cousin who's visiting, or the aunt that they had to bring along, like a chaperone. Otherwise their parents wouldn't let them come out. I dance with the ugly one first and ignore the other conceited princesses. They ain't used to that shit. Believe me, they'll be fightin' each other for my pee-pee after that.

"And another thing - when was the last time any of you *malagradecidos* asked your moms out to dance, even if it's just a *merengue*? You know how proud and happy she'll get when she knows all her friends and neighbors are watching her and her *hijo* out on the dance floor together? It'll make her feel young, too, like she's part of the party. After everything she does for you in your lives it's no big deal to do a little something nice like that for her once in a while. Man, women eat that shit up."

After that there was nothing but silence. Then Mr. Wiseguy spoke up and said "Ey, Salsa, man, if you're so good with the ladies, how come you ain't got a girlfriend?" Johnny was starting to get on my nerves with his ignorant questions.

"Bro', I'm still too young to tie myself down to one chick. I'm only sixteen. I'll dance with all of them all night long, but for me to stay with just one, I don't know. I can't see that happenin' anytime soon."

That's when I saw her walking up the street, the most beautiful girl my eyes had ever seen, man. She was with her family - her parents and two sisters. It looked like they were checking out the building across the street.

"Wow, would you look at that", said Louie. "Who are they?"

Johnny said "I think they're the people movin' in." Johnny lived in that building, his father was the super. "I heard my Pops say that this new family was coming, relocating to New York from Puerto Rico." Johnny always thought he was so smart and he liked using big words like 're-lo-ca-ting'. Maybe he wasn't so smart 'cause from what I heard, all Johnny ended up being was the super of that building after his Pops retired and moved back to P.R.

I couldn't keep my eyes off of this angel. She had curly brown hair hanging around her shoulders, a smooth, milky-white face, dark black eyes. I was looking at her so much I didn't realize she was staring back at me. Our eyes met for the first time and I knew it was love. Without realizing, I said out loud "I'm gonna marry that girl". All my boys starting laughing and fuckin' with me again.

"Marry?!" giggled Louie. "Which one, they's three of them. You gonna marry them all? You're slick, Papo, but you ain't *that* slick. What the fuck you talking about, *marry that girl.*"

"Yeah, *bellaco*, they just got here. Give them a chance to unpack" followed Chico.

Of course Johnny had to say something, too. "Didn't you just finish saying that you're too young to get hooked up with one chick? Or was that just bullshit?"

I didn't care what they were saying. "All of y'all *cabrones* can kiss my ass. I'm talking about the one with the curly hair and the white blouse. Didn't you see her checkin' me out?"

"Oh, she was checkin' you out, alright," cracked Louie. "She's probably thinking it's time to give your hair an oil change." Even I had to laugh at that one.

This angel and her family entered Johnny's building with his Pops, but not before she turned around to give me one last look. Even though my heart was pounding like it never had before, I still managed a little smile, as if to send her a silent message of love.

When I saw the corners of her lips turn up to smile, I could feel my heart ready to burst wide open.

We stayed on the stoop for a while, listening to more music and ranking on each other, playing the dozens. I kept looking across the street to see if my future wife would come back out, but I had to do it on the sly, you know, *bien disimulado.* If the fellas saw that I had a "jones" for that girl they'd start on me all over again. My rep as being the coolest dude in the gang would be ruined.

After about an hour Louie said he had to go over to Dón Marco's *bodega* where his little brother worked part-time. Ricardo – everybody called him Ricky - was more serious than the rest of us. He actually had plans for his life even though he was only fourteen. He wanted to work hard and save some money to buy his own store someday, and Dón Marco was teaching him everything he knew. Ricky was like the son that Dón Marco never had. He never hung out with us or did the crazy things we did. He just went about his business and nobody bothered him. It helped having an older brother like Louie because Louie was big and strong, the best fighter on the block. Even though the two brothers were completely different, they were very close and Louie protected Ricky. Nobody ever messed with them.

I couldn't stall the fellas anymore without making it obvious I was waiting for you-know-who. So we all ran down the stoop and headed down the block towards the *bodega.* I wished I could've waited longer, but I figured her Pops was signing the lease for the apartment with Johnny's dad. If that was true, and I hoped it was, I knew I'd be seeing my angel again.

CHAPTER THREE

We never got into any kind of serious trouble back then. Every now and then we'd play hooky from school when Papo DJ's parents went away and he'd throw one of his parties at his crib. That's right, he was also nicknamed Papo like me, but we called him "Papo DJ" because he had a *bad* stereo. DJ's father had a good job in Manhattan, I think he cut diamonds for the *Judios*, or some shit. He made more money than the rest of the fathers on the block, at least the ones who had jobs. Him and DJ's moms would always be taking trips to the island, or to a house they owned in *Las Villas* in upstate New York where a whole bunch of Puerto Rican families would go in the summertime. On DJ's fifteenth birthday his parents gave him the stereo. *Pa' qué fue eso?* You couldn't walk past his building without hearing the music going full blast. Every week he'd buy two or three new records, so he had all the latest jams of all kinds of music, not just salsa. He had the Temptations, Smokey Robinson, Dion, remember him? He sang that street-corner doo-wop harmony shit. That was still a big thing in the Bronx, even though it was old. At first the neighbors complained about the noise, but after a while everybody got used to it. It gave the block life.

The hooky parties were the best, believe that. We'd all go to school in the morning so we'd be there when the teachers took attendance. If we weren't there for attendance the principal would call home and tell our parents we weren't in school. Nobody wanted a *correaso* from

13

their moms for cutting out. But after one or two classes we'd be able to slip out the cafeteria entrance without anybody noticing and make it up to DJ's apartment. We still had to go one or two at a time so as not to attract attention in case anybody was looking out the window. It was less risky when the weather was a little cold and people's windows were closed. Shit, in the summertime it was like a regular way of life for mothers to be hanging out the window, looking at everything going on down in the street. If we played hooky when it was warm out we'd usually go up to Van Cortland Park and play handball all day. It was safe there. But in the wintertime? *Pa' la casa de Papo DJ*! Good thing his parents always picked the wintertime to go to Puerto Rico.

Other than cutting out of school there was nothing really bad about the hooky parties. Sure, we brought some girls from school with us to have a little fun, usually the easy ones. A lot of us boys became men in those parties. If DJ's folks only knew what went on in their bedroom sometimes they'd kick him *and* his stereo out on his ass. But that didn't happen all that much. It was just us hanging out, listening and dancing to some beat music for a while. Then DJ would turn the lights down and switch to a slow jam by Marvin Gaye. Remember *Distant Love*? That's when things got good. Girls digged Marvin Gaye and didn't mind "grinding" with us fellas when he sang. We used to do a thing called the "500 Grind", where the guy and the girl would hold each other real tight and press their thighs into each other's crotches. As the song got hotter and hotter the couple would grind into each other and try to get as low to the floor as possible without falling over. A good grind would make a dude pop a boner that he'd rub up against the girl's leg when they danced. We weren't shy about that, bro'. A lotta dudes had bulges sticking out of their pants when the dance was finished. Sometimes you'd see a wet spot on a guy's pants. Then you'd know it was a *really good* grind. We'd goof on him for that, but then we'd all be fighting to be the next one to dance with that same girl. A *mami* with a rep for being able to make a guy come while grinding would ALWAYS be invited to the hooky parties.

It was at one of these parties that I got my first real taste of drugs and alcohol. It was no big deal at first. I had tasted wine and beer in my house when I was growing up. My folks had family get-togethers all the time, like for the holidays, an' shit. For the Thanksgiving toast my Pops would serve everybody a small glass of wine, even the kids. Moms would give him a hard time about it, but he would always say that it was good for us, puts color in our blood. "Just look at the *Italianos*", he would say, "they put wine in the babies' *bibí* from the time they are born and there's nothing wrong with them." She would call him a *borrachón* and say that he was raising all of us to be drunks too. So Pops would take a big swig of wine and wrap his powerful arms around my Moms' big waist. When he had her trapped, he would go to give her a big kiss and when she didn't expect it he would squirt the wine from his mouth to hers, filling her mouth until it started spilling off to the side of her chin. "*Mira, cochino!*" she would curse while wiping up the mess on her face. But she'd do it laughing, and all of us would laugh too. As many times as Pops did this, she never caught on and he got her every time. I think deep down she liked it. One thing about my family, we may not have had much by way of money and stuff, but there was beaucoup love among all of us. We really cared about each other a lot. I miss my Moms and Pops. I wish I could see them again.

One day we was all at Papo DJ's house, like always, listening to music and telling jokes. There were a lot more people there than usual, even some kids that I never seen before. The only good thing about letting other people into our parties was that it meant that there might be different girls to make out with. On this day the place was jumpin'! I was listening to Louie tell one of his stupid jokes:

"This gringo is in Mexico on vacation, see? One Sunday afternoon he walks into a restaurant to have lunch and sits down at a table. Not knowing what to order, he looks over to another table and he sees a waiter serving this other customer a plate with two really big, black meatballs on top of some lettuce. It looks pretty good to him, so when his waiter comes

over he asks: 'What's that man over there having? Those are the biggest meatballs I've ever seen.' The waiter says, 'Oh, Señor, those are not meetballs. Those are the testicles of the bull from today's bullfight. Eeet ees our Sunday specialty.' The gringo says, 'Your specialty, huh? Okay, I'll have that.' The waiter says, 'I'm sorry, Señor. There ees only one bullfight on Sundays, and that customer has the only order. If you want to come back next Sunday, I promise to save that plate just for you.' The man agrees to come back again the following week. Sunday arrives, and he is back at the restaurant and asks the waiter for the Sunday special. As promised, the waiter reserved the order for him, and brings out the plate and serves it to him. The man looks down at it, and instead of the big serving he saw the previous week, now there are only two tiny, pink bolitas. So he complains to the waiter, 'What's this? The plate you served that customer last week had bigger testicles than these! What happened?'

'I'm sorry, Señor,' says the waiter, 'but the bull, hee don't always lose.'"

Not all of Louie's jokes were funny, but the way he told them made everybody laugh. I looked around the room and saw this fine-lookin' ass over by where DJ had his record collection. I guess she was lookin' to make a request. I never saw her at one of these parties. I know she wasn't from my school, she looked older. She was a little *trigueña*, pimple-faced, and not too pretty. But, man, what a behind! DJ was playing a Pacheco album - which is my thing, you know - and I could see this *mulatta* movin' her hips to the music. Another victim, I thought to myself, in more ways than one. I started making my way over to her.

"See anything you like?" I asked with a smile. She looked at me up and down, sizing me up, but didn't answer. She went back to studying the album in her hand, still moving to the beat of Pacheco's *tumba'o*. *Que come mierda*, I thought to myself. But I love a challenge, so I tried again.

"Would you like to dance? I could move this coffee table out of the way, DJ don't mind."

She looked at me again and smiled. "Sure, I'll dance. But I gotta feel nice first. Is there anything to drink in this place?" Being sixteen we never thought much about bringing any liquor to these parties, so I didn't know. "Wait a minute, let me see if I can find some Bacardi in the kitchen."

"No, never mind, I got something better", she said. "Come on, let's go to one of the rooms." Not knowing what the fuck she was talking about, I followed her into Papo DJ's sister's bedroom. Chico ran over like he wanted to tag along.

"Where you goin', Salsa?"

"Yo, man, beat it. I'm busy," I told him. "I'll be right back."

He looked at me, then looked at her, then looked back at me with a smile and a wink that signaled *"Vaya! Papo gettin' lucky!"*

We just brushed past him and kept walking to the room. I hated to blow Chico off like that. I always thought he looked up to me like some kind of hero, even though we practically grew up together. But this lady was, like they said on *Laugh-In*, "veddy interesting".

Once we got into the bedroom she told me to close the door. I thought, this chick don't waste no time. "What's your name?" I asked her.

"Why do you want to know my name?" she said mysteriously.

"I'm just makin' small talk, *mami*, I don't really care." I was trying to be even more cool in front of this honey.

She laughed at my audacity. "It's Cookie, that's what everybody calls me."

"Cookie? What's your real name?"

"I thought you didn't care."

"I don't."

"Then mind your business and light this up." With that she took what looked like a bent-up, used lollipop stick out of her pocket. As tight as those jeans were on her big ass I was surprised she could get anything into those pockets.

"What's that? A cigarette?" I asked.

She started laughing at me. "Oh, brother! Ain't you ever smoked a joint before?"

"Sure I have," I lied. "I just never saw one so skinny before." I was talking beaucoup *ca-ca* now.

"Don't let that fool you, baby, this herb'll knock the shit outta you. This is the weed that made Yul Brenner's hair fall off." I forced a laugh to keep myself from asking who the fuck Yul Brenner was. I didn't want her to think I was some stupid *jíbaro* right off the plantain boat, you know what I'm sayin'? In one quick motion she took out a lighter and sparked up a flame right in front of my face. Now I didn't know much about marijuana back then, but I'd seen some junkies smoking it behind the Associated Supermarket up on White Plains Road. I recognized the smell sometimes at the clubs I snuck into when I went dancing. It didn't seem like a big deal to me, so I lifted the joint up to my mouth and let her light it.

"What's the matter?" she said. "Your hand is shakin'. You nervous?" I could tell she was teasing me.

"Nah, I ain't nervous. It's just a little cold in here." She turned one eyebrow up to let me know she thought I was full of shit. Trying to copy how I saw the junkies do it, I took a long drag of the cigarette and immediately began choking and coughing. I didn't expect the smoke to be so rough. The junkies never coughed, they just jerked their heads and shoulders up and down, keeping that shit inside. I handed the joint to her, still coughing like a *puta madre*. I watched as her experienced hand held the cigarette between her thumb and her pointy finger. She took a deep drag and had no problem at all holding the smoke in.

By this time my eyes were watering and I was still coughing. Unbelievably, it was my turn again and she passed the joint back to me. This time it was a little smoother than the first, maybe because I was more careful and only took a short puff. Copying the junkies again, I jerked my body back and forth although I had no idea why I was doing it.

Other than the coughing and the watery eyes, I didn't feel any different smoking that joint. Cookie, on the other hand, seemed to be drifting off into a mellow haze. After she took her tokes she held her breath for a while, closing her eyes. Finally she let the smoke stream slowly out of her lungs through her nose. I kept wondering how she did all that without choking, although years later I became an expert at it myself. I watched her as she went back to swaying her hips to the music that we could hear from the living room. She was moving side to side, like she was doing before, but this time she seemed more relaxed, like she was finally enjoying herself there. Come to think of it, she even looked prettier. Kind of sexy, as a matter of fact. That should have been the first sign to tell me I was fucked up.

There was nothing but a tiny roach in my hand. I looked for someplace to throw it away, but Cookie grabbed it from me and, believe it or not, got another long drag out of it. I thought there was nothing left. I saw this red glow on her fingertips as she held it up close to her puckered lips, the hot flame burning brighter when she inhaled deeper. I would have said something about it, but I couldn't think of anything to say. So I just smiled. I didn't know what I was smiling about, but I smiled anyway. I wanted to move along to the music with her, try and get closer to her so I could cop a feel of that nice *fondillo*. I was feeling bold, Jack. But for some reason I couldn't move at all. I could only lean back against the wall, right next to a poster of the Jackson Five that DJ's sister had put up. I was still smiling like a *mama'o*, getting horny watching this lady swing her hips all around. I had completely forgotten where we were and that there were other people in the apartment outside the bedroom. Then I heard the pounding on the door.

"Ey, Papo, man!! Whatta you doin' in there?!" DJ was pounding on the door like *four* motherfuckers. "What's that smell? You better stop that shit, man. Don't be smokin' that shit in my sister's room, she's gonna be home any minute! If she finds out somebody was in her room gettin' high she's gonna drop a dime on me in a heartbeat. *Puñeta!* C'mon, come outta there!!" I opened the door and could see DJ was really pissed off.

"Yo, 'mano, cool out," I told him as I stumbled out of the room, Cookie following close behind, still dancing.

"Fuck that 'cool out' shit, man! You know my sister's queen of the *chotas*. She'll rat on me as soon as my Pops walks in the door, and laugh the whole time while he's beatin' my ass with the belt." He went in the room to open up the windows, even though it was like 30 degrees outside. Me and Cookie kept giggling like this was the funniest thing we had ever seen. I think that pissed him off even more because he shut off the stereo and began yelling for everybody to get out of the apartment. He ain't never cut short one of his parties before. So we all had to put on our coats and leave.

Chico snuck up next to me as we were walking down the stairs with a wide-eyed look, like he wanted to know all the juicy details about what went on in that room that got DJ so bent out of shape. He was disappointed when I told him that I'm not a man to kiss and tell. He didn't have to know that nothing juicy happened, not after DJ interrupted us. Looking ahead I saw my new get-high partner leaving the building, hanging on the arm of some *cocólo* I didn't know. *Coño*, what an ass!

CHAPTER FOUR

By the time we got to the *bodega,* Ricky was just finishing up and was ready to go home. I remembered that Moms wanted me to pick up some peppers and other shit so she could make some of her homemade *sofrito,* so I gave the list to Dón Marco so he could get everything for me.

"*Bueno*, Papo," he said, "*cómo esta tu mama?* I haven't seen her around the store in a while."

"She's doin' alright, Dòn Marco. I guess she finally figured out that it's easier to send me to the store, since I'm always hangin' out outside anyways. I can't wait until Benny's old enough to go to the store by himself so I won't have to do this no more."

"What's the matter, *hijo.* You don't like to come visit me once in a while? Remember who gave you all those free *bon-bónes* when you were a *mocoso* little kid."

"I remember," I laughed. "It's just that there's a lot of shi-, I mean, stuff happening in my life now, you know. The girls are getting prettier and prettier every day, it's hard for me to keep up. And they're opening up a new dance club around the Westchester Circle that I'm gonna check out tonight."

"Dance club? *Olvídate de eso, muchacho.* You're too young to be worrying about that. How's school, you doin' okay?" Dón Marco was always trying to look out for us. That's why he took such good care of Ricky.

"That's it! Come here, you little shit!" I lunged after him, but the little booger was real quick, man. In no time he jumped off the bed and was running out the room and down the hall, screaming.

"MOMMMY!! PAPO'S GONNA HIT ME!!! MOMMMY!!!"

By the time I caught up to him he was safely on 'base', which was Moms' lap on the sofa in the living room.

"Mommy, Papo's cursin'!"

It's a good thing Moms was too busy concentrating on the *novela* on Channel 47. Otherwise, I would've gotten punished and missed opening night at the new club. I went to get my coat while I still had a chance.

"What's the name of the club, Papo?"

The little creep didn't know when to stop.

CHAPTER FIVE

The name of the club was "Tapestry". It was up on Westchester Avenue, right under the "El" of the 6 train. The lights all around the club were flashing like it was Christmas. The owner had strung up different color flags from the building out to the columns of the "el", like the kind you see at used-car dealers. You could tell that something big was going on because there was a lot of commotion in front of the place, with cars double-parked and taxis coming and going, dropping off loads of passengers. There were about fifty people hanging out right outside the club, all dressed up like they were trying to win a contest. It was common for groups of friends going to a club together to arrange to meet outside and all walk in at once. That way they could get a table for the whole party. Some people were passing joints around, trying to get their buzz outside so they wouldn't have to spend so much money on drinks and *servicios* inside. There was always somebody around selling skinny joints for a dollar, just like the one big-assed Cookie had.

There were two bouncers standing by the door letting people in. I knew most of the bouncers from the clubs I went to in Manhattan, which helped me get in even though I was underage. But I never saw these guys before. One was a short, mean-looking guy wearing a black beret. I guess he thought he was G.I. Joe, or some shit. The other was a big, fat dude with a head twice the size of mine, and no neck. He wasn't as ugly as G.I. Joe, but I wasn't gonna fuck with him either. I hoped they were cool and just worried about fights breaking out. Most bouncers didn't give a shit about underaged kids getting in. But if they asked me for I.D.? M*e jodí*. I figured maybe if I went in with a group they wouldn't notice me. I had to wait for a couple of my friends anyways, so I leaned up against an old Volkswagon that was parked down the block and checked out the talent going in.

To some people, going out dancing is the biggest social event of their lives. They spend their whole week making plans, inviting as many friends as they can to make a big party out of it. Sometimes it'd be for somebody's birthday, but most times it was just showin' off to let everybody know they were going dancing. I guess it made them feel like they were "with it". Problem was that most of these people that went out dancing only a few times a year really had no idea what they were doing. I'm not saying that everybody had to be as good as me, I mean, we're all out there to have a good time, right? But these were the kind of people that would crowd the dance floor, taking up more space than they needed, swinging their arms and elbows around like chickens, stepping on other people's feet. I can't tell you how many times I've gotten kicked on the leg by one of these assholes. They would say 'excuse me' about as often as they would buy a round of drinks, which was never. I hated dancing on a crowded floor. Cramped my style. Sometimes it'd get so bad I couldn't even make any of my simple moves without banging into somebody. I wished all those lames would go back to Queens, man, and leave the dance floor for the real *salseros*.

On these nights ladies used to dress up like they were going to the royal wedding of the Queen of England. Nothing wrong with that. It was "dressin' for impressin'", like an urban-tropical fashion show to see who had the tightest and most expensive looking outfit. It wouldn't surprise me if a couple of them used their welfare checks to buy them clothes. I'd wonder how some of those chicks were able to sit down in them, much less move around to dance. These dresses made all them biddies look like they had big asses, which for a *Latina* is a good thing. All part of the presentation. After all, they never knew when they might meet up with the future father of their next kid out there. These poor girls could never get it through their heads that the *last* place you want to meet someone to get serious with is in a club.

When a guy sees a fine *mami* in a club, his thoughts ain't about living happily ever after in a big house with a white picket fence. Shit, he'd rather not even be bothered with the dancing part. If she's looking that good he'll want to leave with her right away before he ends up spending bucks on drinks for her and her friends. Guys hate spending money on a girl only to end up going home with blue balls. They try to figure out for sure if *la tipa* is gonna put out before he wastes a whole night in the club with her. If they realize the girl ain't happenin', they come up with any excuse to get out of there and move on to another one. Stupid shit like, "Excuse me, baby, I see my cousin over there by the bar, let me say hi and I'll be right back." Then she'll turn around a few minutes later and see him on the dance floor with somebody else having the time of his life.

It went like that both ways too. Sometimes a girl wouldn't want to be bothered with a dude so she'd try to get away from him. She'd excuse herself to go to the bathroom with her girlfriend, hoping the *pendejo* would be gone by the time they got back. A real chump would never catch on to this game, even after the girl's gone to pee 10 times within a half hour. He'd still be at the same spot waiting, smiling, probably with another drink sitting on the table for her. She would see him there and just roll her eyes.

People could get possesive real quick in the clubs too. A girl will meet a guy she likes and think that since she "let" him dance with her she owns him. She plays hard-to-get, you know, so as not to make him think she's that easy. They always gotta be playing games. So now the guy realizes this lady's not gonna give him any play right away, so he'll excuse himself. He'll hook up with another girl and, WHAM! Before he knows it, here comes Miss "I-was-only-playin'" outta nowhere cursing him out, calling him *"un infeliz, desgraciado".* Like that's gonna hurt his feelings. But then the new girl he was dancing with thinks that this crazy *fiera* really is his woman, so she walks away from him too, leaving him alone out there to deal with it. That hurts.

Por *otro lado*, some guys think that just because he bought a girl a drink she belongs to him the whole night. If he sees her so much as look at someone else he goes off, ready to grab this girl and drag her away. Or even worse, he'd be ready to fight the guy she was looking at. I seen fights break out over shit like that even though the two of them hardly even knew each other's names.

And sometimes a couple would hit it off pretty good and exchange numbers at the end of the night. Of course, getting a telephone number didn't mean you were automatically in good with the person. You had to make sure that the number was real. Too many *embusteras* had the habit of giving out wrong numbers just to get rid of you. Guys did that shit too, especially if they were already married or with somebody. A guy wouldn't be interested in anything else other than bustin' his nut that night, and if the girl didn't give it up he had no other ideas. Trouble with that was that you couldn't be a regular at the clubs without running into the same people over and over again. If you met up with a sucker you lied to before, you had to first, remember what bullshit you told her before, and then add on some more bullshit to explain why the number you gave her didn't work, and why you didn't call her yourself:

> *"Bueno, muñeca, what happened was that my brother had to move in with me and he was using up the phone too much, so I had to get it disconnected, you see, he don't got no job, you know, and if he ain't gonna help me pay the bills I'm gonna have to kick him out, you know what I'm saying, I didn't want to bring you down with my problems, but that's my brother, you know, I love him and I can't turn my back on him, it's a bad situation, mami, and I've been going through a lot of shit with him, that's why I haven't called you, and....DAMN, girl, you lookin' really nice in that dress.....!"* Then the lying game would start all over again.

I didn't have to worry about none of that because everybody knew I just went out to dance. I was younger than everybody else so there weren't many girls interested in me like that anyways. That is, until they danced with me. Then I couldn't get rid of them. Still, it was more because they liked to be on the floor with somebody who knew what he was doing. Most of these jive motherfuckers didn't know a *salsa* from a *pachanga*, and didn't care. Chicks thought I was so-o-o cute and mature for my age, and that's what got me over. I knew a lot of people in the clubs, both guys and girls, but it's not like any of them were my friends because I never saw any of them outside the club. A lot of people would say hi to me like they knew me all their lives, but I'll be damned if I remembered any of their names. My boys from the block weren't into dancing like I was, so they wouldn't go through all the trouble of trying to sneak into a club. About the only dude that I hung with from my neighborhood was Big Ray, Ray Rodriguez. He was about twenty-four or twenty-five, and he would help me get into the clubs if any bouncer gave me a hard time.

Speaking of the devil himself, here came *mi pana*, Big Ray, boppin' up the block, dressed to the nines. He must have saved some of his own *cupones* for a new outfit too. He was wearing a powder blue, polyester "dig-me" jumpsuit, with lapels so wide they were blocking traffic across Westchester Avenue. Underneath he had on a flowered silk shirt with the collar pulled out over the jumpsuit. He must have been the one who taught John Travolta how to dress for that movie. The shirt was unbuttoned all the way down to his stomach, with the few hairs on his chest puffed up, like he spent some time picking them out to match the Carlos Santana afro on his head. He looked like a Puerto Rican Q-Tip. He had this medallion hanging around his neck, resting perfectly right in the middle of the opening of his shirt. I had to shade my eyes to protect them from the reflection that was coming from it when he passed under the street lamp. He called it his lucky medallion because he swore that every time he wore it he got lucky with some honey. It never worked when I was with him, because I ain't never seen him leave with anybody from the clubs. I musta been his *un*lucky charm.

"Hey, Ray! Over here!" I had to bite my lip to keep from laughing at his outfit.

"Ey, what's shakin', *chiquito*?" We did our neighborhood dap. Ray called me '*chiquito*' because I was younger than him, and also because he was about a foot taller than me. "How's the action look tonight, any potential candidates?" He rubbed his lucky medallion, as if it needed to be warmed up like a car in the winter.

"Yeah, I seen some new faces. It looks like it's jumpin'."

"It better be. Shit, it's opening night. Have you tried to get in yet?"

"Not yet. I was out here waiting for your skinny ass. There's some ugly goons at the door I don't know. Who knows what they're gonna say when they see me."

"Ey, don't worry about that, *chiquitín*. You know your homeboy Ray finds a way to get you in, right?" He held his hand out so I could give him a 'pound'. Ray was one of those guys who asked for a pound at the end of every sentence. "You seen any of the other fellas?" The other fellas were some friends of Ray who would hang out with us once in a while. They were cool, but since they weren't from the block I wasn't as tight with them. They still looked at me like some little kid who was getting in their way, especially when the girls preferred to dance with me instead of them.

"No, I ain't seen them. By the way, Ray, what band is playin' tonight?" He took out his afro-pick and started to puff up his hair some more.

"The radio said that Joe Cuba and his Sextet were gonna be here. They're alright, I saw them a couple of weeks ago at the Cheetah." Now he was using the palms of his hands to give his 'fro its final shape. Like radar, he turned around and spotted a group of gorgeous girls walking up the block. "Oh, mercy! *Mira, mami!* Here I am, your Prince Charming. I know you been lookin' for me all your life..." He threw kisses at them. I could never believe how he thought that this method would ever work on babes like these, or anybody, for that matter. No wonder he needed a lucky medallion.

"Hey, Ray, man, we been out here long enough. Let's go inside before somebody else cuts in on your action. We can meet up with your boys inside."

"I'm hip, *chiquito*." He gave his suit one final tug to straighten it out, took out a pack of Winstons and handed me one. I didn't smoke at the time. Pops would have kicked my ass if he caught me with cigarettes. But it was our usual routine when going into the club. We figured a cigarette hanging from the side of my mouth made me look older and the bouncers wouldn't stop me. It worked most of the time. Once inside I'd squash that square in the first ashtray I saw. "You ready?"

"Let's go." As we headed up the block towards the club I couldn't hold it in any longer.

"Hey, Ray?"

"Yeah, kid?"

"Man, how many polyesters did they have to kill to make that suit?"

"Ey, you're a funny guy, *chiquitín*. Who writes your material, *Cantínflas*?"

"I.D., please."

Fuck! G.I. Joe was gonna bust my balls. "Perdón?" I asked, making like I was confused with the English language.

"You heard me, shorty, I need to see some identification. You gotta be 18 to get in." The nerve of this motherfucker! I could see the top of his stupid beret and here he is calling *me* shorty'. I was looking in all my pockets, pretending to be searching for something that didn't exist.

"Oh shit, man, I musta left my wallet in my car. But hey, my partner here can vouch for me. He's my cousin."

"Yeah, man, he's twenty years old. We're takin' courses up at Community College together. We're studyin' to be court reporters."

Oh, brother, I wished Ray would keep his bullshit simple.

"Look, *bejuco*, I don't care if you guys are gonna be brain surgeons. No I.D., no get in." Before Ray could say another word, No-Neck stepped up in front of him. Apparently, these guys gave a shit.

"Okay, okay," said Ray, "you don't have to get all *guapo* on us. We'll just go to the car and get his wallet. We'll be back." For all his attitude, Ray could be a real pussy sometimes. We turned and walked away.

"What are we gonna do now, man? I don't want to miss opening night," I said. "Look at all these fine *mamis* around here."

"Relax, kid, I'll think of something. Don't I always?" At that point, a van pulled into the alleyway that led to the back of the building. The band had arrived. Then I remembered.

"Hey, Ray, you said that Joe Cuba was gonna play tonight, right?"

"Yeah, so?"

"His lead singer is Jimmy Sabater. I know his family from the neighborhood. You too."

"I *knew* that dude looked familiar when I saw him at the Cheetah."

"That's right! Maybe if we go around back he'll recognize us and let us go in with him, you know, like we're with the band. We won't even have to pay admission."

"*Coño, chiquito*, for a youngblood you could be pretty smart sometimes. *Vámonos!*" We gave each other a pound and took off for the alley.

CHAPTER SIX

It had been about a month since I seen that cute girl that was supposed to move in across the street. I thought about her a lot, but I started to lose hope of ever seeing her again. Johnny said that they had signed the lease, but that his Dad had to do some work on the apartment before the family could move in. Knowing Johnny's father that could take forever. Not that the old man was lazy, just the opposite. Anytime he had to do something to that building he wanted to make sure everything was perfect, and that would take him longer to finish the jobs. One time the people in the building complained about all the rats in the basement. Instead of just calling an exterminator to come and kill off all them nasty suckers, he began building little traps that would catch them without killing them. Then he'd take them down to Throgs Neck and let 'em loose. Some of those traps looked nicer than some apartments. Mr. DeJesus would say that these were also God's creatures and they deserved to live, too. "That's fine," the tenants would say, "but not in our fuckin' building!"

It was late March and the weather was getting warmer. That meant that everybody was coming out of their homes to be outside more. A lot of people who had moved here from Puerto Rico, especially the older women, never got used to the cold temperatures of New York in the winter. They would stay locked up inside from November to March, complaining about not getting enough heat in their apartments and talking about the good ol' days back on the island. My Moms was one of them. But once the sun started shining again and the snow melted away, the whole *barrio* would come back to life. By summertime the boys would be in the streets playing stickball or 'Ring-o-Livio'. The girls stayed by the curbs, jumping ropes. They did that double-dutch style, which always amazed the shit out of me how they could do that without falling and bustin' their asses. All the mothers sat on the stoops, watching the smaller kids run around, and complaining about the heat. They were never satisfied, no matter what time of the year it was.

I was glad that winter was finally over. Things had been kind of dead the last couple of weeks. I hadn't been out dancing since opening night at Tapestry. That was some night, I'll tell you. The place was jumping, just like me and Ray had hoped. Thanks to Jimmy Sabater, the lead singer of the band, we were able to get in with no problems. I think I got home at five o'clock in the morning, just as Pops was leaving to go to work. He didn't say anything about me getting home at that time because he knew where I was and was glad to see me home safe. We had an understanding, Pops and me. He knew that all I really did when I stayed out late was dance, so he supported me. As a matter of fact, he would always brag to all his friends that he was the one who taught me all I knew. He was part right, though. He always taught me about hard work and how to treat women with respect, the same way I would want any man to treat my mother or my sister. No matter how tired he was from working, he always found a way to do something nice for Moms, to show her how much he loved her. It was also his way of saying thanks to her for coming to this country with him and taking care of the kids while he worked. He wanted all of us to have what he didn't have as a kid. I was very proud of him. For a long time, he was proud of me too.

One of my favorite street games we used to play was a game called "Hot Peas and Butter." You ever play that? It was like a combination of "Tag" and "Hide and Go Seek", Bronx style. The object of the game was for one person to hide a leather belt somewhere on the block, while the rest of the gang would close their eyes so they wouldn't see where the belt was being hidden. The guy hiding it could put it anywhere, under a car, in a garbage can, anywhere. When he was ready, he would give the okay for everybody to open their eyes and spread out, looking for the belt. The best time to play was at night because there were more places to put the belt without it being seen right away, even right out in the open. While we looked for the belt, the guy who hid it would give us clues, like "you're getting warmer," or "you're cold-blooded." The first person to find the belt would have to yell "HOT PEAS AND BUTTER!", then chase down the closest guy to him and beat the shit out of him with the belt. While that's happening, everybody else had to run back to 'base' before they got caught and got whupped too. We had a lotta fun playing that game, even though a lotta times somebody'd get pissed off if he got hit too hard. But instead of fighting, you'd wait. You knew you could get your payback by finding the belt yourself in the next round, and going after the dude who just beat you.

We were playing this game one Saturday afternoon. I was half-way up the block, looking, searching, when I heard someone yell "Hot Peas and Butter!" I recognized the voice to be Louie's, so I took off. You didn't want to get caught by Louie because he was ruthless. He wouldn't say anything until he was close to you, even though he already had the belt in his hands a few minutes. That was allowed. Then he would pounce on you and even hit you with the belt buckle, and then say "oops!", like it was all an accident. I got to 'base' just in time to hear Chico screaming like a bitch. Big Louie was all over him, whackin' poor Chico like he was his son. WHACK! WHACK! I thought I heard Chico crying while he begged for mercy. Me, Johnny, and a couple of the other guys who also made it to 'base' were crackin' up laughing. Finally Louie stopped and headed our way to start the next round. *Pendejo* Chico couldn't leave well enough alone.

"*Cabrón!*" he yelled at Louie. Big mistake. Louie turned around and went after him again, chasing him around the parked cars and out into the street. We were on the ground, hysterical. It was so funny tears were coming out of my eyes. Finally, Chico realized he wasn't going to outrun Louie, so he just dropped to his knees and held up his hands, begging for Louie to leave him alone. Now he was really crying. Fuckin' Louie got a big kick out of that. He helped Chico up and we started the next game. It was Louie's turn to hide the belt.

A few minutes later I was searching around the steps going down to the basement of Johnny's apartment building where the garbage cans were. Louie was saying that I was getting warmer, but I couldn't find shit. I heard the door of the lobby open, but didn't pay it no mind because I was concentrating on finding the belt. With no luck, I started going back up the steps. There she was.

Just like the first time I saw her, it seemed like everything stopped. She stood at the top of the stoop, looking down at me with her million-dollar smile. She was just as beautiful from up close as she was from across the street. I know it sounds corny, but I could swear that there was a soft glow around her head, like in those pictures of the Virgin Mary that Moms had in her bedroom. Her Spring dress waved with the light breeze. All I could do was smile back at her and stare. I wanted to ask her where she'd been for the last month, but all I could do was stand there. I couldn't even get the word "Hi" out of my mouth. Then her eyes seemed to get real wide as she looked up behind me. I thought for sure she was taking a deep breath to say "Papo, I love you."

"HOT PEAS AND BUTTER!!!" Johnny jumped me from behind swinging the belt real high and started whupping me good. He had just found it in one of the small bushes nearby. Picture that, there're only about three bushes in the whole Bronx and Louie had to use *this* one for a hiding place. The rest of the fellas, just to fuck with me in front of this girl, took off their own belts and joined Johnny beatin' the shit out of me. If it wasn't because I was wearing a pair of thick blue jeans I would have gone home bleeding. These motherfuckers - my boys – were having a party on my ass. There was nothing I could do but cover myself as much as I could in case one of these *idiotas* got carried away and hit me in the face. Even Louie, who wasn't supposed to be in on this one, was swingin' away. Finally they stopped and helped me up, laughing and talkin' shit. I had to laugh along with them. I couldn't let on that anything they did hurt me. That would make me look like a punk. I looked up and saw my angel with a worried look, but I smiled to let her know I was all right. The guys led me away to start another game, but I didn't feel like playing no more. All I wanted to do now was talk to this girl before she disappeared on me again. I let the fellas go on ahead and turned around to look back at her. She was sitting on the steps.

"Hi." *Que mama'o!* I couldn't think of anything better to say.

"*Hola.*"

Damn, I thought. I'd forgotten that she was from Puerto Rico and probably didn't know much English. "*No hablas Ingles?*", I asked her.

"*Un poquito.* My *papá* used to live here before."

"Oh, yeah?" That was a relief. Even though I learned Spanish from my Moms and other people in the neighborhood, I didn't want to have to talk it all the time. "My name is Papo. *Cual es tu nombre?*"

"*Hola,* Papo. My name is Esperanza, but everybody calls me Espy." She had a heavy accent, but she seemed to speak English a lot better than I thought she would, which was cool for me.

"Esperanza. That's a nice name. Doesn't that mean 'Hope'?"

"*Si*", she said with another smile. I *hoped* she was impressed that I knew that.

"So, did your family move in yet?"

"Jes, a*noche.*" She pronounced 'yes' with a 'j'. "Do jou and jour friends always beat each other up like that?"

"Oh, that? Nah, we were just playin'. Makes us tough. Don't the boys play games like that in Puerto Rico?"

"No. They're too busy picking *aguacates* and *chinas* from trees. Then they sell them on the street corners for a dollar."

"What town are you from?"

"Humacao. Jou ever been there?" Again with the 'j'.

"No. I've never been to Puerto Rico. *Mis padres,* they were born there, but they haven't gone back since they moved here."

"Jou don't know what jou're missing. It's a beautiful island."

"I heard all about it from my Moms and Dón Marco in the *bodega* at the corner. Maybe someday we can go together and you

I had stood out there long enough, I had to do something. I knocked, but not too hard, in case somebody might still be sleeping. I hoped Espy would answer the door. It swung open. It wasn't Espy.

"Buenas tardes, Señor Malavé."
"Si?"
"Mi n-nombre es Eduardo T-T-Torres. S-s-soy un amigo de Esperanza." Stop stuttering, pendejo. He squinted his eyes when I mentioned his daughter's name and looked down at the flowers in my hand. I had to pee.

"Esperanza? Y qué deseas? What do you want?" He looked like he hadn't smiled since Kennedy was shot.

"I would like very much to visit your daughter, with your permission and *bendición,* of course." He looked at me up and down, as if to say 'look at the balls on this kid'.

"Adelante, come in. ESPERANZA!" He was wearing a T-shirt, but he quickly put on a white shirt as I followed him into the apartment. Respect. Pops was right.

Espy came running out from the room she shared with her six-year old sister, Maritza. Not expecting a visitor, she stopped dead in her tracks when she saw me, her eyes wide open. Little Maritza was running up behind her and crashed right into her. If it wasn't for that, Espy would have turned around and run right back to her room. Just like me, she was trapped now, nowhere to go. She was wearing another nice Spring dress. It was obvious she got dressed up for my visit, but really didn't think I would actually show up. Little Maritza was scopin' me out, too, trying to figure out what to make of me. She was probably thinking I had some pair of balls too.

"Hola, Papo." Oh-oh.

"Papo?" said Espy's father, squinting at me again. "I thought you said your name was Eduardo?"

"Uh, *si Señor. Mi nombre es Eduardo.* But everybody calls me Papo. *Mis padres,* they been calling me that since I was a baby."

"*Siéntese.* Where do you live, er, *Papo?*" He said 'Papo' like he was committing a sin. I sat down thinking that this *viejo* was gonna be tougher than me or Chico could ever imagine.

"We live right across the street, on the fifth floor. I grew up in this neighborhood."

"And how did you meet my Esperanza?" At that point her mother came out of the kitchen. I stood up, like a good *caballero.*

"*Bueno, Señor,* I saw you and your *familia* when you first came by to look at the apartment. Then I saw Espy one day and thought it would be nice to personally welcome her and your whole family to our community. We're always happy to see new faces from the old country join us. We do what we can to make our new neighbors feel comfortable in their new homes. Oh, these are for you, Esperanza." I handed her the flowers. "*Y, con su permiso,* Dón Malavé, these are for your *Señora.*" He nodded and I handed the other flowers to Espy's mother. He might've been impressed, but he didn't show it.

"*Pues,* Eduardo, what do you do with yourself. Do you go to school?"

"*Por supuesto,* Dón Malavé, of course. I graduate from high school next year, and then I plan to go to college."

"What do you want to study?"

I wasn't ready for that question.

"Court reporter!" I blurted out. Damn, I been hangin' around Big Ray too much.

"*Qué?*"

"I mean, lawyer. I want to be a lawyer someday." I wasn't sure if that was a right choice for him, but I couldn't think of anything else.

"*Un abogado.* That's good. You can help a lot of people being a lawyer."

"*Si, Señor.* Like Jesus tells us, we must help all those who can't help themselves." I heard that on an old *Davey and Goliath* cartoon.

"Oh, you know about Jesus Christ?" All of a sudden he was interested.

"Yes, sir. My mother sent me to Bible school when I was younger. We are Catholics, but I respect the lessons of all religions. I believe everyone must have a spiritual guidance in their life, no matter where they are from. After all, it's what separates us from the animals on this earth."

His eyes lit up! He was hooked, so I poured it on.

"I wish I had more time to spend in the church, but I have to help my family around the house when my father is working. It is my responsibility as the oldest son."

"*Eso es maravilloso! Muy bien, hijo, muy bien!* Esperanza! What are you waiting for? See if Eduardo here wants something to eat. *Avanza, darte prisa!*"

After that, I was in like Flynn. Dón Ramón, that's his first name, was still very strict with Espy. Anytime I went to visit someone had to be in the room with us, whether it be him, Doña Carmen, or one of her sisters. Whenever I went over I had to leave by nine o'clock. Dón Ramón didn't want the neighbors to think that I was messing around with his daughter right under his roof. In the beginning, if I asked for permission to take her out for a walk, or maybe to buy some pizza, we always had to bring Maritza along. Espy still wasn't allowed outside too much, just a couple of hours on weekends. He didn't want people to think she was a *cualquiera*. And she could NEVER play music in her house on Sundays. Dón Ramón said that that was the Lord's day, and we should devote it to *El Señor*. It was a bitch, but I had to go along with it.

I didn't mind all that because all I cared about was being with my Esperanza. The guys were surprised that I got that far with her. They used to call Dón Ramón *cara-chocha*, because of the nasty look he had on his face all the time. I still had plenty of time to hang out with them when Espy was inside or doing something with her family. But whenever I could, I would be with her. After a while she was able to come out more often, and he even let her come over to hang out in my house. I had to introduce the old man to my parents first, so he could check out what kind of family I came from. When he saw that they were cool, he let up a bit.

Espy got along real good with my Moms. You know how Moms are, they're always worrying that some girl is gonna come along and take their place in the heart of the *hijo*, and mine was no different. But Espy wasn't like the other girls in the neighborhood. She was very respectful to Moms and was always watching her cook dinner, asking her questions about everything she was doing. Most girls these days don't want to learn how to cook because then they'll be expected to do it all the time. And with that Women's Lib bullshit, girls don't want to be servants to their men anymore. That didn't go over too good with *Latino* men because we liked it better the old way. I remember when Pops would come home late from playing dominoes, Moms would always have something ready for him to eat if he was hungry. Shee-it, nowadays if a man comes home late, all he's gonna find is a cold stove and an empty bed because his woman's gotten up and gone out her damn self, just for fuckin' spite, you know what I'm sayin'?

Me and Espy spent most of our time together in front of her building, just talking. She was helping me speak Spanish better, and I was helping her with her accent. It was the Spring of 1969 and I'd never been happier in my life. We went to the same school, so I got to be with her even more without her Pops watching us all the time. We walked to school together, but she wasn't allowed to hold hands with me out in public. That was cool, we held hands all the time in school. She was a year younger than me, so we weren't in any classes together. But by three o'clock I'd be standing outside her last class waiting for her to come out so we could walk home together. She was smart too, always studyin'. That helped me out too because she'd get me to pay more attention to my schoolwork. She said that I needed a good education to get a good job so I could take care of her. Funny how my Pops been telling me that shit for years and I was like "Yeah, Pop", you know, in one ear, out the other. But when this girl said it, it all kinda made sense.

Another thing that ended once I started going out with Espy was the hooky parties. I stopped playing hooky, no shit. I mean, I didn't play hooky a whole lot before then. Like I told you before, it was only every now and then when Papo DJ had something goin' on. But Espy would not dare cut out of school, and I didn't really want to take her to those parties anyways. She wasn't that kind of girl. Besides that, I knew she'd get pissed off at me if she didn't see me in school the whole day, especially after we walked in together in the morning. I only did it one time in the beginning, and even though she didn't give me a hard time about it, I saw that look of disappointment in her face that I never wanted to see again. So that was that for playing hooky. Believe it or not, thanks to Espy, my grades started getting better.

While other dudes were making out with their girls like they would never see each other again, me and Espy just talked. We talked about so many things when we were together. She made it clear that there were things she wasn't ready to do yet and that she promised her father a long time ago that she wasn't going to let a man touch her in certain places until her wedding night. Imagine that, fifteen years old and she was still a virgin. They must've did things differently down in P.R. You know how it was up here in the Bronx, *everybody* was fuckin'. Everybody except Chico, of course. Yeah, I know, that's cold. (Sorry, Chico, wherever you are.) So I had to accept that then because that's how Espy wanted it. You know what? It didn't matter. I didn't care that we didn't do anything, in fact, I kinda dug it. It became a challenge to wait and it gave us something to look forward to. It's funny that we were even talking about getting married after only knowing each other a few weeks. But that's what teenagers did back then. They'd meet somebody, and BAM! Right away they're in love and talking about getting married. But in our case I knew it was for real, and I knew that someday, someday soon, it was going to happen.

The more I got to know Esperanza, the more beautiful she became. She had a heart of gold and always seemed real happy to see me. I would look deep into her eyes and swear I could see heaven. When I took her hand in mine, she would hold it tight the whole time, and not let go until I let it go. She would tell me stories of life in Puerto Rico, and sometimes even sing me old *boleros* she learned while growing up. I never saw her looking ugly or dirty. Every time

I paid a visit, she always had a nice dress on and the curls in her hair were just right. When Moms taught her a new dish, Espy would try to prepare it for me. Sort of like practicing for when we got married. It never came out as good as Moms, but I didn't let her know that. I told her it was BETTER than Moms.

At night I would look out my bedroom window towards her building, wishing that her room was on the same side as the street so I could wave to her goodnight. It wasn't, but I'd wave to her anyway and go right to sleep. That way, the morning would come faster and I could run down to meet her for our walks to school. It's like what they used to tell the kids on Christmas - the quicker you go to bed, the sooner Santa Claus comes.

All my boys liked Esperanza, even though they complained that she took up all my time. She tried to fit in too, doing whatever she could to make sure the guys liked her. That was important to her. One day we decided to have a track meet on the block, with everybody taking turns racing each other. Espy took the job of saying "Ready, Set, Go!" That was pretty cool, especially since the other girls on the block never bothered to play our games with us, not that we wanted them to anyways. But Espy was an exception. She was disappointed to find out I wasn't the fastest kid on the block. That title went to Louie and this little *moreno* kid named Papo *Cocólo*. He was half-Cuban, another kid named 'Papo'. I don't know why we let him race with us because he was only eleven years old. Nobody wanted to get dusted by a little kid. But it was alright, we was all just having fun.

My seventeenth birthday was coming up soon. Usually I would already be making plans to celebrate by going dancing, like I did when I turned sixteen. But I didn't want to be without my girl on my birthday and I knew there was no way in *hell* Dón Ramón was going to let her go. Even if he did she was too young to get in the club anyways. With that innocent angel face, she would've gotten busted in a minute. So instead of going out, we all decided to get together and have a party at home. Moms was going to cook, Papo DJ was bringing some records over, and all the fellas were gonna try to find dates. To make more room for everybody, Pops moved all the furniture from the living room into my bedroom. My pain-in-the-ass brother Benny was throwin' a shit fit over it because he slept in that room too. To make him happy Pops made sure his bed was clear and piled everything up on my side of the room. That was fine by me. I figured, if anything, I could just go and sleep over Chico's house like I'd done a million times when we was kids. *Pero se jodió* Benny, you know, because we ended up using his bed to throw everybody's coats on. The way he was carrying on about that you'd think we were throwing garbage on his fucking bed.

A lot of people from the block came to the party. Chico was there, so were his mother, Doña Hilda, and his sisters Yolanda and Yvette. His Pops didn't come. He had a drinking problem, and even though him and my father were close friends, he usually stayed away from these family get-togethers so as not to get drunk and make trouble for everybody else. Louie came, and so did Johnny and his girlfriend, Brenda. There were even some other chicks from the neighborhood there. Everybody had somebody to dance with. Out of respect, I invited Esperanza's parents. I didn't expect them to come, them being all religious, an' shit. But surprise, surprise, Dón Ramón and Doña Carmen showed up too, along with Lourdes and Maritza. Lourdes was about three years older than Espy, and she was pretty cute too. But she was already into that Pentecostal stuff, so she didn't do much to make herself look better. She never wore makeup and she always had her long hair pulled back in a ponytail or in a bun. I don't know how she expected to find a man lookin' like that, especially in the Bronx. I guess Dón Ramón was happy about that.

When Esperanza got to the apartment with her family, she was carrying a birthday cake she had baked all by herself to surprise me. It was chocolate with different color sprinkles all over it. You could tell that she didn't have much experience in baking cakes because it was small and lopsided to one side. It didn't matter, though. As far as I cared it was the most beautiful cake I'd ever seen, and it made me very happy that she went through all that trouble to make it. I put the cake right in the middle of the table that Moms had decorated with all kinds of birthday ribbons and balloons. It was kid's stuff, I know, but that was alright. We was all family there and I didn't feel embarrassed.

The party was going real good, everybody was joking around, having a good time. I saw Espy's parents sitting on the sofa next to Pops. They weren't drinking anything and poor Pops was stuck there, forced to listen to Dón Ramón talk about Jesus Christ and the church. Every now and then Pops would excuse himself and sneak into the kitchen where Moms had a cold beer stashed away for him. He didn't want to drink in front of Dón Ramón, I guess even Pops was afraid of him. But I knew it was more out of respect to his guests. To help me score some points he played the good host and made sure to keep them company most of the night.

Papo DJ was playing some great music, lots of *salsa* for me and *merengue* for the older folks. He didn't have his stereo system there so we had to use our old Hi-Fi. It was one of those big suckers that was a combination stereo and TV, I think they called them consoles. It didn't sound as good as DJ's system did, but it was what we were used to and nobody complained. Already Benny and Maritza had become buddies, if you could call it that. They were chasing each other all over the apartment, sometimes playing, mostly fighting. Every ten minutes one of them would come in crying because the other was playing too rough. I remember Maritza tried to sit down on one of the chairs and Benny came up from behind and pulled the chair away from her. Her little butt hit the floor and she started screaming bloody murder. Pops gave Benny the 'eye', which meant "Stop fuckin' around, *pendejito*, or I'll put the belt on your little ass". Benny hardly said a peep the rest of the night.

One of my favorite Eddie Palmieri songs came on and everybody jumped up to dance. I went to grab Espy, but she pulled me back.

"*Qué pasa?* C'mon, *vamos a bailar*, let's dance." I had told her how much I loved to dance, but she never saw me.

"No, Papo, I don't know how to dance *salsa*." I guess she wasn't perfect after all.

"C'mon," I begged her, "you could do it. Just follow me."

"*No me atrevo.* I'll get embarrassed."

I knelt down in front of her and tried to talk her into it. "C'mon, you'll do alright. We're family here, nobody's gonna laugh at you. Look at Chico, even *he's* up there." Chico was dancing with Jeanette, one of the girls on the block. He heard what I said and gave me the finger.

"*No, por favor*, Papo, don't make me. I promise I'll dance the next one. Dance with somebody else, I want to see you."

I realized it was no use. Not even if the building caught on fire was she gonna get up from that sofa. I squeezed her hand and gave her a little smile. I couldn't kiss her, not with *cara-cho..*, I mean, Dón Ramón in the room. "Are you sure?" I tried one last time.

"*Si*, Papo. Dance with somebody else for now, I want to see if you're as good as you say you are."

She shouldn't had said that. A challenge! I got up and turned around looking for Chico's sister, Yolanda. She was by the door to the kitchen, stuffing a hunk of *pernil* in her mouth. I grabbed her by the hand and dragged her to the middle of the floor, barely giving her the chance to put her plate down. Right away people started spreading out, making room. They knew we could really go off when we wanted to. Palmieri was just getting into one of his piano solos that went on forever. It was showtime!

For starters, we just moved around the floor holding each other without doing any turns. I always liked to start slow, just to get warmed up and let my partner get used to the beat. Some dummies want to show off right away and start doing crazy shit before the girl even gets in step. Those are the kind of dudes who never get to dance with the same chick twice. Not me. I try to make things as easy as possible for my partner, depending on how good they are. Yolanda was good, but she still had a forkful of food in her mouth. I had to give her time to swallow it.

Now we were really getting into it. I started her off with some simple one-handed turns, first in one direction, then the other. Then I made it so that I turned Yolanda, then I turned myself. We did that back and forth a couple of times. Now it was time for the heavy duty shit. I held both her hands over her head and spun her around, wrapping my arms around her as she turned, then spinned her back towards me so that she landed right up close to my body. People were beginning to cheer us on, clapping to the *clave* of the song. I could imagine Palmieri's sweat rolling down his face while he played on and on. I turned Yolanda three times in a row, non-stop. On the third turn, she did her famous shoulder-shake and hand wave, just to let me know she was still hangin' with me. The crowd loved that. I broke one of my rules and peeked over to where Espy was sitting and saw her with a smile on her face from ear to ear. She looked so happy watching me, her eyes were sparkling. I winked back at her, then me and Palmieri went for the big finale.

As the trumpets and the *timbales* joined in for the final *descarga*, me and Yolanda were twisting our arms around each other so fast you'd think we'd get tied up in knots. But no matter what, we'd always end up facing each other, without missing one single step. We did one more turn and calculated it so that we stopped just as the last note of the song was played. It was perfect. My people were cheering and applauding. We bowed to all of them, like we just finished a command performance in Carnegie Hall. Even Dón Ramón dug it. I glided over to Espy and she got up and gave me a big hug, forgetting that her Pops was there.

"You were wonderful, Papo! How do you expect me to dance with you like that? You're too good!" She gave me another hug.

"Don't worry, *mami*, I'll teach you." This was getting to be a better party than I thought. People were fanning themselves from the heat in the apartment, others were refilling their drinks. Even Louie and Johnny were drinking rum and cokes from cups, *guillaito*, like camouflage, so that nobody would realize what was in them. I think Chico was drinking too, because his face was all red. I heard some noise coming from the front door.

It was my big sister, Elizabeth. She had just arrived with her fiancé, Alberto. He was alright, I guess, but too uptight for me, with his gold-wire glasses. He was nothing like my sister. The Odd Couple, I called them. She met him in high school a few years before and they'd been together ever since. He was about to graduate from college, one of the few kids in the neighborhood that could say that. Elizabeth was holding a big box, and being the rowdy chick that she was, was making all kinds of noise about clearing the table. She put the box down and opened it up.

"Happy Birthday, Papo! Check this out, me and 'Berto picked it out." Everybody gathered around to see that my sister had taken it upon herself to provide the birthday cake for my party. It was a big, beautiful cake, one of those *Valencia* cakes, remember those? It had flowers made from white cream frosting all over it, with silver leaves for decoration, and those tiny little silver balls that would crunch in your mouth when you ate them. I never understood why Valencia put those shits on the cakes and wasn't sure if we were supposed to eat them. The cake part was angel-food, and the filling was all pineapple. Everybody was going "ooh" and "aah". Any other time I would have been very happy about this. But when they put Elizabeth's fancy cake on the table next to the one Esperanza had especially baked for me, it made the chocolate cake look like an old, stepped-on Hostess cupcake. I looked up at Espy. God bless her. It was obvious she had a *complejo* about her cake, but she was doing her best not to show it. She was smiling and trying not to let people see her feelings. I had to think quick.

"Thanks, Lizzie." I gave her a kiss. "Thanks 'Berto." I gave him a handshake and a hug. I was really grateful to them, but Espy's cake still meant a lot more to me. "But I think that if we leave this cake out here, somebody is gonna bump into it and mess it up. Let's take it to the kitchen and put it on top of the refrigerator, so nobody can get to it. You know Benny, he'll stick his finger in it as soon as everybody turns around."

"He better not!" said Elizabeth, "I'll cut his little booger-digger right off!" Benny gave that look like *What the fuck did I do now?*

"But you're right, Papo. C'mon Louie, help me take this thing to the kitchen." They both picked it up and went off to the other room, leaving my special home-made birthday cake back in the middle of the table where it belonged. I looked at Espy. She was happy again.

The rest of the party was boss, man. People kept coming and going, it's a miracle so many of them fit into the apartment. I got presents from everybody, mostly clothes. Moms and Pops gave me a new pair of shoes to wear for when I went out dancing. Speaking of dancing, I finally got Espy to dance with me, but it was a *merengue*, real simple shit. She said that that's all they dance in Puerto Rico. I told her someday we'll go there and show them how it's really done. I was surprised that she was a pretty good dancer when she wanted to be. She didn't know all the crazy turns and all that shit, but she was graceful and light on her feet. And she felt real good in my arms. After a while Moms got everybody together to sing "Happy Birthday" and cut the cakes. I thought it was corny at my age, but what was I gonna tell Moms, you know what I'm sayin'? She been doing that for us since we were little.

I took two big pieces of Espy's chocolate cake and led her by the hand out to the fire escape outside the kitchen window. I was sweating from all the dancing and I wanted some fresh air. Plus, it gave me and Esperanza a chance to be alone. We sat down on one of the stairs that went up to the sixth floor and started eating the cake.

"Do you like it, Papo?" Espy really wanted to have everything perfect for me.

I took a big spoonful, which from prior experience took a lot of courage. Believe it or not, it was pretty good. "*Es delicioso, mi amor.* The best birthday cake I ever had."

"*Ah, no séa embustero.*" She said that and I made like I was shocked and hurt.

"You callin' me a liar on my birthday?" I took a piece of the cake and smeared it on her nose. She laughed and threw a piece back at me, and we went at it back and forth, chocolate frosting all over the place. It looked like one of those scenes in a wedding when the bride and groom cut the cake and smash it into each other's faces. It seemed so right.

After there was no more cake to throw around, I got my Moms to throw me a towel from inside so we could clean up. We sat back down on the stair and looked up at the clear spring night.

"Papo, *te tengo una sorpresa*, a special birthday gift." I was wondering when she was going to get around to that. She reached into a small pocket in her dress and took out a small figurine wrapped in tissue paper. She presented it to me with both hands. I opened it up and saw that it was tiny and green, it looked like a frog sitting on a leaf.

"A frog? Um, thank you, Espy." I didn't get it, but what else was I gonna say?

"It's not a frog, *loco*. It's called a *coquí*."

"Oh, yeah, a *coquí*. That's what I meant to say." She hit me on the arm knowing I had no clue what this thing was.

"A *coquí* is a small animal, much smaller than a frog, that lives in the forests of Puerto Rico. It is symbol of the island's innocence and natural beauty. They call it a *coquí* because that is the sound it makes at night: *Co-Quí, Co-Quí*. You should hear them right after it rains, it's like a symphony of millions of tiny musicians playing nature's, how do you say....lullabye. It is what I used to listen to every night when I was a little girl. Their song would help me fall asleep."

"*Gracias*, Espy." It started to mean a lot to me now. "I wish I could hear them."

"You will. Remember? I'm going to take you there someday. *Mientras tanto*, I want you to hold onto this *coquí*, it is your little piece of the island. Promise me you'll keep it until we go to Puerto Rico together?"

All I could do was look back and forth at my angel and the figurine. It was really the most special gift I had ever gotten. She knew this, so there was no need to say thank you anymore.

"Promise?" she said again.

"I promise, with all my heart and soul." We kissed lightly and hugged. Then, from inside, I heard the beginning of the next song that Papo DJ played, a slow *bolero*.

"*La, la, la, la, la-la-la*" It was one of my favorites, "To Be With You", by Joe Cuba, the band I saw at Tapestry. I took Esperanza, my Hope, by the hand, and right there on the fire escape, we held each other close, and danced. Not a grind. Just a tender embrace by two young kids in love.

It was the very bestest birthday I ever had.

CHAPTER EIGHT

Summer finally arrived, which meant no more school and more time to be with Esperanza. With her help I passed all my classes and now only had one more year left in high school before graduation. We spent almost all of our time together, talking about how it was gonna be when we got married. I would have a job and we would buy a house, and we'd have lots of kids. She told me she wanted to be the mother of my children, and promised that the first one would be a boy. I don't know how she was going to make sure of that, but it felt good hearing it anyway. Too bad it was gonna be a long time before we could get started on that project.

The biggest thing happening around New York in the summer of 1969 was that those scrub Mets were on their way to winning the World Series in baseball. That didn't mean *jack* to us in the Bronx because if you're from the Bronx you had to root for the Yankees. A Met fan didn't dare show his face around our neighborhood. The bitch about it was that the Yankees really sucked that year. Mickey Mantle quit the year before and there was nobody good enough to take his place. That gave all those faggot-ass Met fans the chance to come out now and talk a lotta shit. Still, if you were a real fan you stuck with the team, in good times and bad. But boy, those Yankees were bad that year.

The other big thing that happened that summer was when the United States sent a man to the moon. I remember all of us going over to Johnny's apartment to watch it on TV. That was some unbelievable shit, man. It made everybody feel real proud being an American. Even Chico was saying he was going to be an astronaut, the first Puerto Rican in space. Louie said he already was a space cadet and everybody cracked up. It was so hard to imagine that we had actually put somebody on the moon. I sat by the window as I watched it on TV so I could look outside up to the sky to see if I could see those dudes walking around up there. Maybe if they waved or something....

I started giving Esperanza serious dancing lessons. I wanted to make her my permanent partner so that when we got the chance to go to the club I would dance with her and only her. I knew the club girls would be upset about that, but they'd get over it.

At first it was pretty frustrating, not because I thought she wasn't as good as me, but because she felt embarrassed every time she messed up. Then she'd get discouraged and wouldn't want to do it anymore. I had to beg her not to give up. I remember one time....

"C'mon, *nena*, you can do it."

"No, Papo, I don't want to. I'll never be as good as you."

"*Nobody* will ever be as good as me." I know that sounded conceited, but that's how you gotta think when you're on the dance floor. "You don't have to be as good as me. You just gotta try, that's all I'm asking."

"But if you see how much I mess up you won't want to be with me anymore." She was pouting, but I knew this was just a little game she was playing to test me.

"That will never happen, *mi amor*, I promise. But you know how much I like to dance, right?"

"*Sí.*"

"And you know someday you'll be able to go to the clubs with me, right?"

"*Sí.*"

"So what happens when we go out to the club together, do you expect me to just sit there next to you all night long?"

"What are you saying?"

"Well, if you won't dance with me, would you want to see me dancing with anybody else?"

"I let you dance with Chico's sister."

"Who, Yolanda? That's different. She's like a sister to me too. I'm talking about all the *chicas* I know in the clubs. They're always willing to dance with me. They even take turns."

"*Pues*, if you want to dance with them....." She folded her arms and looked away with *mucho* attitude.

"That's just it, I *don't* want to dance with them. I want to dance with *you*. I want us to be the best. But if you won't dance with me, I'll have to take someone else out. And there are some bee-u-tee-ful women that go to these clubs, *mami*."

Worked every time. She got up right away and was ready to try again. No matter how young and innocent Espy was, she was still a *Latina*, jealous like a motherfucker.

It wasn't that long before Espy started getting pretty good at following my moves. She was a quick learner, even though sometimes I'd get carried away with the music, not realizing she was just a beginner. That's why I always liked better dancing with somebody I knew instead of a stranger. A steady partner knows my style and knows ahead of time what I'm gonna do. You didn't necessarily have to be a great dancer to hang with me, just a great follower. Espy was picking things up real fast. With days and days of practice, she was learning all my tricks. My girl was turning into a *salsera* herself, right before my very eyes.

The only chances we'd get to show off was when we hung out in front of the building or down by the schoolyard. She wasn't allowed to go anywhere else. Somebody always had a radio and we listened to Radio WADO on AM, especially DJs like Dick Ricardo "Sugar" and "Symphony" Sid. That was before they came out with cassettes and eight tracks, so we had no choice but to listen to whatever they played on the radio. It was cool, though, because you had a lotta groups from around New York like Joe Bataan, Larry Harlow, Tito Puente, Johnny Colon, Willie Colon, Rafy Pagan, and the Lebron Brothers. *Salsa* was just beginning to get noticed around the city.

Most people were used to hearing those groups from the island, like El Gran Combo, Ismael Rivera, Ralphy Levitt y La Selecta, Pacheco. It didn't matter to me, *salsa* was *salsa*. I didn't give a damn who played it.

Elizabeth and Alberto finally got married that summer. We had the reception at the community center in the Soundview projects not far away. It was the first time me and Espy got a chance to dance in front of a lot of people and she did great. Of course, she had to share me with Moms, Yolanda, Chico's mom, and some of the other girls who were my sister's friends. Espy didn't mind too much since everybody there was family and they all knew that she was my girl now. We did so good that this dude who always used to call me the "Fred Astairs of Soundview" started calling her "Ginger Rogers". *Bendito séa*, Espy never heard of Ginger Rogers before, but she took it as a compliment anyway.

Alberto must've had a pretty good time on the honeymoon, because within a month Elizabeth announced to everybody that she was going to have a baby. All of a sudden I felt grown up, I was gonna be a *tio*. It didn't hit me when she was making all the preparations for the wedding, especially since she was still living at home. Alberto would only come around a couple times a week. But after they got married, and after she found out she was pregnant, I started to realize that things were changing, not only for them, but for all of us.

Dig it, when you're young you get used to living life a certain way. You see the same friends every day and you play the same street games all the time. In the wintertime you have snowball fights, maybe play a little football. In the summertime you play stickball all day and hang out on the stoop all night. You cool yourself off by opening the Johnny-pump and spray cars as they pass by, hoping you can get one schmuck who left the windows open. The whole family is always there, together. Your moms and pops look the same. You think that life is going to be like that forever. Then something happens, even if it's something good like a wedding. All of a sudden it's not the same anymore. At home it felt like something was missing with Elizabeth being gone. Everything got quiet. Even Benny stopped acting like a brat. I kind of hoped that eventually Elizabeth would walk back through the front door with all her stuff and say "Okay, that was fun, but I'm back!", and everything would go back to normal.

But everything didn't go back to normal. Elizabeth never came back. Yeah, she was around all the time, talkin' about "My husband this, and my husband that..." But it just wasn't the same. She never slept in her room anymore. Instead, Benny moved in. Even though Moms and Pops were happy about the baby, they started to look older, like from one day to the next. I never pictured them as *abuelos*, but now that it was happening they started to look it. It was the hardest thing to accept that things would never be the same again, no matter how much I wanted them to be. I should've kicked Alberto's ass. It was all his fault. If he hadn't come along and taken our Lizzie away, everything would still be like it used to be.

Now that I had a steady girl, I had to start thinking of things to do with her, with her Pops' *permiso*, of course. This meant that I had to have some money. I wasn't used to having money in my pocket before that and I never really needed any anyways. The only times I had to have money was to get into the clubs. That was usually only about five or ten dollars, and I got that from my Moms for doing stuff around the house. Once I made it inside the club I didn't need any money because I didn't drink back then. I was just a kid, you know? Besides, if I wanted something there was plenty of older honeys who loved to buy me drinks, even if it was just a soda.

I wanted to take Esperanza to nice places, like the movies, or maybe out to dinner. I wanted to be able to buy her things too. Her birthday was coming up soon, so I had to think of something nice. I went with Louie one day to the *Casa Pepe* Jewelry store up on Fordham Road. I saw a nice 14 carat diamond ring that cost about five hundred dollars. I knew no way Pops was gonna give me that kind of scratch, so I figured I needed a job so I can buy that ring for Espy. It would be kind of an engagement ring. Dón Ramón would have a titty attack if he knew his little girl was thinking about getting married. She was only going to turn sixteen, but when you're that young and in love you don't care what people say.

I started asking around to see if anybody knew somebody who was looking for summer help. I also went door-to-door all over the neighborhood, asking storeowners if they was hiring. I thought of Dón Marco, but he already had Louie's brother, Ricky, helping him out. I knew he couldn't afford to hire anybody else. My Pops suggested that if I want to get somebody to give me a chance I gotta look serious and professional. So I went up to Westchester Avenue dressed up in some nice good clothes, the kind I used to wear to go dancing. Pops must've been right because I lucked out at a discount store, what they used to call a "five and dime". I don't know why they called it a five and dime, because wasn't shit in there that cost only a nickle or a dime, unless you were buying bazooka gum.

I introduced myself to the owner, Mr. Kohler. He was an old Jewish dude who lived over in the Bronxville section of the Bronx. He was cool, you know, didn't talk much, but he was a smart businessman. When he first opened the store it was just a small space in the middle of the block. He started his business finding old broken-down shit, like radios and furniture. He'd fix them up and sell them cheap to the poor people in the neighborhood. It didn't take long for him to save up and buy the space next door, making it all into one big store. Then he was able to fill it with all kinds of stuff, a little bit of everything, like Woolworth's. He was doing pretty good.

Mr. Kohler liked me right away because I showed respect, not like some of them coolies back then who thought nobody could tell them shit. I told him I needed the job to help out my parents, so he hired me on the spot. He started me off stocking shelves with all the new shit he stored in big boxes down in the basement. I remember after going up and down those stairs all day long I'd get home too tired to do anything else, not even dance, if you can believe that shit. The only thing that I didn't like about doing that stock work was that in the beginning people would come up to me asking me where could they find this and that. I was new to the job, so I didn't know where anything was. I felt stupid telling them I didn't know all the time. What I really felt like telling them was "look for the shit yourself, you lazy motherfucker, can't you see I'm busy!" Mr. Kohler would have fired me as quick as he hired me if I said that to one of his customers. So I made it a point to memorize where everything was as I put it up on the shelves.

When it wasn't so busy and all the shelves were stocked and the floors were swept up, I'd just hang out with Mr. Kohler learning all about the business. Now I knew how Ricky felt working with Dón Marco. Mr. Kohler even started teaching me how to play chess. He said that his father taught him when he was a kid in Germany. They had a business together over there too. Then the Nazis came around startin' shit and he had to get out and come to New York. He didn't talk much more about that and I didn't ask him. Little by little he let me take care of customers at the cash register, which made me feel pretty good, like I was the owner myself.

One day, while Mr. Kohler was in his office, I was sweeping the floor behind the counter near the register. Right there on the floor in plain view was a twenty-dollar bill. I picked it up and thought about it for a while. You know, back then I was making less than minimum wage, being a young kid working part-time. Twenty dollars was a lot of money for me. But I didn't want to step on my dick, so I went to the office and gave the money to the boss, told him I found it on the floor behind the counter. Mr. Kohler made like he was surprised, thanked me, and took the money. I didn't think nothing of it. But as I was leaving the office to go back to my sweeping, for some reason, I decided to look back at him. He was just sitting there, peeking over his glasses at me with a little smile. Mr. Kohler never smiled. He didn't say anything else about it. It was a long time before I realized that he put that twenty-dollar bill on the floor himself to test me. By me returning it to him proved that he could trust me with the store's money. I passed the test with flying colors.

The next time I got paid I saw that he had given me a raise, $1.50 an hour. You can say what you want about them Jews, but they's really smart when it comes to running a business.

Esperanza's birthday was coming up and I was pissed that I still didn't have enough money to buy the ring. Being the kind of chick she was I knew she wouldn't complain about that. Besides, I also knew she probably wouldn't dare wear it in front of her old man, so I had to think of something else. It was the middle of August and the weather was as hot as it had been in years. I got the idea of taking her out to the beach, like I promised when we met. She hadn't done that since she moved here. I told everybody about it and we all decided to make a big day of it out at Orchard Beach, the "Rican Riviera". We were going to give Espy a beach birthday party. We packed a cooler with soda and sandwiches. Johnny brought his radio. Chico, Louie, Yolanda, Yvette, Jeanette, and some other kids from the block went. Even Ricky took the day off from the *bodega* to come with us. But the biggest surprise was that Espy's older sister Lourdes came too. She *never* hung out with us. Then again, without her, maybe Espy wouldn't have been allowed to go either.

We started the day off early one Saturday morning. I didn't have to work at the discount store that day because Mr. Kohler, being Jewish an' shit, never opened on Saturdays. We all got together in front of my building. Everybody brought something to eat and drink. Louie asked if my sister was going to show up with another Valencia cake. We got a good laugh over that one, but I knew that wasn't going to happen. Lizzie and Alberto had moved to a house in Elmont, out in Long Island. They needed the extra room for the new babies. That's right, *babies*. The doctors told her she was gonna have twins. When Chico heard that news he tried to be funny by saying that 'Berto must have fucked her twice in one night. He felt like a shithead when nobody laughed.

We checked to make sure everybody had enough money for the bus ride, and, like Jackie Gleason, away we went. We got on one bus that took us to Fordham Road and 188th Street. Then we switched to the BX12 bus that went on the New England Thruway right out to City Island and Orchard Beach. Once we got off the highway it was like being in another part of the world. You ever been up to Orchard Beach? It's like being in the country. Long, winding roads, trees everywhere. In those days they used that place as a city dump, so when the bus passed by there it stunk so bad it was like everybody threw one big, juicy fart at the same time. Nowadays you go there and you see nice green hills and the air smells fresh. If you didn't know better you'd never believe that under all that nice green grass lies buried all of the Bronx's garbage from thirty years ago.

As the bus continued on it passed a golf driving range. Picture that, bro'. Who plays golf in the Bronx? Not us. Further up was this big circle, people used to call it *"La Curva".* There was a softball field off to one side, and a picnic area where, if you went by there often enough, you'd see the same group of *boricuas,* week after week, cooking barbecues and playing volleyball and softball. One time I walked by there and these old men in *guayaberas* were playing a game that looked like baseball. But instead of a bat and ball, they used sticks and this little piece of bamboo wood that stuck out of the ground. With the stick, one guy would tap the piece of wood to make it bounce up, like Laurel and Hardy did in "The March of the Wooden Soldiers". Once the wood was in the air, he would try to hit it just like we did playing stickball in the streets. The other team would have fielders who would try to catch the wood before it hit the ground. Nobody ran any bases. I still don't know exactly what the object of this game was, but these *viejos* seemed to take it very seriously.

Once you pass that you see a road going off to the right. That road took you over a bridge to City Island. That's a nice seaport, right? You'd never think that that is part of the big, bad Bronx. You ever been to the seafood restaurants over there? They're the best in New York, better than Sheepshead Bay in Brooklyn. I never been to Sheepshead Bay, but that's what people said.

Finally, the bus pulled up to the beach. It was about ten-thirty by the time we got there and already there were crowds of people everywhere. We piled out of the bus, me and Espy leading the way carrying bags with blankets and towels. The other girls carried the munchies, like potato chips and cheeze doodles. Johnny had his radio blasting already. He had to compete with the other thousand radios already there. Chico and Louie carried the cooler.

I remember one time when I was about six or seven years old. I had some stupid fight with Lizzie, I can't even remember what the whole shit was about. We was just kids, you know? Anyways, I get in trouble with my moms and she punishes me. She made me kneel on the floor facing the corner for two hours. The worst part, though, was that she poured some rice on the floor and made me kneel on that. Think about it, man. Imagine kneeling down on hard rice for two hours. That shit started hurting after about five minutes. When I finally got up my knees looked like two golf balls, you know, with all them little holes on 'em. So now I'm really pissed off, especially because Moms didn't do nothing to Lizzie.

I decided to run away from home and never come back. I was gonna make Moms pay for punishing me. I packed some stuff in a little bag and waited until Moms went out to the store. As soon as she was gone, I walked out the apartment and went downstairs. But once I got outside I didn't know where to go. So I turned around and went upstairs to Chico's house. I knocked on the door and Doña Hilda opened it and let me in. Chico was taking a nap, so I started telling her that I ran away from home and I was never going back. She listened to everything I was telling her, giving me a chance to spill my guts out about why I hated my sister and my mother. She even made like she agreed with me on everything. She fixed me something to eat and said I could stay there with her forever if I wanted to. She even promised to hide me from Moms if she came by looking for me.

After I ate, me and Doña Hilda sat together watching TV for a while until I got sleepy. Next thing I know I was waking up the next morning in Chico's bed, with him snoring next to me. I wasn't so mad anymore. In fact, I kinda missed my moms and was sorry for the way I acted. I got scared too because I knew they would be worried sick looking for my ass all night. Pops was gonna be *real* pissed.

Doña Hilda offered to go with me back home, if that's what I really wanted to do. I felt safer with her next to me. We walked into our apartment and my mother ran to me and made like she was really happy to see me. She said she panicked when she came home and I wasn't there. She told me they were looking for me all night long. They even called the police, she said. I told Moms I was really sorry for the way I acted and I promised I would never be bad again. I was crying, but I was happy to be home.

What I didn't find out until years later was that while I was sleeping, Doña Hilda had secretly called my Moms up and told her the whole story. Her little Papo had run away from home and traveled all the way to the apartment next door. They decided to have some fun with it, and maybe even teach me a lesson. Chico's Mom agreed to let me stay there a while until things had calmed down, all the time making believe she was on my side. It must've worked, because after that night I didn't fight much with Lizzie anymore. And never, ever again did I run away from home. I was just a little kid, but I'll never forget what Doña Hilda did for me that night when I really needed somebody just to talk to.

Plus, she kept me from getting my ass beat with the belt too.

When she came home from the hospital the doctors told her to stay in bed for a while. That was good for her because she was too weak to do anything else. Everybody took turns watching over her. Most of the time Dón Guillermo, Chico's dad, would be there to help her out of bed, make her breakfast and lunch and all that. When he had to go off to work, Yolanda and Yvette would stay with her. For a while Chico hardly came out much. He was helping with the house cleaning and going to the store for food shopping.

Moms was over there almost every day too, keeping her best friend company. I could tell Moms was hurting, but she was a very strong woman and she didn't want to upset Doña Hilda or anybody else by showing her emotions. Sometimes I could hear Doña Hilda through the walls of my room, moaning from the pain she was feeling all over her body. Yolanda told me that it was her stomach that hurt the most and she couldn't eat anything without throwing it up. It gave me the creeps. I started thinking about what if that happened to somebody in my family, how would I deal with it. If anything, I learned early on how to appreciate the things we got, 'cause, you know, they ain't gonna be around forever.

Pretty soon they had to take Doña Hilda to the hospital more and more. First it was for a couple of days, but then each time she would have to stay longer and longer. Sometimes she'd come home feeling better, and me and Chico would hang out in her bedroom trying to make her laugh with all our stories of stuff that happened to us on the street. I don't know if it took the pain away, but it was still a good thing seeing her smile again. It was coming close to Christmas, but not too many people around our way were in the mood to celebrate like we used to. All anybody cared about was how Doña Hilda was doing, and what could we do to make her feel better.

When Doña Hilda first got sick, she weighed something like 160 pounds. She was a nice healthy Puerto Rican momma. Now, just three months later, she was down to about 110 pounds. That shit was eating her up from the inside and we had to watch while it took her over. Her night table was filled with bottles of pills that she had to take all the time. Those pills weren't meant to cure her, it was too late for that, but they were supposed to make the pain easier to deal with. She was getting dizzy all the time, like when she had to get up to walk around. She had pills for that too. It got to the point where she couldn't even get up to go to the bathroom, she was so weak. Yolanda and Yvette took turns cleaning her up, which was a bitch because she couldn't control herself anymore. Poor Doña Hilda felt really embarrassed when that happened and she didn't want people to come to her room anymore. We all visited her regardless, we didn't care. We felt like we was all in this together.

The situation with Chico's mother took a lot of the fun away from Christmas. We all tried to go on like normal, but the spirit just wasn't there. The holidays meant I was busy at the store, so that's where I spent most of my time. There was not much else going on. It was like a cloud hanging over the block, everybody was hoping for the best, but preparing for the worst. Doña Hilda was spending more and more time in the hospital. It was too much to try to take care of her at home.

The doctors decided to put Chico's mom in that big hospital in the city that specializes in cancer treatments, what's it called? Sloan Kettering, or somethin' like that? It gave us hope that maybe there they could find some way to cure Doña Hilda. I saw when they brought her down on the stretcher from Chico's apartment. It was weird, man. Doña Hilda was about two years younger than my Moms. But when they brought her downstairs to put her in the ambulance she looked like she could be somebody's grandmother. She looked so old. By now she was down to maybe 80 pounds, real skinny.

Chico didn't want to get too close to her because he didn't want her to see him crying. Before they put her in the ambulance, she called him over, along with Yvette. She gave them both a kiss and told them not to worry, that she was going to be okay. She made them promise that they would behave themselves with their father. She tried to convince them that deep down he was a good man. She also made them promise to do good in school. She said she wanted to be proud of all her kids.

They put her in the ambulance and drove off. There was a small crowd of neighbors outside by this time. These were people that lived for many years on that block together, they all treated each other like family. And now a member of the family was really sick. Some of the older ladies were making signs of the cross, mumbling "*pobresito niños*" in low voices. Everybody was crying.

Two weeks later, the day after Christmas, Doña Hilda died. She was only forty-two years old. Chico and Yvette were not allowed to go to the hospital, so they never got to see their Moms alive again. Maybe that was for the better. The body I saw at the funeral didn't look anything like the lady I grew up with and lived next door to all my life. At least they got to say good-bye when they had the chance.

There must have been hundreds of people in the *velorio* for her. The funeral parlor was crowded from wall to wall. Some people even flew up from Puerto Rico to see her. I was there with Esperanza, my parents, and Lizzie and Alberto. I asked Lourdes if she could stay

Another reason we never worried about the war was because they kept talking about ending the draft and bringing all the boys home as soon as possible. The only way to go into the Army would be to enlist, you know, sign up. I know ain't none of us were stupid enough to sign up while a war was going on. That's like volunteering to get your ass blown up on purpose. But those politicians in Washington could never make up their minds about how they was going to end the draft, so they just kept calling dudes in, whether they liked it or not.

They ran the draft like a lottery back then. First they assign you a number from 1 to 365, depending on what day your birthday is. Then they put all these numbers in a big drum and mixed them all together. One by one they would pick out a number, and all the guys whose birthday fell on that number would be called in. Poor Louie's number was 27, and that was one of the first numbers called up that year. He got the notice that he was to report to Fort Hamilton in Brooklyn right after he finished the year in high school, whether he graduated or not. In the meantime, he had to go a couple of times for physicals and evaluations. Every time he went in for one of those tests he would come back all excited and gung-ho, like they was already eatin' his mind about that *serving your country* bullshit. Louie didn't seem worried at all, or at least he didn't show it.

Louie Jimenez was always a good fighter and never scared of shit around the block. The few times we had rumbles with kids from other neighborhoods, Louie led us in and would challenge the biggest dude on the other side. Everybody on both sides respected that. We was lucky that in those days gang fights in our neighborhood was just a bunch of kids playing tough guys. A lot of times, the same kids you fought one day were playing football against you the next day. It was never about fighting for your turf, protecting your colors, or any of that stupid shit. You didn't have to worry about someone getting shot or stabbed to death like you do now. We fought like men, and the best man always won, and that was it. Everybody went home and ate dinner. These gangbangers today who don't dare do shit without having their posse gettin' their back with guns and knives are pussies. They'd piss in their pants if they ever had to fight by themselves. I'd like to see these punks out here today spend one day in the Nam, just one. They'd cry for their mommas like the bitches they are.

Now that Louie was going into the Marines we all started paying more attention to the news about the war. We kept hearing about small battles here and there with a couple of G.I. casualties, but at the same time they'd say that about a hundred of the enemy got killed too. They made us think we was kicking ass and didn't have anything to worry about. The United States never lost a war and we sure as hell weren't gonna lose to these little jungle bunnies and their home-made slingshots. A lot of people around the country were protesting the war, but not around the Bronx. If we got called, we went. Simple as that, there was nothing we could do about it. We had to do what the government told us to do. It's how we were brought up.

Growing up in the *barrio* we never knew about the things that rich people were doing to get out of the draft. None of us went to college, so we didn't know that by going to college you could get a draft deferment. That meant you didn't have to go in as long as you stayed in school a certain period of time. Nobody in our neighborhood could afford to go to college, so that option was out even if we *did* know about it.

We heard that other dudes were running to Canada and having their parents send them money to support themselves. I thought that was a *cobalde* thing to do. If the country needed you, you had to go. You couldn't punk out. We were still caught up in that John Wayne-patriotic shit, where we go off to war like it's okay because we were the good guys and we never lose. We thought war was like that TV show *Combat*. Nobody ever got killed in that show, except the Germans. You never even saw any blood. Vietnam was the same, right? We had to stop Communism no matter what, and when we came home we would get a parade and be treated like heroes. What a bunch of stupid, fucked-up, senseless bullshit *that* turned out to be.

Louie decided not to wait until he graduated from high school. He dropped out and went right into the Marines. He kept saying that when God says it's his time to die, he'll die, whether he's in the boondocks in Vietnam, or taking a piss in the bathroom at school. There was nothing he could do about it. My man had heart, I'll tell you that. He made me proud. We threw a nice party for him before he left for boot camp, just the guys. Ricky snuck some beer out of the *bodega* and we even got some smoke from a spot a few blocks away that Big Ray knew about. We got *fucked* up. Chico got all sentimental about his Moms and drank too much. He threw up all over the place. Louie didn't want to spend his last hours in the world sleeping, so we all stayed up and broke night, drinking, smokin' herb, and telling stories of all the funny things that happened to us growing up.

After Louie left things got real quiet around the block. He was our best athlete and the life of the party with all his jokes and put-downs. Even Chico missed him. He said there was nobody who could goof on him the way Louie did. With him gone, nobody felt like doing anything anymore. Ricky was even more distant without his brother around, so he stayed at the *bodega* all the time with Dón Marco. When Johnny wasn't with Brenda he spent his time helping his old man running the building. I was always with Espy, or at the store with Mr. Kohler. Chico had to help out more around the house after his mother died. His Pops was still messed up over losing his wife. He was drinking more and talking to people less. Everybody pretty much stayed out of his way.

Since I had a girl now, I didn't go out dancing much anymore. I managed to sneak out a couple of times to check out the scene, but without Espy, it wasn't no fun at all. I kept thinking about how much better it'd be if she was there. Instead, all I did was hang out by the stage to watch the musicians play. Once in a while one of the babes I used to dance with before would come along and drag me out to the floor. I did alright, but I wasn't into it like before. Don't get me wrong, I still loved the music and I was dying to dance. But the only person I wanted to dance with was Esperanza. Dancing with another girl was like jerking off. It was alright if you had to do it, but it just wasn't the same.

Ain't nothing I wanted more than to be able to take Espy out to the clubs. We got real good as dance partners, but there was nowhere for us to show off. Nobody on the block was in the mood to party anymore, nobody was hangin' out. Only place to go was the clubs, and I was sure old Dón Ramón wasn't having any of that with Espy.

I knew I could sneak her out, but she didn't want to disrespect her father that way. She was always afraid of how hurt he'd be if she got caught. I was more afraid of how hurt *I* would be if she got caught. Besides, I had his *confianza* now. It took a while to get in really good with him and when I finally did, I didn't want to mess it up.

We finally got some good news to put everybody in a better mood. In March Elizabeth had the twins, a boy and a girl. I went with Moms to the hospital when we got the call that Lizzie went into labor. The hospital was in Queens, so we had to take the subway to Jamaica, then take a bus. It took us about an hour and a half. The trip was so long I told Moms that by the time we got there those kids were gonna be in kindergarten. When we finally got to the hospital, Alberto was in the waiting room looking like he was having a nervous breakdown. Lizzie wasn't supposed to have the babies for another three weeks, so he thought something was wrong. Moms was trying to calm him down, telling him that it was normal for twins to be premature. That's the same shit the nurse told him, but I guess Berto felt better hearing it from someone he knew and trusted. He said that he was in the ward with Lizzie for a while, but that every time she had a pain she would scream and curse him out. She called him a *pato* and blamed everything that was happening to her now on him. She even swore that she was never gonna let him touch her again. Moms laughed and put her arm around the poor guy, then sent me out to get him a cup of coffee. When I came back with the coffee I handed it to him and said, "Here ya go, *pato*." I was havin' a goof with him.

After a few hours the doctor finally came out and congratulated Alberto, he was the father of two beautiful healthy babies. Doc reassured him that Lizzie was doing fine. I called Pops at work and told him he was an *abuelo*. He was really happy to hear that, especially when Berto told him that the boy was gonna be named Jorge, after his grandfather. They named the girl Jessica. I was an uncle. These tiny little things were gonna be calling me *Tio* Papo someday. I couldn't believe it. I remember when Benny was born, but I was just a little kid then. This was different. Georgie and Jessica, the new members of the Torres family. *Chévere!*

83

For the first couple of weeks Moms stayed at Lizzie's house in Elmont to help her with the babies. She took Benny with her. I was goofin' on Lizzie because for a few days she was walking around bowlegged, like she had just finished riding a horse a thousand miles. She told me to cut the shit, that she was hurtin' but she could still kick my ass. Besides, she knew if she wanted to get rid of me all she had to do was whip out a tit and stick it in one of the babies' mouth. I didn't want to see that nasty shit, especially when it's my sister. So I stopped making fun of her and went back to the Bronx.

Back home it was just me and Pops for two weeks. We had the whole apartment to ourselves. We joked about throwing our own little party and invitin' all kinds of women. We were just kidding around, but it was cool that my Pops was looking at me now like a grown man instead of some little kid. We talked about a lot of things. We even went to the movies together, just the two of us. We never did that before. I was always close to Pops, but in those two weeks, we got even closer. I was a little sad when Moms came back and ended our little vacation. But she brought the babies with her, so that brought some excitement to the house. Everybody came around to see them.

By now Benny was getting jealous of all the attention the babies were getting. He had been the baby in the family for so long that he was used to everybody spoiling him. Now he was just another kid hanging around and he didn't like it. I told him to join the club. While everybody went crazy over Elizabeth and the twins, me, Pops, Berto, and Benny just hung out on the stoop. Nobody gave a shit about us, but we understood.

Soon after I got my first letter from Louie. He was writing from boot camp in Parris Island, where, as he put it, "The baddest dudes on earth are born". They musta been drilling that shit into his head from day one. I remember the letter went something like this:

April 15, 1970

Camp Lejuene
United States Marine Corps
Parris Island, North Carolina

Dear Papo,

Qué pasa, homie! It's your old buddy Louie, still alive and still *loco*. I finally got a break from all this crazy training here to write you a few lines. You wouldn't believe all the shit they got me doing down here. They make us get out of bed every day at 4:30 in the morning, even on Sundays. And they don't just come knock on your door and ask you nicely. These big dudes wearing Smokey-the-Bear hats come in yelling and screaming, banging on garbage cans, beds, and anything else that makes a lot of noise. Everything we do and everywhere we go we got to do it running full speed. Before we even have breakfast in the morning we have to make our beds, clean the barracks, pick up cigarette butts all around the compound, and do PT. Then we only get about ten minutes to get our food and swallow it down real quick. If you're too slow in following orders, the whole platoon gets punished. Nobody likes that shit, because then you get your ass kicked at night by your own guys when the Drill Sergeants leave.

Our Drill Sergeant is this big, black, ugly *cocólo*. He looks like a gorilla. His nose is so big that I swear he'll drown if he tilts his head back too much in a rainstorm. He's already done two tours in Vietnam and he's always saying he'd rather be back there with real men than wasting his time with us "pasty-faced momma's boys". Hey, I wanted to take up a collection to buy Mighty Joe Young his plane ticket back to 'Nam, but I couldn't get nobody to go in with me.

We train in the snow, the rain, the mud, whenever. We don't get a break for shit. I've been learning how to shoot a rifle and take it apart to clean it. I'm pretty good at it too. I already earned me a marksman medal. Maybe when I get to 'Nam I can just show those VC there the medal and they won't fuck with me. Then I won't have to shoot nobody. What do you think?

That's all anybody talks about around here. The instructors are always yelling about how important it is what we're learning, that someday it will save our lives. They keep saying we're going to be scared shitless when we finally get there because we're all a bunch of pussies. Dudes here, especially the *blanquitos,* are believing that shit. I could hear them crying in their beds at night. I'm scared just like anybody else, but I know there's nothing I can do about it. So I just do whatever they want me to do, and be ready to go when my time comes.

How's Espy? Give her my regards. I hope your family is okay. Ricky told me about Lizzie and the twins. Congratulations, bro'! As soon as I can get to the PX I'll buy them a card and send it to them.

With all this running around and humping heavy equipment, my knee has been killing me lately. I tried to complain about it, but instead of sending me to get checked up, they made me jump up and land on my knees on a footlocker. I had to do that shit over and over again. Can you believe that shit, bro'? They said I was trying to get out of training by making like something's wrong with my knee. So now I just keep quiet and deal with the pain, just like I did at home.

Well, Papo. I got to go now. Lights out is in five minutes and I still got to spit shine my boots. Say hi to Johnny, Chico, Papo DJ, and everybody else. I love you, man, and I hope to see you real soon.

Your panín for life,

Louie

Leave it to Louie to find a way to brighten up my day like he always did, even when he wasn't around.

Believe or not, my birthday was coming up again pretty soon. So many things happened in the last year that time flew by fast. I was gonna be eighteen and this time I wanted to party at Tapestry. I had to figure out how to get Espy to go. Not only that, I had to find a way to sneak her into the club too. Remember the problem I had with G.I. Joe and his faithful sidekick, No-neck, from the last time I went there? Well, I didn't want any hassles with those two assholes. It'd be a bitch if they messed up my birthday plans with Espy.

I tried to get Moms and Pops to come with us and act as chaperones. I figured with them around Dón Ramón would feel that it's alright to let his daughter go. But Pops had to work early the next day and couldn't go, and Moms hadn't been out to a club in years. She didn't want people wondering what this *vieja* was doing in a dance club. I tried to convince her not to pay no mind to those idiots, but she just laughed and said she'd pass on the invitation. She'd never go without Pops anyways.

Johnny agreed to go with his girl Brenda, so that made it a double date. Then Yolanda said she wanted to go with her new boyfriend, so now there was six of us. Still, I had to come up with something to get Espy to go without worrying about getting busted. I thought of asking Lourdes to come along, but she didn't fit into these places any better than my moms did. Chico came up with a brainstorm of inviting Espy's parents to go and let them be the chaperones themselves. I almost smacked him upside his head with my baseball hat for that one. But Espy said to ask them, at least I was being honest and up front about it. I looked at her like "Why do *I* gotta be the one to ask?"

That year my birthday fell on a Sunday, so I decided to celebrate the night before. The previous Sunday I went with Dón Ramón, Doña Carmen, Espy, and her sisters to the worship at the Pentecostal Church. I did that a couple of times, just to show the old man that the story about me being into Jesus Christ wasn't all a sack of shit. He appreciated that, but he understood I wasn't crazy into it like he was and that was okay too. After the service, which took most of the day, for Christ's sake, we all went to their house to have Sunday dinner.

While Lourdes and Espy helped their moms with the food, I sat in the living room talking to Dón Ramón. I hoped I had heard enough about Jesus Christ for one day.

"*Pues*, how did you like the sermon today, Eduardo?" He still had trouble calling me 'Papo'.

"It was very interesting, Dón Ramón." I left out the fact that I thought it was just long enough to help me catch up on some sleep. I had hung out the night before and was tired.

"*Si. El Hermano* Perez can recite passages from the Bible better than anyone in the Church. But don't you think he talks too long?"

I almost jumped out of my seat reachin' for a pound, sayin' '*YES, BROTHER! We finally seeing things eye to eye!*' But I chilled.

"Well, sir, whatever it takes to get the message across to the people." That was jive, but when he laughed at that I felt for the first time like me and Dón Ramón had something in common. It gave me the nerve to try Chico's idea and bring up my plans for my birthday. I cleared my throat.

"Dón Ramón?"

"*Si?*"

"I don't know if you know it, but my birthday is coming up again."

"*Otravez! Como pasa el tiempo.* I remember it was like yesterday that you had that party in your house. I saw you dancing around with that girl, *cómo se llama?*"

"Yolanda. She's my *vecina, mi amigo* Chico's sister."

"Oh, yes, Yolanda. Their mother died recently, *no?*"

"Yes, sir. I took Esperanza to the funeral to pay her respects on behalf of the family."

"Yes, very good. It is sad for us when a loved one dies. But if you have faith in our Saviour, *el Señor Jesus Cristo*, you are happy to know that death is just a passing from this life to the next one. He promises it will be much, much better."

I had to get him off the subject quick or I was gonna lose him.

"*Si, señor.* I believe that with all my soul. But still, I hope that we don't suffer another loss like that of Doña Hilda around here for a long time. About my birthday......"

"Are you going to have another *fiesta?*"

"Well, not exactly. My parents want to show respect to our neighbors, since they are still in *luto*. Instead some friends of mine want to get together at a dancing club not too far from here. They want to sing me Happy Birthday there."

"Dance club? You need to go to a dance club to sing Happy Birthday? Why don't you do it in the church basement?"

"Um, well, different people go to different churches. I don't know if they all would want to come to the Pentecostal Church. Anyway, we must respect the house of the Lord also. I wouldn't feel right using it to have a party, *no?*"

"*Tienes razón.* When is this party?"

"It's next week, on Saturday. I was hoping I could invite you and your *Señora* to join us, if that's alright with you. Maybe Esperanza and Lourdes could come too."

Dón Ramón looked at me real serious. I thought he was gonna spit fire and smoke out of his mouth, like the dragons did when they got pissed off. I decided right there that if I lived through this I was gonna go across the street and kick Chico's ass. This was all his idea.

He opened his mouth like he wanted to say something, but before any words came out he started laughing. I didn't know what to do, but I wasn't going to laugh with him until I was sure what the fuck was so funny.

"*Hay, muchacho.* You are a clever one." A nervous smile creeped onto my face. "It is very nice that you want to include me and Doña Carmen in your plans. And since we had such a good time at your house last year, it may not be such a bad idea."

I heard that and it occurred to me that I was gonna be the first *pendejo* in the history of Tapestry to bring his *suegros* along to keep an eye on him.

"But don't worry, Eduardo. I don't think a nightclub is the proper place for us. We don't drink, we don't dance, and we have to be up early on Sunday to go to church. Thank you for the invitation, but we can't go. Besides, don't you think I know that the only reason you are inviting us is so that Esperanza can go with you too?"

Busted.

"Um, no sir, I was....." He held his hand up and, like magic, my mouth shut tight.

"*Esta bien.* I know what you want. *Vamos a ver.* You have always treated my daughter and I with respect. I admire you coming to me man-to-man, instead of sneaking around behind my back. I trust you, Eduardo. I know you will look after my daughter and make sure nothing happens to her."

"Oh, *si,* Dón Ramón, I......" The hand went back up and my mouth shut tight again. How'd he do that?

"Who is going?"

"Well, let's see, me, my friend Johnny and his girlfriend, Yolanda and her boyfriend, and Lourdes, if she wants to come too.

"How are you getting there?"

"We can take a bus, or the subway."

"You may take Esperanza with you. But she is not to drink. I don't want her getting drunk. Remember, she's still only sixteen. I will give you money for a taxi, *ida y vuelta.* Call it my birthday present to you."

"Thank you, Dón Ramón, thank you very much." From the kitchen door, I saw Espy quietly jumping up and down with happiness.

Then the old man looked at me straight in the eyes, squinting like he always did.

"I am putting the light of my life in your hands. The truth is I don't agree with this nightclub business. It is where the devil lives. I know you, and I know you will take good care of my Esperanza. But if something happens to her, you will meet the devil himself in me. *Comprendes?*"

"*Si, señor.* I will guard her with my life. Thank you for putting your faith in me. I will not disappoint you. I promise."

"*Muy bien.*" We settled back in our seats. My palms were soaked with sweat, but I was relieved, man. Turned out Chico was right after all. But just when I thought the coast was clear I heard him mumble, "*Espera*, you said Yolanda and her boyfriend were going? I thought they were in *luto?*"

"DINNER! *Vén, siéntense!*" The cavalry of Espy, Lourdes, and Doña Carmen came to my rescue with big plates of food.

The rest of the week could not go by fast enough. I went and bought a new shirt and some sharkskin pants. I whipped out those shoes my folks gave me for my last birthday that I hardly had a chance to use until now. Yolanda took Espy up to Fordham Road to shop for dresses. I told her to pick out something nice, but to make sure the dress ain't too flashy. I didn't want Dón Ramón to change his mind at the last minute if he saw his little girl lookin' too *putita*, you know what I'm sayin'? I even called the car service to make a reservation for that night, just to make sure I wasn't gonna be left hangin' without a ride. It felt like I was ordering a limosine, but I knew all I was gonna get was some dude named Cheo and his gypsy cab.

Saturday night finally came and I went over to pick up Espy. Johnny, Brenda, Yolanda, and Hector were waiting for me at my place. Hector was Yolanda's new boyfriend. *Otro pendejo.* He tried to be cool, but something about him I didn't trust. He always looked like he had something else on his mind, like a schemer. But this was my night and I wasn't going to pay him no mind. I was taking my queen out big time for the first time. Our debut. Roll out the red carpet, man, 'cause we was coming through!

When I got to Espy's apartment Dón Ramón wasn't there. He was helping out with something over at the church. All the better. That way he didn't have to see his little girl looking all grown up, ready to hit the town. Doña Carmen let me in and said that Esperanza would be out in a minute. She didn't look too happy. I waited in the living room playin' around with Maritza. She was showing me her new Barbie Doll. Then I heard some footsteps coming down the hallway and turned around to see Lourdes walking towards me with a big smile. Behind her was someone who looked a little like Espy, but at first I wasn't sure.

"*Hola*, Papo."

She was wearing a shiny blue dress that was just long enough to cover her knees. It was a little low cut in the front but not too much. No straps. Her beautiful white shoulders were bare, and she had a black velvet choker with a diamond in the middle wrapped around her neck. It was a fake diamond, but I didn't give a shit, it looked classy anyways. The dress was real tight and I could see the same curves of her body that I remembered checkin' out when we went to the beach. Her hair was rolled up in a *moño* on top of her head, with a couple of curls hanging on the side of her face. For the first time I saw my Espy with makeup on. Her lips were cherry red and she had some light blue eye shadow over her eyes. It wasn't too much, but just enough to make her look like a grown-up, sophisticated woman. If it wasn't for the hard time she was having trying to walk on those high heels, you would never believe she was only sixteen.

"*Cierra la boca*, a cockaroach might fly in." That was Lourdes breaking me out of my spell. I was speechless.

"Well? Do you like it, Papo?" Espy made one of those turns models do in fashion shows. She musta been practicing that all week.

"I, I..., you look beautiful. I can't believe it's you."

"*Gracias*. You look very handsome yourself. *Bien guapo*."

"Thanks." I couldn't take my eyes off her. "These are for you." I handed her the corsage I bought for her. The buzzer from the downstairs door was ringing. That was Johnny letting me know the cab was there.

"Your carriage is waiting, your Highness. Ready to go?"

"But of course." She held out her hand so I could take it, *bien* Grace Kelly-like. Espy was playin' this off real good and enjoying every second of it.

"*Tengan cuidado*," said Doña Carmen. I don't think she was in agreement with Dón Ramón about all this. "*No vengan tarde. Esperanza...!*"

"*Sí*, Mamá. I know. Don't worry." She gave her Moms a kiss. I'm sure the old woman gave Espy one of those mother/daughter lectures on how to act like a proper lady.

We went downstairs to join the others.

The cab dropped us off right in front of Tapestry. It was nine o'clock, and already there was a crowd hangin' by the entrance waiting to get in. I took a quick look and was glad to see that those two bouncers from the other time, G.I. Joe and No-Neck, weren't at the door. Whoever was there probably was cool because people were just walking in easily. Nobody was getting stopped. That was good because only me, Yolanda, and Hector were old enough to be allowed in.

Just as we were heading into the club Hector tells Yolanda, "*Mami*, you go on ahead, I'll meet you inside."

"Why? Where you goin'?" asked Yolanda.

"Nowhere, baby. I gotta see a friend of mine who owes me money. He said he would meet me out here. Go ahead, I'll only be a couple of minutes." Yolanda gave him a look that could kill, but she went inside with us anyway. Of course, she ended up having to pay her own way in. That was chickenshit on his part, but I wasn't gonna let anything mess up my night with Espy. Besides, I knew Yolanda could take care of herself with this turkey.

I walked in arm and arm with Espy. I could feel all eyes turning to check us out. Guys trying to be cool and *disimulado* scoped out Espy real quick, then turned away so as not to disrespect. That was a common move for dudes in the clubs, on the make, looking to see who's alone and who's with somebody. People I knew looked surprised to see me with somebody, since I always went dancing alone. I was hot shit, you know? *Lookout!*

We stood at a spot not far from the bar, next to these poles that held the ceiling up. It was still too early for the band, so the deejay was spinning some records, *Tony Pabon y su Orquesta* I think it was. Espy was so nervous she was holding on to my arm for dear life. Yolanda was kissing people left and right like she knew everybody in the place. I guess they were happy to see her start going out again.

Johnny was just holding Brenda's hand and boppin' his head to the music. He'd hadn't been out much either.

I had just come back from the bar, buying myself and Johnny rum and cokes, and soda for our girls. All of a sudden here comes Hector to join us. Now he was walking with a little more life to him than before, shakin' around like he was ready to start partyin' hearty. He suggested getting a table down by the dance floor, the ones with signs that always said "Reserved", except ain't nobody ever had reservations for them. They was just saving them for people who had money to throw away. The trick with the tables was that if you sat there, you were obligated to buy what they call a *servicio*. This was a tray with a bottle of the liquor of your choice, some cans of Coke and Seven-Up, cups, and a bucket of ice. You make the drinks yourself all night. Only problem was that they charged you $80 dollars for that shit, plus a tip for the waiter even though he wasn't doing *jack* once he brought the tray over. It was a ripoff. Everybody knows a bottle o' Bacardi and a couple of sodas cost only about ten bucks around the 'hood, and you get the cups for free.

Hector was talking about all of us chipping in for a *servicio*. In fact, he thought it was a good idea that one of us buy the first round and he would buy the next. This guy musta thought I was some kind of *bobo*. I told him it wasn't necessary for us to get no *servicio* because that's for people who drank a lot of that hard liquor, and we weren't going to be drinking that much. Especially not the girls. Disappointed, he took Yolanda's hand and went to get their own drinks.

I saw a big sign behind the stage that said they were holding a dance contest that night. First prize was fifty dollars and a free pass for a future date. Couples that wanted to participate had to give their names to the deejay. I showed the sign to Espy and she said no way. She tried to use the excuse that she could barely *walk* in those shoes, much less try to dance in a contest. I went and signed us up anyway. I told her we were going to dance regardless, so what's the difference. It didn't take much to get her to change her mind. After all, it was my birthday, right?

We spent the next couple of hours dancing, goofin' around making fun of each other. Johnny was an okay dancer, better than the other guys on the block. That wasn't really saying much, but he did alright. Espy loosened up and got used to dancing in her high heels. We took it easy at first, I wanted to save all the good stuff for the contest. Yolanda made like she was mad because she wasn't going to have me as her partner for the contest. She was stuck with Jughead. She knew that me and her were a cinch to win. Too bad, I told her, I was spoken for. She faked a grab at my balls and I jumped back. She said "I taught you everything you know, *mamaíto*." Everybody was cracking up.

It was time for the contest to start and all the contestants were told to go out to the dance floor. The deejay announced the names of all the couples so that people could clap for their favorites. The final decision was going to be made by a couple of judges that were picked from the crowd. Regulars, I guess.

Once the contest began, the people who really sucked were told to leave the floor right away to make room for the rest of us. The song they chose was Larry Harlow's *"Abran Paso"*, one of my all-time favorites. The music started and everybody began staking out their spots on the floor, moving around and getting into the rhythm of the song. I knew this one by heart, so I knew when to make certain moves that matched good with the beat. Espy had that confident look on her face, just like I taught her. My girl was a good student. People who weren't in the contest were gathering around the dance floor to get a better look. It was time to go *off*.

We might as well have been on that floor all by ourselves. Me and Espy looked into each other's eyes and felt alone to the world. We began just spinning around together, holding each other tight. At the exact moment when the song changed beat, I spun her out towards the middle of the floor, holding on to her hand. And when I yanked her back towards me she blew me away by doing *two* complete turns - *Pow! Pow!* - with her arms high over her head like Cyd Charisse, landing right in my arms, her face inches from mine. I looked at her bug-eyed as if to say "*Damn*, girl! Where'd you learn *that* shit?!" She smiled real cool-like and I knew there was no *way* we was losin' this contest.

95

Already couples were being told to get off the floor. On one turn I looked over and saw Yolanda walking away *pissed* off, with Hector following behind her holding his hands out like, "Hey, I tried." Poor Yolanda, they had been eliminated right off the bat. She was too good for that. Oh well....

It was down to about four couples, with me and Espy getting the most attention. People were whistling and shouting. Johnny and Brenda weren't in the contest, but I could hear him cheering us the loudest. The song was about half-way through, with the best part yet to come. The deejay called out our names one by one so that people could cheer the ones they liked best. Me and Espy did a couple of double-turn combinations, falling right in step each time. The cheering kept getting louder. The judges told two other couples to leave. Now it was down to us and one other couple. I had seen them before, I think the dude's name was Victor. His partner was his girlfriend. He was one of the best dancers around too. I'd say we were in the same class, except he was older, and he always had his girlfriend for a steady partner. It was a lot easier lookin' good with a steady partner.

The big finale was coming up, the final *descarga*. Listening to the reaction of the people I knew it was gonna be really close. Victor and his girl were smokin', and so were we. I had to do something big to put us over the top. Out of the corner of my eye I noticed a familiar figure. Long and lanky, smooth and doofy at the same time. There was a glow around his afro from the light on the wall behind him. He looked like Jimi Hendricks. *Mi pana* and club partner, Big Ray Rodriguez. He was spraying Binaca in his mouth.

I got his attention and made a little move with my head for him to come over. He caught the sign, palmed his 'fro one more time, and bopped his way over to us. Espy never saw it coming.

In one motion, I spun her around one way, while I turned around the other way and took a step to the side. When Espy came out of her turn, she found herself in the arms of Big Ray. She looked up at him with surprise or horror, take your pick. Without missing a beat, Ray went into his own shit with her and she just went along with it. She looked over at me like she wanted to kill me and I smiled to let her know it was okay. Let's do it! She broke into a smile and went to work.

Ray was pretty good too, it's just that he had a different style than me. But Espy picked up on it easy. He spun her around a couple more times and she landed back in my arms. Then we did some more turns and I spun her back to Ray. It went on back and forth like that. Me and Ray made it look like we were trying to outdo each other to impress her, doing something fancier each time. Espy never missed a step, we were all perfect. Harlow's band was going off with the music and the crowd was going wild.

When the song was over there was no doubt that with Ray's help, me and Espy had won that contest. Even Victor came over to compliment us and ask me for permission to dance with Espy later on. I told him it was cool. Everybody was applauding for the show we all put on. When the deejay went to announce the winner, he declared that only one person deserved the award as the best dancer. That person was....ESPERANZA MALAVE! The judges decided that since Espy did so good with *two* partners, she earned first prize all by herself. Me and Ray had helped each other, so it didn't count. Everybody agreed with that decision and they were clapping and cheering. Espy jumped into my arms and I hugged her tight. We were both so happy. People were slapping me on the back. I was so proud of my baby.

They presented her with the first prize. Espy handed me the free pass so I could put it in my pocket, since her dress didn't have any pockets. Then she used the fifty dollars to buy a round of drinks for our group. She bought drinks for Ray, Victor, and his girlfriend too. We toasted her victory, and my birthday.

We decided to end the night at about two o'clock. Me and Johnny had to have our girls home early. We got a cab outside the club and headed home. We had a really great time that night, bro'.

The cab dropped us off and I walked Espy up to her apartment, safe and sound, just like I promised. Johnny took Brenda home to the building next door. Yolanda and Hector stayed at the club. We got to the front door.

"Thank you for a wonderful time, Papo." She did one last pirouette, right there in the hallway.

"I should thank you. You gave me another perfect birthday. You were great."

"Was I, Papo?"

"Of course you were, *mami*. Didn't you see how all the people were talking about you. You were a star."

"I met so many of your friends there. You know a lot of people, *no?*"

"Ah, those are just people you see all the time when you go out dancing. I don't know them that well."

"*Pues*, I can't wait until we go again, can you?"

"No, baby, I can't wait either. I got the free pass right here in my pocket."

"That's right. Oh, Papo, *te amo*." She gave me a long kiss.

The sound of fifteen locks disturbed the moment.

"*No se preocupe*, Doña Josefa," Espy called out. "It's only us."

Patrolwoman Josefa Sanchez peeked her little head out the door to make sure. Then she closed the door, and all them locks.

I gave Espy one last kiss goodnight. She went inside and I headed across the street. I spent an hour looking out my bedroom window towards her building until I finally fell asleep.

CHAPTER ELEVEN

I was working at the discount store one afternoon about a month after my birthday. I was in the back loading a shipment of garden supplies up on the shelves. From the front of the store I heard somebody come in and bang real hard on the counter with a stick or something, yelling shit like "WHO'S IN CHARGE OF THIS CLUSTERFUCK!" I turned and walked towards the front, picking up a shovel along the way, you know, just in case I had to go upside some stupid nigga's head with it. As soon as I got a clear view of the area by the counter I yelled really loud *"NO ME JODA!"*

There, standing by the counter, was Ricky. And next to him was my boy Louie, all decked out in his fancy Marine dress uniform. I ran to him like a little kid who found his mom after being lost in the woods all night. We jumped into each other's arms and hugged real tight. I didn't care what people thought, this was my boy, MY BOY!

"What the fuck are you doing here, motherfucker! I had you down in them rice paddies in 'Nam, *cagándote en la madre de* Nixon!"

"Nah, boy, not me. They let me come home for a couple of days on leave."

"No shit! Look at you, lookin' all Gomer Pyle an' shit. Check you out." I stepped back while Louie modeled his uniform. He looked *good*. I looked over at Ricky and could see the pride for his big brother was shining all over his face. "When did you get in?"

"This morning. I would have gotten to New York last night, but I had to report to my base first."

"What do you mean, your base?" I was picking at the medals Louie had pinned on his chest, trying to figure out which one was for marksmanship that he had wrote to me about.

"Dig it. I'm stationed at the Philadelphia Naval Yard. That's in Philadelphia."

"In Philadelphia, huh? Like, no shit. What happened to Vietnam? I thought they were pumpin' you up for that shit."

"Can't go."

"Why not? They scared you might hurt somebody? I thought that was the whole idea."

"No, it's not that. Remember my bad knee? The one I hurt running around at the beach with Chico? It got so bad they finally had to check it out. Turns out that all this time I had torn cartilage and ligaments in there."

"Damn, man. How bad was it?"

"Real bad, man. Remember, I never went to the doctor or anything. I just dealt with the pain thinking eventually it would go away. Since I didn't take care of it, it kept ripping up more and more. Jumping on the footlocker didn't help much either. The shit was so torn up that they couldn't sew it back. They had to operate and remove all the cartilage completely. Check it out."

Louie pulled up his pants leg to show me the scars on his knee. His leg looked like a subway map.

"They just took the bandages off this week. My knee is just bone on bone. I'm not even supposed to be walking yet. That's why I got the cane."

"I thought you were making like Patton. So this keeps you from going to Vietnam?"

"Square business. I can't stay on my feet too long, so I can't be depended on out in the field. I'm a little bummed, but I ain't gonna bitch about it. I'd rather have a bad leg than no legs at all."

"So what they gonna have you doin' over there in Philadelphia?"

"The only thing I'm cleared to do is clerical work, supplies, you know, pussy shit like that. They gave me a choice to get out, but I still wanted to do my part for the war."

"John Wayne to the end, right bro'? Hey, man, it's good to see you. Things ain't been the same since you been gone."

"Thanks, man. Too bad I'm only gonna be home a couple o' days. I got to be back in Philly by Monday morning."

"Oh, that gives us enough time. Maybe we can go to the beach."

"Very funny, *maricón*." We hugged again. Seeing Louie made it seem like things could go back to normal again, if that were possible.

"Hey, Louie, why don't you go on home and get out of that costume. I'll ask the boss if I can get out early so we can hook up later on and do something."

"Sounds good to me. Besides, I gotta go find Chico. If it wasn't 'cause he was chasin' me I never would have hurt my leg. I'd be in 'Nam dodgin' bullets right now. I want to give that boy a big kiss, right on the mouth. Where is that *pendejito?*"

"Ey, I'm sure he'll be real happy to see you too." We all laughed.

"Lemme go," said Louie, "I gotta visit some family. Later, bro'." Him and Ricky turned to leave. He was limping real bad.

"Hey, Louie?"

He stopped and turned. "Yeah, Papo?"

"What's a clusterfuck?"

That night we all hung out in front of the stoop, just like the old days. It's funny how one guy can be the difference between old friends staying together with the same routine, or going their separate ways. We spent the next couple of days going around visiting different people. Louie got to New York on a Thursday, so the next day he came with me to school to check up on the fellas we used to hang out with. He dressed up in his uniform again to show off for the girls. He wanted to see some of his teachers too, just to let them know he was alright and that he was planning on taking some courses on base to get his GED. They were happy to hear that, especially since he was only four months short of graduating when he left. School was almost finished for me too, I was graduating in three weeks. I had Espy to thank for that.

On Saturday, we got Big Ray to drive us out to Long Island to visit Lizzie and the twins. Louie bought some stuffed toys for them. My sister went crazy when she saw him. Of all my friends, Louie was always one of her favorites. I think she was the first girl he ever kissed when we was about nine. They always got along real good. He held court while everybody listened to him tell stories of the things they made him do in boot camp. Alberto went out and bought beer for all of us and Lizzie made lunch. We didn't get back to the block until about eight o'clock.

On Monday morning me and Johnny cut school so we could help Louie take his stuff on the subway to Port Authority. He was taking a bus back to Philadelphia. It was great having him around for the weekend and we was sad to see our boy leave again. But we knew he was only a couple of hours away and he would be coming around a lot more now. We dapped and hugged and said our goodbyes. Me and Johnny stayed around until the bus took off. While I was there I noticed a whole bunch of dudes in uniform, coming and going to different places. I wondered how many of them were as lucky as Louie and got stationed so close to home. We hung out for a while on 42nd street, then headed back to the Bronx.

On my way home I thought about going straight to the discount store and put in the hours that I missed over the weekend hangin' with Louie. But I decided to stop by the house to see if Moms needed anything. When I got there she was sitting on the sofa with a real worried look on her face. The TV was on, but she wasn't paying attention to it. I hardly ever saw my Moms nervous about anything. She had been a rock when Chico's mother was sick. But now she didn't look too good.

"*Que pasa, mamá?* You burned Pops' toast again?"

She just looked at me real sad.

"*El cartero ya llegó.* There is something for you, a letter from the Department of the Army."

I went to the kitchen where we usually kept the mail. Right there on top of the pile was a yellow envelope. It was addressed to Eduardo J. Torres, that's me. "Department of the Army, Selective Service Division" was printed on the top. I remember feeling all the blood rush out of my face. For a minute I thought of not opening the letter, that maybe that would save me from what I knew was inside. I could see my hands shaking as I held it.

Finally, I took a deep breath. Let's see what Uncle Sam has to say to me. Maybe he wants to thank me for showing Louie a good time over the weekend. I opened it slowly. The words were clear and simple.

"In accordance with Article IV of the United States Code of Civil Defense, you are hereby instructed to report to Fort Hamilton, Brooklyn, to begin the induction process into the United States Armed Forces. You will report to the Post Processing Center at 0800 hours on the morning of July 2, 1970. Failure to report will result in you being designated absent from your assigned duty, and you will be apprehended and prosecuted to the full extent of the law, as authorized by Congress and the President of the United States of America."

What a kick in the ass. My number had come up. If I'da known this I would've gotten on the bus to Philly with Louie and saved my subway token back home.

Once Moms knew for sure what the letter was about she started crying, even though she was trying hard not to. I tried to play it off and be cool.

"Check this out, Moms. Nixon figured he can't win that war without me. He knows I'm bad. He needs me."

"*Hay, mi hijo. Dios te bendiga.*"

to meet up with everybody at Orchard Beach over the summer. This was it, and life would never be the same.

It finally came down to the day before I was supposed to leave. Some sergeant from the base was coming to pick me up the next morning and personally drive me and a couple of other dudes to Brooklyn. That way nobody could use the excuse that they got stuck in the subway and couldn't make it. I made my rounds of goodbyes, starting with Mr. Kohler at the store. He gave me some advice about working hard, just like I had done for him. He said he would say a special prayer for me at the next *minion*.

From there I passed by Dón Marco's *bodega*. He told me he was proud of me and promised to send me some cans of *Goya* food so I can show all my buddies from around the country what good Puerto Rican food is. I said goodbye to Ricky and he shook my hand real tight. That kid was getting strong like his brother, probably from all the work he did for Dón Marco.

We didn't have a big hangout party the night before I left like we did for Louie. Chico and Johnny came over to the house for dinner. Moms was making my favorite dish of rice and beans, *chuletas fritas*, and *tostones*. Lizzie and 'Berto came over with the twins, so did Yolanda and Hector. He looked like he was already high on something when he got there. Pops was there, but all he did was stare at the TV all night. I guess he didn't know what else to do. Of course, Espy was by my side the whole day. I don't think she smiled once the whole time.

Everybody was wishing me well, telling me to be careful. Johnny was making jokes, trying to put everybody in a better mood. He said "Don't be no hero, Papo, 'cause a hero ain't nothin' but a sandwhich". He must've heard that from somewhere else. Nobody got it anyway. Chico took out the baseball bat that Benny got on Bat Day at Yankee Stadium and said "Hey, Papo, it ain't too late. Let me give you a good whack on the knee!" Everybody laughed and that made us relax. I was fine. It was everybody else who was worried. It should've been the other way around, right?

When the night was over I walked Espy back to her apartment. When Dón Ramón heard me at the door he called me inside, he wanted to talk to me. Espy waited for me in the kitchen while I sat in the living room with her father.

"*Pues, hijo*, you are leaving tomorrow, eh?"

"*Si, señor*. They are coming to pick me up at 6:30 in the morning."

"How do you feel? Are you ready?"

"Well, sir, if I had my choice I would rather stay here and make your daughter happy."

He laughed a little. "Don't worry. There will be plenty of time for that. You are both still young. Listen, Papo...." He called me Papo for the first time in a long time. "I want to thank you for the respect you have showed my daughter since you first met her. I know in the beginning I was very strict with her, very careful. Someday you will understand that a daughter is the most precious gift God can give to a man. It creates a special love you will never find anywhere else. At the same time, the biggest fear a father has is that someday a man will come along and want to take that little girl away from him. Fathers pray that when that man does comes along, that he is a man of honor and respect. We hope that this man, this man who dares to come and rip our hearts away, is a man who will love and cherish our little flowers as much as we do.

Me? I have been blessed three times with three beautiful daughters. But at the same time, my fear and worries are multiplied three times over. It is enough to make me old before my time. Fortunately, my Esperanza has been lucky enough to meet a young man like you. Hard working, intelligent, brave, devoted to his friends and family, as well as to her. Even though you are both very young, I am happy that in you she is learning at a young age what a good man is. There is still plenty of time for you to think about building a life together. Papo, you are a good man. I thank you for proving that to me each day since the first time you walked through that door."

"Thank you, sir. I care for Esperanza very much."

"Yes, I can see that. I have a going-away present for you."

Dón Ramón reached into his jacket and pulled out a small pocket Bible. The New Testament.

"I want you to take this with you wherever you go. If you can take some time to read it, I'm sure it will give you the peace and guidance you will need to get you through this very difficult journey. I have selected a very special passage for you. I wrote it down on the inside cover. You don't have to read it now. But as soon as you can, take a look at it. *Cuídate, muchacho. Y que vaya con Dios.*"

"*Muchas gracias*, Dón Ramón. Thank you very much. I will carry this Bible with me always. I feel like it will protect me."

"*Espero que si, hijo. Espero que si.*"

I went to say my last goodbye to Espy. She was in the kitchen, already crying her eyes out. I took her by the hand and led her back outside to the front stoop. I turned to face her. For the first time I was crying too.

"How am I supposed to live without you, Papo?"

"Don't worry, *nena*, I'll be back before you know it. We'll have that big wedding we been planning and invite all our friends and relatives."

"You promise?"

"I promise. You just wait for me. I love you, Espy." She said she loved me, too.

We hugged for what seemed like forever. I finally had to let go and go home to bed. It was almost midnight. We kissed one last time, and I turned around and walked slowly across the street. Climbing up the stoop, I looked back towards her building. She was still standing there, still crying. I blew her a kiss, and then went inside.

Before I went to sleep I took out the Bible that Dón Ramón had just given me. Inside the front cover he had written "Timothy II, 1-13". Espy had taught me how to look things up in the Bible, so I flipped through the pages until I got to that part. I've read it so many times over the years that I know it by heart. It said:

"So, my son, be strong in the grace that Christ Jesus gives. Everything that you have heard me teach in public you should in turn entrust to reliable men, who will be able to pass it on to others.

Put up with your share of hardship as a loyal soldier in Christ's Army. Remember: 1. That no soldier on active service gets himself entangled in business, or he will not please his commanding officer; 2. A man who enters an athletic contest wins no prize unless he keeps the rules laid down; 3. Only the man who works on the land has the right to the first share of its produce. Consider these three illustrations of mine and the Lord will help you to understand all that I mean."

There were so many people processing in at one time that we had to wait hours for everything we had to do. Still they made us run to each station. There's an old Army saying, "Hurry up and wait." That was us. There were long lines for everything. When we finally got the chance to eat lunch, we had to wait an hour on line in the mess hall. I knew not to expect no rice and beans, but the shit they gave us was awful, man. Cold mashed potatoes that tasted like cardboard, and dried-up meat loaf. I asked the guy next to me if these people didn't believe in salt. He said he heard that instead of salt, they put something called 'salt-peter' in the food. That was something that was supposed to keep your dick from getting hard so you wouldn't be getting all *bellaco* while you were in training. I didn't see any women around anyways, so it didn't matter to me. Besides, I was set on waiting to bust my nut for the big night with Espy, whenever *that* was going to be.

We were there a whole day before it was my group's turn to get our haircuts. I'd seen those other guys marching around with their heads all bald an' shit. They looked like a bunch of *Mr. Cleans*, all marching in a row. I wondered how I was going to look without my famous shiny, black hair.

They did everything in alphabetical order, so I had to wait a while for my turn. When I finally sat in the chair the barber, a soldier himself, says "What'll it be, one, two, or three inches?" I asked him what he meant by that. He said "How long do you want your hair to be, one, two, or three inches?" I thought "Bet!" I get to choose how long I wanted my hair to stay! I didn't want to look like a *Mr. Clean*, so I says "Make it three inches."

Next thing I heard was the sound of the electric razor humming up against my head. In thirty seconds this asshole shaved every bit of hair off my head. Three inches, my ass. I heard him laugh, like "Got me another sucker!" When I got up I caught some of my hair before it fell to the floor and put it in my pocket. My head ain't never been that clean, not even when I was born. Even though it was July I felt a cool draft. I got back in line with the rest of the guys. They were rubbing up their heads and goofin' on each other. I didn't want to

112

touch mine, much less look at myself in the mirror. I finally put my hand on my head and all I felt was stubble. I promised myself I was never gonna let Espy see me looking like this.

It took another day before we finally got our fatigue uniforms. For two days we had to wear the same clothes, even our underwear. They gave us ten minutes each night to take a shower, and we had to put the same clothes back on. It was nasty, bro. Once we got our fatigues - which didn't fit right, by the way - they gave us each a box so we could put our civilian clothes in and send them home. They said we wouldn't be needing those clothes anytime soon. They had a guy from supply come in and collect all the boxes after we put our addresses on them. They would mail them home for us.

I took my hair, which was still in my pocket, and put it in a separate envelope in the box. I figured Moms would get a kick out of it, maybe even keep it as a souvenir. But she wrote me and told me that it scared the shit outta her, she thought it was a rat. I shoulda put a note.

Louie was right about the way they woke people up in the morning, with all the screaming and noise. I thought the building was on fire. You know how sometimes in the morning, when you're groggy, you can't really tell where you are right away? Some of these guys must've forgotten they was in the Army because they didn't get up at first. They tried to roll over and cover their heads with their pillows. These dudes ended up on the floor when Drill Sergeants picked up their mattresses right up over them. That cement floor was cold and hard, Jack. I made it a point to jump out of my rack as soon as I heard them coming down the hallway. I wondered when these Drill Sergeants ever slept. They were there at night to make sure we were in bed, and they were already dressed and ready to go when they woke us up in the morning. I thought, "Don't these *pendejos* got families?"

We never got a break from anything from that point on. From the moment you wake up at 4:30 in the morning to the time they turned out the lights at nine o'clock, every minute was planned. If we weren't running and doing exercises, we were picking up paper and cigarette butts off the ground. That's when I realized why the fort was so clean all the time. I didn't smoke, so it kinda pissed me off having to pick up butts. But I knew better than to complain.

They had us running like three or four miles every morning, right off the jump-street. Some of these guys were so out of shape you could tell they never ran more than half a block before in their lives. You ever try running four miles with combat boots on? They's a lot heavier than the "Cons" I wore back on the block.

Before we were allowed to eat we had to cross over this long horizontal ladder hanging outside the mess hall, like the ones you see in the monkey bars in the park. Hand over hand, one time across and one time back. If you couldn't do it you had to go back to the end of the line and start all over. My hands got blisters that peeled off and started bleeding. You think they cared about that shit? Hell no. Each week we had to do it more and more, two times, then three times, and so on. You either got stronger, or you starved.

For the first time in my life I got to meet people from other parts of the country. In my company we had dudes from North Carolina, Ohio, even this one cowboy from Texas. It was the first time they met any "Porto Reecans", too. That's how they pronounced it, "Porto Reecans". They kept saying they had to be careful with us because we always carried knives. I said "Whatta you think this is, 'West Side Story' or some shit?" I started hanging with some Ricans from New York. There was Angel Martinez from the Lower East Side, Ralfy Rosado from Bushwick, in Brooklyn, and a couple of other guys, I can't remember their names now. We never really had time to hang out because we was always busy training. And them fuckin' Drill Sergeants didn't want us together anyways because they didn't want us talking Spanish. They figured we was talkin' shit about them and they couldn't understand. They said we's in America now, leave that "*Kay Pasa*" shit back home. These ignorant jerkoffs didn't want to believe that we was born and raised right here in the good ol' U.S.A.

Once we got used to the routine of basic training it wasn't so bad. The hardest thing for me was going to sleep at nine o'clock. The last time I went to bed that early was when I was, like, five years old. I laid in my bunk thinking that back home even Benny was still up watching TV at that time. And then getting up the next day at four thirty was a bitch too. But after about a week my body got used to it. I learned how to catch a snooze with my head staying straight up without nodding in classroom sessions. You didn't want to get caught sleeping, 'cause if you did they'd make you stand up in front of the class next to the instructor for the rest of the session. That shit was embarrassing. And if that wasn't bad enough, they'd make everybody else run an extra mile.

With all that running around, and carrying heavy equipment on our backs all day, I was ready to jump into bed at eight. But that stuff helped me, man. I was doing sit-ups, push-ups, climbing ropes, hand-to-hand combat. All kinds of crazy shit. I was pumped up. You see me all skinny now, but back then I was solid, man. They drilled all that fighting shit in us and we swore that NO-body was gonna fuck with us. We was ready to go kick ass anywhere they wanted to send us.

The only thing I had trouble with was shooting. I couldn't shoot for shit. They trained us on M-16 rifles. These things looked like toys, but they could fuck you up if you got shot by one of 'em. They took us out to the rifle range every other day to practice shooting at different targets. The targets were these plastic boards shaped like humans. They would pop up at different distances, like the enemy when he jumps out at you. When you see one pop up, you shoot it. If you hit the target, it would fall back down and then you wait for another one to pop up. Real easy, right?

I was pretty good with the ones up close, about twenty-five yards away. But as they popped up further and further away, I would shoot and nothing happened. They stayed standing. I could swear I saw some of these targets standing out there laughing at me while I shot round after round at them, missing every time. I'd get so pissed off I felt like running out there and beating the shit out of them with the butt of my rifle. *Tóma, puñeta! Don't fuck with me, I'm from the Bronx!* I thought I was going nuts. How Louie ever got a marksmanship medal, I'll never know.

At first they sent me to get glasses, thinking maybe I couldn't see that far. But they issued me these black-rimmed glasses that made me look like a Puerto Rican Clark Kent. I said fuck that, I looked doofy enough with that haircut. So I kept trying, day after day, but it was no use. And I had to learn quick because I wouldn't get through basic training if I didn't pass the shooting tests.

It got to the point that when they started testing I tried to get out of it by volunteering for KP, working in the mess hall. Washing all those nasty pots and pans was bad, but at least I didn't have to get embarrassed by being the last dude on the rifle range trying to hit a target 500 yards away. They didn't fall for that shit, though. I still had to take the test, even after I did the KP. I washed all those pots for nothing.

Lucky for me that the guys they had scoring us on the tests weren't Drill Sergeants. They was just regular soldiers who happened to be stationed at Dix. I saw one dude that looked pretty cool, so I managed to get in the line where he was at. When my turn was next I asked him, kidding around at first, how much it would take for him to pass me regardless of how I scored. Without even taking his eyes off the guy ahead of me, he says "Ten dollars." We had just gotten paid, so I took a ten dollar bill out of my pocket and folded it in my hand, *guillaito,* of course. I didn't want the both of us to get busted. When it was my turn to shoot, he came over to make sure I was in the proper shooting position and took the ten dollars out of my hand.

After wasting all my ammunition, not hitting shit, he handed me my scorecard and congratulated me for passing the test. No other words were spoken. It wasn't a high score, we didn't want to make the sergeants suspicious when I turned in my card. But I passed. I didn't care that this wasn't gonna help me much if I got sent to 'Nam, but I figured I would worry about that some other time. I just wanted to get through this basic training bullshit. I wondered if that's how Louie got his medal too.

When we first got to Fort Dix they made us fill out these cards with the address of our company so we could send them home to our families. That's how they would know where we were. No more than a week later I got my first letter from Espy. She went on and on about how she missed me and wished she could come to New Jersey to visit me. Soon after that I was getting letters and cards from her every day. Guys were goofin' on me at Mail Call because it never failed that my name was called each and every day, sometimes two or three times. Mostly it was Espy sending me letters, but Moms and Chico wrote me too. My sister Elizabeth also wrote me once while I was at Dix.

But my favorite letter was the one that Espy sent along with a picture of herself sitting on a swing in the schoolyard near the block. I kept that picture taped on the inside of my locker in the barracks. I showed it off to my homies and they said she was *fine*. After the first week we were given more free time at night to write home, so I used that time to write to Espy and tell her everything I was doing. I built it up a little to try to impress her. I wanted her to be proud of me, maybe even get hot for me, her very own U.S. Army soldier man.

A lot of the guys were talking about Vietnam because that's what the Drill Sergeants kept talkin' about. Some guys were ready to go and kick some ass, other guys were shitting in their pants about it. I didn't care either way. I felt like Louie did, whatever happens, happens. Most of the Drill Sergeants had already been to 'Nam, so they was already a little crazy. I guessed that's why they screamed at us so much. Still, they said that we shouldn't worry because Nixon was in the process of bringing the troops home and that not many more were going to be sent back over there. They said that out of about a hundred and fifty guys in our company, maybe only ten of us would be sent. The rest would be staying stateside. They must've said that to calm us down and keep those pussies who might've been thinking about cuttin' out to stick around.

Towards the end of basic training six weeks later they got us all together in a classroom and passed out these forms. I didn't know what this was all about since I thought we had already given them all the important information about ourselves. An Army lawyer came in from JAG to explain it to us. Those forms were our last will and testament. We each had to make out a will and the lawyer had to witness and notarize them.

That story about only ten of us being sent to Vietnam was bullshit, man. On graduation day, the day we should all have been proud and happy over having completed training, we got our orders. We were all being shipped to the war.

They gave us a choice whether we wanted to take two weeks off to go home on leave, or report straight to 'Nam. I decided I didn't want go through another tearful goodbye with Espy and the family, so I told them I was ready to go right away. The next day I was landing in Travis Air Force Base in California to wait for the flight that would take me to rice paddie country. The fun was about to begin.

CHAPTER THIRTEEN

The flight from California to Japan took eleven hours. I was sitting for so long I lost all feeling in my legs. Even my ass was numb. I swear if I farted I wouldn't have known it until the smell hit me. Since so many of us were going at one time, they crammed us into a military transport plane the whole way. Most of the guys spent the time sleeping, other guys were too nervous to even move. I was hoping that once we got to 'Nam they would give us some time to freshen up a bit before sending us out to the jungle to kill anybody. Dig it, bro', I was still taking it as a goof.

There was a group of guys on the plane who had been to Vietnam before and were on their way back. Some had volunteered for a second tour, others had been home on emergency leave and were coming back. Those guys were relaxed enough that they spent the time telling jokes and playing "Tonk". I thought them dudes who volunteered to go back must've been crazy, man. Or maybe Vietnam made them crazy, who knows.

Angel and Ralfy, my buddies from boot camp, chose to go home on leave before shipping out. I never heard from them again after we said our goodbyes at Fort Dix, so I don't know if they survived the war or got blown away somewhere in the sticks. For all I know they could have lost themselves in New York and said fuck it. I know they joked about doing that shit all the time, but I didn't think they was serious because they both did pretty good in basic training.

After sitting around the Okinawa Airport for like five hours, we boarded another plane headed for hell. That trip took two more hours. I should've been real tired by then, but the excitement of what was waiting for us kept me up. As we headed for the landing, everybody crowded around the windows checking out what we were getting ourselves into. I was looking for explosions or fires, *something*. That's what you expect to see when there's a war going on, right? I didn't see nothing, though. In fact, it looked like we were flying into some tropical island, like what Puerto Rico must look like from what Espy told me.

The pilot was playing around over the loudspeaker, saying shit like "Welcome to the beautiful Republic of Vietnam, where the temperature is a humid 85 degrees, with light to moderate ground fire." Funny guy.

To say that it was a 'humid 85 degrees' was like saying that Nat King Cole had a suntan. When I stepped out of the plane in Da Nang Airport and caught my first whiff of Vietnam, I almost fell to my knees. Imagine yourself walking into a huge wall of hot toilet water. You didn't breathe the air, it smacked you in the face. It made that dump in City Island smell like a walk through a rose garden. It was late August, 1970, the dead of summer. I hoped they had air-conditioning in them tents. I was sweating by the time I got to the bottom of the stairs from the plane.

We walked across the tarmac towards the trucks that were going to drive us to our assignment. Most of us new "boots" thought that once we got off the plane we would have to run around looking for cover to keep from getting shot up. We expected them Viet Cong to be in the bushes all around us, layin' for our ass. Instead, it was pretty calm and we were able to take our time with our gear. I had a chance to look around at the rice fields and mountains in the distance. All I could think of was that this was going to be home for the next thirteen months.

I saw my first Vietnamese working in the rice paddies, they were wearing those funny little triangle hats to protect them from the sun. I thought of Chico's *pava* at the beach. The civilians weren't paying no mind to us, they were going about their business as if we weren't even there. From what I heard from the Vets on the plane, they didn't want us there. Hey, all they had to do was say the word and I woulda gladly hopped back on that plane and said "Later!" It made me wonder for the first time why we were there. It seemed like these people didn't give a fuck one way or another. You know what? Neither did I.

I was sent to the 90th Replacement Battalion near this town called Bien Hoa. I was made an infantryman, a "grunt". On the ride from Da Nang to Bien Hoa I looked out the truck and saw that we were being followed by helicopters. They were escorting us in case some shit broke out. Machinegunners were hanging over the side of the choppers ready to blow Charlie away. I thought that could have been a cool job, but just thinking about hanging out an open door 250 feet in the air made me want to throw up. I decided it was better to keep m'damn feet on the ground.

We got to the camp around lunchtime. Me and the other boots were just coming out of basic training. We was all spit-shined and strack. You could cut your finger on the creases in my pants from all the starch I had on them. That's the way we always had to be around Fort Dix, or else we'd get in trouble. Now I looked around and these dudes looked like a bunch of bums dressed in mud. Some guys had their shirtsleeves cut off at the shoulder, makin' them look tough. That didn't seem like a bad idea in that fucking August afternoon heat. Other guys were wearing Australian bush caps, with the brim bent up on one side. They wore that instead of a helmet. Fuck that. I wasn't taking NO chances, my helmet wasn't comin' off my head for shit.

Forget about shined boots. These dudes looked like they shined their boots with red slop. It's like nobody gave a fuck what they looked like and nobody said anything either. What asshole was gonna come out to the boonies and give a guy a hard time about being clean? There were more important things to worry about. Like stayin' alive. I wondered why they made such a big deal about it at boot camp.

There were ten other guys besides me arriving at the camp on that day. We barely hopped off the truck when about eight other guys that looked like they been to hell and back jumped on, throwin' what little personal shit they had in the back. Their tour was done and they were on their way home. We were replacing them. These guys were going straight from the camp to Da Nang, then on to the states. They weren't even going to stop to change their uniforms. It's like they felt if they stayed a minute longer to clean up, it might be their last. I did a quick calculation and noticed that eleven of us were arriving as replacements, but only eight of them were on the truck ready to leave. I asked the driver about the remaining three guys, were they running late? He said they had already left the night before. In bags.

Holy shit. Welcome to Vietnam.

The Top Sergeant told me to drop my gear off in this big tent near the motor pool, then I could get on line for chow. As soon as word got out that a new boot from New York had arrived at camp - a Puerto Rican at that - guys there came by to check me out. Just like basic training. Homies always looked for each other. There were five of them. Two brothers - Lipscomb and Jenkins, and three Ricans - Frankie Garcia, David Velez, and a guy they just called "Chito". He looked a little crazy to me. But then again, everybody there had a strange look in their eyes.

This camp was a permanent base, even though it was nothing but a bunch of big tents with dirt floors. It was there that everybody lived most of the time and from where we would be sent out to set up temporary bases. I thought, damn, if this was a permanent base, I'd hate to see what the temporary base looked like. It was probably just a bunch of tired soldiers leaning up against a tree. The shower tent, which by now was calling my name, was off to the side next to a water buffalo that pumped water in through rubber tubes. The biggest tent belonged to the brass. They had their shit filled with radio equipment for relaying messages back and forth between the patrols out in the perimeter and the generals giving orders in the safety of the rear. It must've been easy for those two-star pussies to order young men out into battle from where they sat. From there, they didn't have to worry about being hit.

Lunch was some roast beef and more mashed potatoes. Now I know why they served us so much mashed potatoes in boot camp. It was all part of training, to get us used to the shit we'd be getting every day in 'Nam. I couldn't wait for Dón Marco's first shipment of *Goya* beans to get there. That's if he could find my ass. The way I saw it, I was in the *cúlo* of the world. Not even Columbus could discover me here.

I got my food and looked for a place to sit, a picnic table or something. I noticed that except for a few small groups, each guy was off on his own, eating separately from one another. I thought, "don't these dudes get along?" Then I remembered that they made us do that in boot camp when we trained out in the field. Whenever we were standing around not doing much, we had to keep a distance from each other. The logic behind that was that if the enemy dropped a mortar or grenade in the area, it would only get one or two guys. If everybody was hanging around bunched up together, one little hand grenade could wipe out a whole platoon. I should have taken more notes. Now it made sense, this shit was for real.

I picked a spot under a shade tree to sit down and eat. The first guy to come over was Frankie Garcia. He was a shit-talking *títere* from the Bronx, but he looked right at home out here in the jungle. He was from Gun Hill Road, not too far from where I grew up. Even though we were homies, he didn't get all emotional over meeting me. I mean, he was happy to hear about stuff going on back home, but he seemed more interested in teaching me about what to expect out there. He was lookin' out, just like a buddy should.

Frankie only had a couple more months left in-country, then he was heading home. He didn't seem all that anxious about that, which surprised me. I was only there two hours and I was all ready to pack it in and call it a day. But he said he didn't have much family back in the Bronx. Besides, the only reason he was in 'Nam was because a judge gave him a choice: Five years for Grand Theft Auto, or two years in the service. He said he been to jail already, done that. But he ain't never saw Southeast Asia before. So he took the offer as a way to travel, see the world. I looked at him and thought, "this motherfucker was crazy before he even got here."

Frankie introduced me to Velez, Lipscomb, and Jenkins. Unless you had a nickname, everybody called each other by their last names. I was Torres, or "T". I didn't want to mention any of that "Papo Salsa" crap. I was in a different world now. How good I danced didn't mean shit to these rats. They waited until I finished my food, then Jenkins took out this bomb of a joint. These days you might call it a spliff or a blunt. I panicked.

"Man, put that thing away! Top is right over there, he's gonna see it."

They all looked at me and broke out laughing. I just kept looking around, scared that the Top Sergeant was coming over.

"Man, relax, dude," said Jenkins with a giggle.

"Relax? I don't want to get in no trouble. I just got here."

"Man, nothing's gonna happen. Here, take a puff. You *do* get high, don't you?" He held that bat out in front of me. I had my first Vietnam flashback, and it wasn't of a battle. It was of big-assed Cookie.

Lipscomb spoke up, "Shee-it, he's *got* to get high. He's from the Bronx. Everybody in the Bronx smokes weed."

I kept looking around.

"You gonna take this? My arm's getting tired."

"We gonna do this here, out in the open?"

"No, man, we're gonna go to the bathroom behind the gymnasium. Fuckin'-A, we gonna do this here."

"What about Top? Or the Lieutenants?" I was being a real punk.

"Top? Man, who do you think *sold* us this shit?"

The look on my face made them bust out laughing some more. I could tell this wasn't going to be the first joint they smoked that day, and it was only one-thirty in the afternoon. I grabbed the joint from Jenkins and took a deep drag. It was good shit, let me tell you. After we passed it around a few more times, I leaned back against the tree and looked up at the sky. Maybe this Vietnam gig might not be so bad after all.

I spent the rest of the day meeting the other men in my company. I also had to be briefed by the lieutenants so they could explain to me what their mission was there. They threw a lotta shit at me that I had to learn right away, and being already fucked up on some crazy pot I never tried before wasn't making it any easier. I couldn't wait for the mess tent to open up again. I was getting hungry.

I was told that I was lucky because by now the strategy for winning the war had changed. In the sixties, the United States thought they could fight the war the same way they fought World War One and Two. That was to send thousands of infantry ground troops out on reconnaissance patrols until they met up with the enemy troops, and then just duke it out. Whoever was left standing won the battle. That formula worked before and we always won.

But these Vietnamese were smarter than people thought. They knew they couldn't match up with the kind of technological firepower that the United States had. They understood that there was no way they could win going *mano-a-mano* with the great United States Armed Forces. So they used the two things they had to their advantage: Fierce nationalistic pride for their country, and the knowledge of their own land. These people weren't afraid to fight to their deaths for the land of their fathers and ancestors. There was nothing they wouldn't do, no sacrifice too great. Women, children, old people. Everybody did their part. They just weren't scared of shit.

So instead of coming out and fighting us straight up, they hid in the jungles until the right time. Then, BAM! They would strike quick, and then run back into the jungle. They knew those jungles like I knew the alleyways back on the block. There were hidden trails up in there that to this day we could never find. They also had underground tunnels that took them from position to position, and even from village to village. No matter how much the U.S. tried to get them to come out and fight in the open, they wouldn't bite. Most of the time they struck at night, when we least expected it. Before we knew what the fuck was going on, they had done the damage and were gone.

By the time them geniuses in Washington figured it out, we had lost thousands of men. Soldiers would be out on patrol, looking for some action, and walk right into ambushes they never saw coming. I heard stories where they would come across a little kid with a shoebox, maybe eight or nine years old, offering to *"shine G.I. shoe, one dallah"*. To give the kid a break, suckers would stop to get their boots shined. It was only a dollar, what could it hurt? Before the kid got to the second boot, the shoebox, the kid, and any G.I. within ten yards would get blown up to bits. It got to the point where you couldn't trust anybody over there, no matter how innocent they looked.

When I got to 'Nam they weren't sending ground troops out to fight much anymore. Maybe to get intelligence, you know, spy on the bad guys, but that was it. The war was being fought from the air. That's why they began calling Vietnam the "Chopper War". Helicopters called "Jolly Green Giants", Sikorsky HH-3's, would fly around and destroy whole areas of the jungle if we thought some VC were hiding in there. Gunships and fighter planes fired fifty caliber bullets that could rip your arm off by just nicking you. You heard of Napalm, bro'? That was a kind of jelly-like shit that we'd fire at them from the planes. Once that jelly was exposed to air, the oxygen would make it ignite into a burst of fire that could wipe out entire villages with just one blast. That Napalm was a motherfucker.

Basically, what my company was assigned to do was support the Air Force. We'd tell them where the enemy was and they would go in and fuck 'em up from the sky. When they needed more firepower, rounds, supplies, and shit like that, they'd get it from us. We hardly had to go out and engage Charlie head on. Of course, if they came around the camp we had to be ready to take care of business. But I was told they only came around at night to piss us off.

Sometimes we had to send out rescue patrols to look for pilots who got shot down on a mission. That's the only time it got dangerous going out into the jungle. You never knew what kind of booby trap was out there. When they told me that, I hoped I wouldn't get picked to do that too often.

That night, after chow, we gathered around in our bunkers to get high and talk more shit. As a new guy I had to do guard duty on the perimeter for a couple of hours, but I had to be accompanied by a veteran. Frankie volunteered to go out with me. The whole compound was surrounded by strands of barbwire and constertina, which was the same thing as barbwire but the points were sharper. Frankie said that when he first got to 'Nam, every morning they would find at least three or four dead VC hanging on this wire. They would try to sneak in at night and attack us, but the guards would pick 'em off before they got too far. They did this every night. Stupid sons-of-bitches.

Once nightime came around I couldn't believe how dark it got. I couldn't see my hand in front of my face. Back home we had streetlights everywhere, so it never really got that dark. But in 'Nam, it was pitch black and scary like a motherfucker. From far away I could hear the sounds of artillery fire. Somebody was getting their ass kicked tonight, I thought.

Me, Velez, Frankie, and Chito smoked our last joint after my guard shift was over. No VC tried to jump the fence that night. My first day and I'd been high practically since the moment I jumped off the truck that afternoon. I was hoping the whole Army wasn't like this, or we'd never win this thing. When the joint was squashed, Frankie and Chito decided to head into town to get some more smoke, and maybe get themselves a hoochie-girl. That was a Vietnamese prostitute. They wanted me to come along to pop my Vietnam cherry, but I said no thanks. I didn't want no part of that *bacalao*-smelling gook shit. Besides, I was going to be faithful to my Espy no matter how hard up I got. Frankie said that was cool and headed out the door, telling me he would see me at breakfast the next morning.

Before he left he said "Hey, Torres. Tomorrow, at breakfast, *cuidado con el visco.*"

"*El visco*? What're you talking about?"

Both him and Chito laughed. Too many people were laughing at me since I got there. It was making me mad.

Frankie said, "*El visco, tén cuidado.* You'll see."

I was too fucked up to care what he was talking about, so I just waved him away and went to sleep.

The next morning I was one of the first to get up for breakfast. I washed up with water I poured into my helmet. It was the first time I was out in the open without it on my head. I made my way to the mess tent and got on a short line. There was a different crew cooking and serving the food at breakfast than there was the day before. They worked different shifts.

I was waiting on line for my turn and I could hear this nasty sounding voice of one of the cooks, asking people in line ahead of me "How do you want your eggs?" You could get your eggs scrambled, fried sunny-side up, or fried hard. I already decided I wanted my eggs scrambled, and waited until it was my turn. I was still a little sleepy. That smoke had knocked me out.

"How do you want your eggs?" I waited for the guy in front of me to answer.

"How do you want your eggs?" The nasty-voiced cook was looking at the guy in front of me and I could tell he was getting a little annoyed, but the guy in line wasn't saying anything. I wished he would hurry up and decide, I was hungry.

"MOTHERFUCKER! HOW DO YOU WANT YOUR EGGS, GODDAMMIT!!" The cook kept staring at the guy in front of me, but the guy still wasn't answering. There were some eggs frying on the grill, but I thought they were for the guys further up.

"LISTEN, YOU PISS-ANT NEWBIE COCKSUCKER! I'M TALKING TO YOU! HOW DO YOU WANT YOUR EGGS, YOU SHITHEAD?!?" The cook was almost foaming at the mouth. I looked around to see what was the problem. I heard people around me laughing again. Damn.

Then I realized. The cook, the meanest son-of-a-bitch in the whole camp, was talking to ME! I thought he was looking at the guy in front of me. The COOK was *"El Visco"!* This guy had to be the most cross-eyed dude I'd ever seen in my life. Fuckin' Frankie. This is what he was telling me to watch out for the night before.

My biggest mistake was looking around to see who this cook was talking to. I shouldn't have done that. That offended him and really pissed him off. I thought I had gotten yelled at and cursed out in boot camp by the Drill Sergeants, but this *cabrón* called me every name in the book, even some I never even heard before. It was the first time I heard the word "Goat-Fucker". People do that, bro'? Maybe where he comes from, the fat fuckin' redneck.

I was getting a little upset at the way this dude was carrying on. I was ready to jack him up. Finally he told me I wasn't getting shit for breakfast and to get my spic ass off the line. He was a Sergeant First Class, a crazy motherfucker on his third tour in-country. He outranked me, and nobody else fucked with him. That's why he was a cook. Even HE was too dangerous out in the field with a weapon. Believe it or not, bro', I had to get off the line without breakfast. By now the whole tent was filled with guys laughing at me. I was the new guy, the biggest joke of the whole day. I didn't hear the end of it.

Good thing by lunchtime that cock-eyed *loco* had finished his shift and gone back to bed. I didn't want to run into him again.

CHAPTER FOURTEEN

There wasn't much static around camp for the first few weeks I was there. I was learning the routine of being in-country, getting used to living in bunkers and dealing with the dirty conditions. Breakfast was still a problem with *"El Visco"*, but most of the time I had a buddy bring me bread or something. Sometimes I just didn't eat at all. I didn't have to worry much about being clean either. It was more important to have my weapon clean than my body. Even a little speck of dirt could cause the M-16 to jam, and you didn't want that shit happenin' at the wrong time, like in the middle of a firefight with the Viet Cong comin' at you.

They sent me out on a few patrols when I first got there. When reports came in that the VC might be in the area we'd send people out to try and find them. Most of the time we tried *not* to find them so we could go back to base without any problems. They knew where we were, and we knew they were out there. But as long as nobody fucked with each other, everything was cool and we could all go home in one piece.

Frankie was showing me things to look out for in the jungle, the kind of shit you only learned with experience. They didn't teach you everything in basic training. The VC were good guerilla fighters, which meant surprise ambushes, booby traps, and snipers. Even though things were quiet, I knew it was only a matter of time before I got my first taste of action.

Some of the guys were getting restless because nothing was going down. They said that when things got too quiet for too long it meant Charlie was planning something big. That's why we still had to go out on patrol all the time, to try and catch them before they had a chance to get us. Other guys just wanted go out and kill something, anything. VC, civilians, farm animals, they didn't care. These are the guys who had been there a little too long. They needed help.

I remember one of the first patrols I went on. I was with Frankie, Velez, Jenkins, and a couple of other guys. Frankie was a Sergeant, so he was in charge of our squad. All we had to do was check out a village nearby where we heard some North Vietnamese soldiers were hiding. That was the hardest thing for me because all these people looked alike. How were we supposed to tell the difference between a South Vietnamese civilian and an NVA soldier? That's why you hear stories of G.I.'s killing entire villages, even the women and children. They didn't know who was who, so they'd just wipe out the whole town. Your life was on the line, you didn't take no chances.

I was walking point through the jungle, with Frankie walking along close by. It was the middle of the afternoon, hot as hell. My eyes were wide open, looking up every tree, behind every bush. I was ready to open up on anything I saw move. I'd ask questions later. I was coming into a clearing in the jungle, not far from the village we were sent to check out. It was hot, so I thought maybe we could stop there for a rest before going ahead. I dropped my guard and started looking to cop a squat when I heard Frankie.

"TORRES! Don't move!" He didn't have to tell me twice, I froze right there. The rest of the guys crouched down in the bushes. I looked around the clearing, but I didn't see anything strange or dangerous. Frankie walked over to me, real gentle, looking down at the ground.

In a low voice I whispered, "What's the matter?" Frankie didn't say anything. He handed me his rifle and took out his bayonet. I watched him as he got down on his hands and knees and slowly began crawling around the area where I was standing. He was looking for something, but I didn't know what.

The only noise I heard in the jungle was of the birds. Maybe they were chirping to warn Frankie. I looked up and saw a couple of bush monkeys jumping from tree to tree, like in the old Tarzan movies. The only other time I seen a monkey was in the Bronx Zoo, sitting quietly in a cage. These motherfuckers here looked like they were in a hurry to go somewhere. This shit was getting me nervous.

Frankie finally found what he was looking for. On his hands and knees, he used his bayonet to move some dirt from a small lump on the ground. At first I thought it was one of those land mines they warned us about. Very carefully, Frankie used the bayonet to dig up the lump. He pulled out what looked like a big bullet, and then a bamboo stick about five inches long. He sat back on his heels and looked up at me.

"What's that?" I asked him.

"*Dap Loi.*"

"Dap, what?" The only dap I ever knew was the handshakes we did with our boys.

"*Dap Loi*. It's a booby trap. Probably wouldn't have killed you, but it most definitely woulda ruined your day, maybe even your lovelife. Not only that, the blast would've sounded an alarm to Charlie that we were coming."

I was one step away from stepping on it.

Frankie took one more look around the clearing and decided everything was cool. The rest of the squad sat around to take a break. I wanted to know more about these booby traps, so I went over to Frankie. He was on the radio to base camp to report what happened and wait for orders on what to do. I went up to him while he waited.

"Thanks, Frankie."

"Thanks for what?"

"You saved my life, didn't you?"

"I didn't save your life, I saved mine. If you would have stepped on that thing, you woulda screamed like a bitch and let the whole North Vietnamese Army know where we are. This squad woulda been dog meat."

"Well, *gracias*, anyway. Tell me, how does that thing work?"

He began explaining what a *dap loi* was. It was made from an empty .50 caliber machine gun shell, which is about three or four inches long. The shell was refilled with more gunpowder and chunks of scrap metal and resealed with wax. Then, the refilled shells were placed in a bamboo tube with a nail on the bottom. They would bury them along the trails in the jungle so that only the wax tip was above the ground. When some *pendejo* like me stepped on one, the shell case would push down onto the nail and activate the gunpowder primer, just like in a gun. It would cause an explosion that'd shoot all those metal scraps into your foot and even up to your crotch. Like Frankie said, it wasn't enough to kill you, but it sure would piss you off.

Frankie got word to move out of our position and head back to camp. By finding booby traps, that meant the NVA was active in the area. Choppers and gunships were already on the way. We loaded up to move out. That's when I heard the first gunshot. Jenkins went down, and all hell broke loose.

Charlie had gotten hip to us. They were firing at us with machines guns and AK-47's. It was non-stop, *RATTA-TATT!-RAT!-TATA-TAT-TAT!* We all hit the deck. Velez was the M-60 gunner. An M-60 is a kick-ass machine gun you could carry around with you. He hit the ground with it and started shooting everything in sight. He was tearing up the whole jungle, empty shell casings clinking all around him. The smell of burnt gunpowder filled the thick air. No wonder those monkeys were hauling ass. They knew what was coming. Frankie ordered the squad to set up our positions and spray them cocksuckers with automatic fire.

I found cover near Velez and took my potshots. I didn't want to run out of ammo on my first firefight, so I just fired one bullet at a time, aiming to knock out their machine position with one single shot. Yeah, right. Jenkins was Velez's A-gunner, he was supposed to make sure the M-60 always had a steady supply of ammunition feeding into it. Velez was screaming for another ammo belt, but since Jenkins was down, I was the closest to him. I grabbed the can of ammo from Jenkins and ran over to Velez and started feeding him his shit. He was blowing everything away. POW! POW-POW-POW!! That shit was awesome!

Frankie heard the planes coming so he shouted out for us to get the fuck out of there. He stayed behind to cover us while we got up to retreat back down the trail towards camp. I saw Jenkins laying on the ground as I ran by, so I stopped to pick him up. Velez was carrying his M-60, so he couldn't help me. And Jenkins was a heavy Negro, but I was so scared I wasn't even thinking about it. I just grabbed ol' Jenkins and took off as fast as I could. Every so often one of the other guys stopped to return some fire back at Charlie. We kept doing that until we heard the helicopters zooming down, firing rockets into the jungle. The force of the blasts almost busted my eardrums. Trees were falling down. As one chopper swooped down and back up with guns blazing, another would come along right behind it.

We were about a hundred yards from camp. Behind us we heard more explosions and could see the jungle was on fire. I'd hate to be caught back there, I thought. Those chopper pilots weren't fuckin' around. A rescue squad from camp led by Sergeant Grimes finally got to us. Lipscomb and this dude named Jones got ahold of Jenkins and carried him back to camp. The rest of the men set up positions along the perimeter.

"Where's Frankie?!?", Chito yelled hysterically.

"He's still back there. He was covering us," I shouted as I helped Velez get his machine gun together for the next assault. Before anybody could stop him, Chito took off down the trail, screaming at the top of his lungs. More helicopters flew by us. I could see the gunners checking their sights from the side doors. There must've been a whole battalion of them gooks out there for that kind of shit. Sergeant Grimes yelled for Chito to stop and come back, but he wasn't hearing it. Him and Frankie was tight, and his boy was down there catching hell.

For the next half hour all we saw was fire and explosions. One plane came by and sprayed Napalm on them motherfuckers. There was nothing for us to do but watch it all from far away. Me and Velez laid low, ready to fire the M-60 if we saw any gooks coming through the bushes. We were safe from our positions, but we couldn't stop thinking about Frankie, and now Chito. I know I wanted to see some action, but I wanted to be able to sit back, smoke a joint, and talk about it with everybody afterwards. Nobody was supposed to die.

A radio message finally came through announcing that the Viet Cong, or whatever was left of them, had run back into the woods like the punks they were. My first firefight was over, and I didn't have a scratch. The boys from Air Support flew back to their base. Sergeant Grimes ordered us all to police our area of whatever equipment we had and head back to camp. Me and Velez didn't move. We kept looking out towards the trail, praying. I was rubbing my Bible from my shirt pocket.

The rest of the squad had walked about halfway to camp. Velez eventually reached down to pick up his M-60. He must have been in a few of these fights, because the way he handled himself and that machinegun was something I'll never forget. This dude was bad, and I was glad he was with me, on our side. But we were bummed. I bent down to pick up an ammo can, taking one last look down the trail. It wasn't windy, so it surprised me that some of the bushes were moving around. I squinted my eyes and called to Velez. He turned to look down the hill too. I thought I could see a tiny trail of smoke coming up from the brush, moving along like a slow locomotion train. Then the figures came into view.

Me and Velez screamed at the same time. Coming up the trail, with their arms around each other's shoulders like a couple of lovers, was Frankie and Chito. They were boppin' like hot shit, laughing and giggling like a couple of schoolgirls. The smoke was from a fat spliff they were passing back and forth. They were celebrating another victory. They were alive. They were nuts.

Back at camp we surveyed the damage. Luckily, all the choppers and planes returned to the air base okay. Nobody got killed. The only blood spilled was Jenkins'. He got shot in the ass, I guess when he turned around to look at the monkeys. He was going to be alright, but they still had to Med-Evac him back to a field hospital.

135

I went over to the medic's station where they were patching him up. Lipscomb was there, having a good time with his buddy.

"Hey, homie, I can't believe you let them shoot you in the *ass*." Lipscomb was laughing so hard, it made the medic laugh too.

"Hey, man, fuck you. I didn't see *your* black ass out there."

"Man, if I was there ain't no *way* they gonna shoot ME in the ass!"

"They woulda as soon as you started running, with your punk-ass." Jenkins saw me walking into the tent.

"There's MY man. Come on over here, 'Newbie'."

I walked over to him. "Ey, Jenkins, how you doin'?"

"Man, I'm alright. They just got a little piece of my ass, that's all. My ol' lady back home shot me in the ass once. Ain't no big *thang*. I'll be okay."

"You sure? Is there anything I can get you?"

"Nah, man. You done enough. I wanna thank you."

"For what?"

"For saving me, man. When the shit went down, everybody else was haulin' ass outta there. You the only one who stopped to help me. You saved me, man."

"Aw, c'mon, Jenk'. Frankie gave the order to beat it. With all that shit goin' on, nobody was gonna stick around to discuss it. Besides, they must've thought you were dead. You dropped like a rock."

"What'd you expect me to do, stand there so the mo'fucker could shoot the *other* cheek? Fuck that. But even if I *was* dead, ain't no G.I. wants to be left out here in this motherfucker. We all want to make it home one way or another. I'd rather go home in a bag than let these maggots out here eat up my rotting ass."

"Your bullet-ridden rotting ass...," Lipscomb added.

"I said FUCK you, Lip. Anyway, Newbie, thanks again. I'm finally getting outta here. And when I get home, I'm gonna smoke me a bomb of the purest Panama Red I can find. And I'm gonna think of you and salute you."

"You do that, Jenk."

"You bet I will. And when you get home, you better come around my way. I'm gonna tell all my people about you, and we's gonna party, party, party! You hear me? East New York, Pennsylvania Avenue. Look me up."

"I will. Be good, my brother." We dapped, and then the medics came in with the stretcher. The chopper was ready to go.

Once Jenkins was gone, me and Lipscomb headed back to our bunker where everybody else was hanging out. Radio Saigon was jammin' some Motown, guys were laughing and talking loud shit. It's funny how being so close to death can get some dudes excited. Escaping with all your shit in place will help a little too. I saw Frankie in the corner cleaning his weapon, so I went over to sit with him.

"Man, Frankie, it was *chévere* to see you coming back okay. I thought they had you, man."

"Shit, they need more than a battalion to catch me. Once the choppers got close, I just laid low until everybody stopped shooting. I got outta there just in time before the Jollies came and blasted them. You shoulda seen them VC gooks getting their shit blown up. Hearing them scream was music to my ears."

"Where did Chito find you?"

"Chito. That's my boy, man. At first I couldn't get my bearings. When I took off I wasn't sure if I was running in the right direction. Then I heard Chito's stupid bird calls and I looked up. There he was, climbed up a tree looking down at me. That boy is crazy."

"Why? 'Cause he went in to get you?"

"Yeah, that, too. But that didn't surprise me. That's how we've always been out here. We all get each other's back. Like what you did with Jenkins."

"You're right. You just don't think about it, right? You just do it."

"Show your right. *Pero, ese tipo Chito es loco*, man. He's crazy."

"Why you say that, Frankie?"

"In all that commotion, with shit exploding all around him, he still managed to roll up a fat joint while sitting up in that tree. You believe that shit? He felt like getting high on his way back. *Tipo es loco*." I looked over at Chito. He already had another joint in his mouth and was dancing with Velez.

"Hey, Torres."

"Yeah, Frankie?"

"Velez told me what you did out there. The way you came and fed him his ammo after Jenkins went down. And then when you carried Jenkins back all by yourself. This was your first fight. You did pretty good with yourself. You graduated, man. You ain't no 'Newbie' no more. Good job. I'll see to it that it gets in your record."

"Thanks, Frankie. But remember, if you didn't find that booby trap, none of us would be here now."

"Just doin' a job, man. In this hellhole, that's what it's all about, *hermano*. We all got each other's back. It's the only way we're ever gonna get home safe. Here, light this up." He tossed a joint at me. We spent the rest of the night in our bunker, cooling out, gettin' high. Frankie paid a houseboy to go into town and bring back a case of beer. It was warm, but nobody cared.

I know how close I was to my boys back home - Chico, Johnny, Louie. But that was because we just happened to grow up in the same neighborhood, on the same block. You can't help but get close to someone if you live with them your whole life. But out there, in a jungle thousands of miles from the real world, there's one thing that brings total strangers together. The one thing that can make grown men develope a love for each other they'll never be ashamed to show. That one thing is survival, man. That night, in Vietnam, I learned that we was all we had, and without each other, there was no way we could survive. These dudes were from different parts of the country. But that night, I felt a love for them all just the same as I did for my boys back home.

Word spread quickly around camp about our firefight. The next morning at breakfast, the cook made me a special Spanish-Style omlette, just for me. I don't know where he got the green and red peppers, but they tasted good.

After that, I never had a problem with Sergeant 1st Class Larry Blanton - a.k.a. *"El Visco"* - again.

CHAPTER FIFTEEN

Mi querido Papo,

Cómo estas, mi amor? I hope that when you receive this letter you are safe and that nothing bad has happened to you. I spend every day worrying about you, and pray that you don't get hurt. I hope you don't have to hurt anybody else either.

I am sad that we could not go to your graduation at Fort Dix. I really wanted to see you and hold you real tight. You look real handsome in the picture you sent me of you in your uniform. I am so proud of you. I wish I could have seen you in person. Do you still have the picture of me? I promise to send you more. I don't want you to forget what I look like (ha! ha!).

How is Vietnam? Is it hot over there? I keep watching the news on T.V. to see if I can see you. They say that it is getting close to the end of the war, and that all the soldiers will be sent home. I hope you are the first one they send back. I miss you so much.

Lourdes, Maritza, and Mamá and Papá all say hello. The house is too quiet since you've been gone. I saw Chico the other day. He said to tell you hi too. School is starting next week. I am going to be very lonely walking to school by myself. Remember when you used to walk me to school every day? I have to think of something to do to keep busy in school. If I come straight home every day Papá will make me stay inside all the time. Then I will think of you and miss you even more.

Papo, I can't wait for you to come home. Please don't do anything crazy and get yourself hurt. I want to marry you as soon as you get back. I love you. Write to me soon with your new address.

Te quiero mucho,
Esperanza
X O X O X O

P.S. Send me more pictures of you and your new friends. I love the uniforms.

I was in Bien Hoa two weeks before I got the first letter from Espy. Since she didn't know where I was, she sent her letters to Fort Dix, and from there they forwarded it to Vietnam.

After the first letter a whole bunch of stuff started coming in. It was all the mail people sent me since I left Dix. I got a big stack of letters from Espy all at once. I could see that she was still writing to me every day because each letter had a different date on them. She sent me cards, poems, letters, even a picture of us together at Tapestry on my birthday, when she won the contest. Johnny's girl Brenda had taken the picture, but I had never seen it. The picture brought back memories of that night, of how fine my baby looked all dressed up. I couldn't wait to take her out again.

I was only in-country for two months, but I felt like a veteran already. Besides that one big firefight, the only action we heard was at night when perimeter guards would shoot into the jungle thinking they had seen something. When it's so dark and you can't tell what the fuck is out there, you don't wait around for an introduction. You shoot first, worry about it later. When I knew I had to pull guard duty at night, I tried to stay away from any light during the day as much as possible. That way my eyes would be used to the darkness and I could see better once I got out there. That's another thing Frankie taught me.

We had to come up with all kinds of shit to keep busy. The boredom was driving us crazy. When you're so bored that you wish Charlie would attack, then you know you're a few dominoes short of a set, you know what I'm sayin'?

Chito came by the tent looking for me one day. I think Frankie was busy in town with one of *Mama-san's* girls.

"Hey, Torres, you like fish?"

"Eh. It's okay. Moms used to make *bacalao* with onions and *aguacates* for my Pops when I was little. He made me eat it sometimes. It was alright. Too salty, though."

"C'mon. Let's go fishing."

Here we are, in the middle of a fuckin' war, and this nut wants to play Jacques Cousteau.

"Fishing? Where we gonna go fishing at?"

"Down by the river, a few klicks from here."

"Hey, man. I ain't goin' nowhere far without a squad and a couple of choppers backin' me up."

"Don't sweat it, 'T'. We do it all the time. It's safe. It's on the other side of the village. Our boys got the area surrounded. It's okay."

"We ain't got no fishing poles. What are we gonna stick in the water, our dicks?"

"Let me worry about that. C'mon."

I don't know what made me agree to go along, but I went. Like Louie always said, "if they're gonna get you, they'll get you no matter where you are."

We walked away from camp along a narrow trail that led through the bushes down a hill. We both carried our M-16's, but Chito had a grenade launcher attached to his. You had to be ready for anything in those sticks, boy. I let Chito lead the way. If any booby traps got tripped up, he would have to deal with it first, not me.

We hiked through them woods for about fifteen minutes until we got to a riverbank. The currents looked powerful as white foam clinged to jagged rocks while the water rushed over them. It was a beautiful sight. Dig it, I hadn't taken a decent bath since I been in-country. Quick showers, yeah, but I never really felt clean. The first thing we did was strip down to our drawers and jump in. Man, that water felt good. It felt like I had washed about ten pounds of dirt off of me. I was a new man.

Then Chito said it was time to do what we went there to do, to fish. I figured I had to cut down some bamboo trees to use as poles, so I got out of the water and dried myself up. I assumed he brought some string or something to make a line, but I had no clue what he was going to use for bait. I hoped he didn't ask me to dig up any worms. I wasn't about to dig up something I didn't want to see. Like somebody's bones.

"You ready for some *pescado,* homie?" Chito came over to me with his pack.

"Ready? Where're the poles?"

"We don't need no poles. Check it out." I watched as Chito reached into his pack and pulled out extra hand grenades. What the fuck was this guy up to?

He said, "Put your earplugs on."

"What are you gonna do, *loco*?"

"You'll see." We both put on our earplugs.

Facing upstream, Chito pulled the pin out of one of the grenades. I said "Oh, shit!" and hit the deck. He heaved the grenade as far upstream as he could throw, then dove to the ground next to me. We peeked up and watched the grenade splash in the water, and a split second later the loud boom of the explosion shattered what had been a peaceful afternoon in the woods. Birds scattered everywhere, making screeching noises like they were cursing us out for scaring the shit outta them.

"Let's go!" Chito obviously did this before. He took out an empty sandbag from his pack and ran back into the water. Me, like a *pendejo*, ran in after him.

I couldn't believe what I saw. Flowing downstream towards us were dozens of fish, floating on top of the water. The explosion in the river had knocked them out, or killed them, who knows. Chito was bending over holding the sandbag, and them fish were floating right into it. In minutes he had enough fish in that bag to feed half the platoon. He threw another grenade in the water, and we filled three more bags with fish before heading back to camp. Fish dinner for everybody.

"Chito, man, you're crazy."

"All in a day's work, *Compy*. All in a day's work."

On the way back we made a pit stop so Chito could roll up another doob. I always wondered where this guy got so much herb out there. If you sent him to the moon he would *still* find a place to cop.

We dropped off four bags of fish over at the mess tent. The cook was happy with the catch, said he was gonna have a fish-fry for dinner. He asked Chito how many grenades did he have to blow up for this batch. Apparently, everybody knew this was a regular thing. I still had so much to learn.

One day we were sent out to one of the villages near the camp to check out if anything suspicious was going down. The village was not that far from camp and we knew there was no VC there. Still, we had to take a look every now and then to make sure, keep the two-stars happy. Wasn't much else going on.

Frankie led the squad there, including crazy Chito. Frankie was carrying a bag with products he ordered from the main PX in Saigon. Stuff like shampoo, Tang, toilet paper, and bottles of liquor. The mail truck brought it to him that morning.

We got to the village and all the civilians stopped what they were doing to watch us march in. They knew us and we knew them, so it wasn't a dangerous situation. Some kids ran up to us, calling us *"Wacky"* and asking for cigarettes. A "Wacky" is what they called Americans. These *pives* couldn't have been more than eleven or twelve years old and they were bumming squares from us. I didn't smoke cigarettes, so I had nothing for them.

After a quick look around we all split up to find places to relax for a while. The civilians went back to doing whatever the fuck they do all day. Frankie walked directly towards the biggest hooch down by the end of the main road, carrying that bag with him. I went with him, but he told me to stay outside. I copped a squat on a wooden deck outside the hooch and waited for Frankie to do his business. All that stuff he had in the bag was worth a lotta money in the Black Market. Shit we take for granted *Mama-san* was paying beaucoup money for, and Frankie was her favorite supplier. He got paid, plus he got to fuck any of Mama-san's girls that he wanted.

As I was sitting there fanning myself with my baseball cap, I felt like somebody was watching me. I looked over to the side of the hooch. Whoever was there had ducked back out of sight. I didn't see anybody. I leaned back against a wooden post, checked my watch, and kept on waiting for Frankie. I felt somebody staring at me again. From the corner of my eye I saw something move. I wasn't scared because I was positive that it was safe in that village. Those people were our friends. I turned towards the corner of the hooch, and whoever it was was gone again. Somebody was playin' games with my head.

I made like I was turning my attention towards the main road, then took a quick look back. Got 'im! It was a little kid, not more than five or six years old. I figured he must've been Mama-San's grandson or something. He was Vietnamese, but his eyes weren't like the others. They were rounder. He only had a little bit of hair on his head and it was curly, almost nappy. A war baby. The kid must've been left behind by some *hijo puta* who didn't give a fuck about him or his moms. Then again, his father coulda been dead for all I know.

Once he knew he got busted he didn't try to hide anymore. I motioned for him to come over to me. He walked over slowly, but I knew he wasn't afraid of me. He was just being careful. That's some shit when a kid grows up in a place where they start off not trusting nobody, not even the people that are supposed to be there to help him. I guess not all G.I.'s treated the Vietnamese the same. Those *cobaldes* gave the rest of us a bad name.

This kid reminded me of my little brother Benny. Not that they looked that much alike, but in a way they did. I guess it was because they were about the same age. Maybe Benny was a little older, but I remember when he was that age.

They had taught everybody basic Vietnamese when we got there, so I tried asking this kid his name.

"Em tên gì?" He looked at me funny. I wondered if I pronounced the words right. I tried again.

"Em tên gì?" Still nothing. Maybe he couldn't talk. I took out a candy bar from my C-Rations and held it out for him. He tried to grab it but I pulled it back.

"Em tên gì?"

"Le Vien."

"Bueno, Le Vien. Nice to meet you." I smiled and gave him the candy bar. Kid almost took my hand off snatching it. "My name is Eduardo. But you can call me Papo. Can you say Papo?"

He tried to say something, maybe it was Papo, but his mouth was full of candy. It sounded more *like "Pfunh-Pfonh."* He made me laugh. I picked him up and sat him on my lap. It brought back memories of when Benny used to sit on my lap while we watched cartoons on Saturday morning. We had to be quiet so we wouldn't wake up Pops.

"Tell you what, Le Vien. You can call me Papo, and I'll call you Lee. How's that? Me, Papo. You, Lee." This was Tarzan and Jane, Vietnam style.

He finally swallowed his candy and tried once more to say my name.

"Papo?"

"Yeah, that's it! Very good. You, Lee." I pointed to his chest. He pointed to my chest.

"Papo." He pointed back to his. "Lee"

"You learn fast, kid." We had our first lesson in communication. After that he made himself comfortable on my lap, touching all the equipment I had hanging on me. I tried to explain to him the name of each piece he was curious about. I made my first Vietnamese friend. All of a sudden I didn't feel like I was in a war at all. We hung out together for another half hour until Frankie finally came out. By this time everybody else had taken care of their own business and were ready to leave too.

When I got up it looked like Lee didn't want me to go. He had a sad look on his face. I bent down and told him not to worry, that I would be back to visit him real soon. I took my baseball cap and put it on his head. It was way too big, so I flipped the front bill up like we used to do playing baseball back home. I'd be wearing my helmet for the hike back to camp, so I could go without the cap until I got another one back at the supply tent. Lee looked up at me, still trying to see from underneath the oversized cap. He said *"Papo, Numba 1 Wacky."* At least this kid knew *some* English. Maybe it's all he got from his father.

On the way back Frankie took out some Vietnamese money and handed me a couple of bills.

"What's this for?"

"That's your cut, *'mano.*"

"For what? I didn't do anything."

"You kept me company. That's enough. Besides, if anybody asks, you ain't seen nothing, right?"

"Hey, I ain't no *chota*. You don't have to pay me to keep quiet."

"Don't sweat it. Everybody out here is into the Black Market. Only a *pendejo* from I-Corps in Saigon will ever come snooping around here. But that never happens, they know better than to come out here and fuck with us. Oh, and another thing. One rule about being here in the 'Nam: Don't get too close to anybody."

"Whatta ya mean, that kid?"

"Yeah, that kid. And anybody else out here, including me."

"Why's that? I thought we all had to be tight out here. It's the only way to survive, you said that yourself."

"Yeah, for survival. But people here come and go. Some get to go home alive, others get sent back in bags. When you get too close to somebody, it only makes saying goodbye that much harder. It'll be tougher to get over it. Trust me."

I thought about what Frankie said, about him and the rest of the guys in the platoon, about Lee. I thought about my boys back home. About Espy. What Frankie just said made a lot of sense. But I was afraid it was too late for me to think like that.

I started going with Frankie to that village on a regular basis. While he conducted business, I played with Lee. Each time I went I made sure to bring him something from camp. Sometimes I'd sneak out food from the mess tent, sometimes I'd bring him an extra blanket, or a pair of fatigue pants. One time I gave him a couple of Spiderman comic books that Espy had sent me. She knew Spiderman was my favorite. I knew Lee couldn't read them, but he got excited when he saw all the colorful pictures.

Frankie kept trying to fix me up with one of the girls in the village. I told him no thanks. I was determined to stay faithful to Espy. Besides, didn't want to bring any wild diseases back to the world that would fuck things up for my big night with my baby. It had been almost two years since I got laid, but fuckin' was never a big part of my life before anyways. I was smooth with the girls, alright. But other than a dance, I didn't get anything more out of it. I wasn't missing a thing.

On one of our trips to that village, Chito came back with a joint that he said was special. He said he bought it from one of the old men in the village and he wanted to share it only with me. Like always, I didn't know what the fuck he was talking about. I looked at the joint. It was fat, but *all* of Chito's joints were fat. The paper was dirty, though, like it was smeared with *mierda*. We waited until late that night and went to our bunker. Lipscomb and Howard were on guard duty. Who the hell knew where Frankie was.

Me and Chito brought a couple of beers from the mess tent, turned the radio on, and got comfortable. Chito fired up his monster joint. Right away the smell told me something about this was going to be different. It smelled sweeter, stronger. For the first time since I met Chito I saw him coughing on a toke. He passed the joint over to me, still in the middle of his cough attack. I took a drag and my head almost exploded. In no time the room was filled with smoke.

"What's *in* this shit?" I asked Chito, trying to get myself together again.

"It's regular weed, bro'." He was already giggling like a girl.

"Nah, man, this ain't no regular weed. There's something in it."

"Opium."

"What?"

"Opium. The old man laced this thing with opium."

"What the fuck is opium?" Not waiting for an answer, I took another long drag. Stuff was pretty good.

"It's some shit that grows wild out here. Some of these *viejo* gooks live on this stuff. It mellows them out, let's them deal with their pains."

It must've been true because by now I wasn't feeling shit. I had to take a swig of beer to clear my throat.

Between tokes Chito kept giving me a new lesson on opium.

"I heard there's even a religion somewhere in this country where they smoke opium all the time. Brings them closer to God, or whatever they call Him."

"Buddha."

"What?" Chito was already fucked up.

"Buddha. Isn't that what they call God here in the 'Nam?"

"Who fuckin' knows. All I know is that if there's a religion that lets you smoke this shit, then sign me up and praise the Lord!"

We laughed and gave each other a pound, then sat back to enjoy our head.

"Hey, Chito, you got a girl back home?"

"Nah. Used to."

"What was her name?"

"Miriam. She's the mother of my son."

"You got a kid?"

"Yeah. He's about three years old now."

"No shit. What happened to Miriam?"

"'Jody' got her. She sent me my 'Dear John' a week after I got here."

"Man, that's messed up."

"Yeah, I know. That's why I don't give a fuck about nothing over here. Ey, if it wasn't for Frankie, I'd *really* be fucked up. He helped me get through it. He's my main man, for all time. How about you?

I see you been getting letters from home all the time. What's her name?"

"Esperanza. I call her Espy. Here, check her out." I took out the picture of her I had in my pocket and handed it to him.

"Mmm. *Esta buena*, Compy. Kinda young, ain't she?"

"She's seventeen. But she's nice, man. I love her a lot. We's gonna get married as soon as I get back to the world."

"Ey, man, good luck to you. I hope she don't do the same thing to you that that *puta* Miriam did to me."

"Nah, bro'. Espy's different. She loves me like crazy, man. She'll be waiting for me as soon as I get off the plane. That's square business."

Pretty soon we were slowing down, mellowing out, until we were laying back on our bunks, staring at the inside of our eyelids. I can't remember at what point I nodded out.

The sand under my feet was hot, but the ocean waves splashing against the shore cooled them off. I looked up at the sun peeking through light clouds dotting a pale blue sky. The breeze seemed to weave in and out among the long leaves of the leaning palm trees. I could hear sea gulls in the distance, and the smell of salt water easily made its way up my nostrils.

Up ahead was Espy, walking towards me slowly. We had agreed to meet here on this beach on a deserted island where nobody could find us, where nobody could stop us. Her light skin blended in with the white sand, the wind blowing her curly hair away from her face. She was also walking along the edge, letting her feet kick water in front of her as she neared. She was wearing an old undershirt, one I might have given her to hold for me while I played handball in the schoolyard. The undershirt was wet, cut off above her waist to expose a hard, flat stomach. The roundness of her hips were barely covered by a long sarong she had wrapped around her legs, tied in a knot on her side. The breeze pressed the wet undershirt against her, showing off her erect nipples.

As she got closer her dark eyes stared deeply into mine. She held out her hands and I took them in mine. We kissed, tenderly at first, not wanting to rush into what was about to happen for the first time. Soon passion took over, our mouths opening, our tongues taking each other hungrily. She took a step back. I watched as she delicately grabbed the bottom of her shirt and lifted it up over her head. I was finally getting my first look at her firm white breasts. They weren't large, but more ample than I had imagined before. Her pink nipples grew from the touch of the cool air. As she held her arms over her head I cupped each breast in my hands, bending over to kiss them, one at a time. I nibbled on them gently, then ran my tongue down the front of her body. The only sounds I heard were the endless waves crashing against the shore, and her muffled moans coming from deep inside. She clutched the back of my head, running her fingers through my hair. I undid the sarong, allowing it to fall gracefully to the sand. She stood before me, totally nude. It was my first glimpse of the beauty I had waited to see for so long.

Espy wrapped her arms around my shoulders as I picked her up and carried her to a nearby palm tree. I laid her down on the sand and stood over her. She reached out to me, as if to beg me to come down to her. I knelt down and caressed her trembling body. Her heavy breathing told me it wouldn't be long before she would open herself up to me, and share with me her most intimate possession.

With little difficulty, we began to make love. We moved together in a natural rhythm that many lovers need years to master. Slowly at first, then faster and faster. The relentless waves assaulted the ocean shore. The wind blew harder; the sea gulls cheered us on like approving spectators at a sporting event. Espy and I were grunting and moaning, fucking for the first time. It was everything I hoped it would be. I could feel the hot sensation surging from inside, my body convulsing powerfully. As we got closer to the magic moment, our ultimate climax, I could hear explosions from a distance. The explosions grew louder and louder until....

I woke up drenched in sweat. For a second, I wasn't sure where I was. I looked over at Chito, but he was passed out, snoring like a pig with a cold. My hard joint was poking its way through the buttons in my pants. The shots I heard were coming from the perimeter. Lipscomb and Howard were having visitors. I didn't give a shit. I pulled a blanket over my head, hoping I could fall asleep and pick up where I left off in my dream with Espy. But my erection wouldn't let me. I took off my pants, and with the sounds of a firefight not too far away, I closed my eyes and thought of Espy, of the beach, of the sarong wrapped around her waist. In no time I exploded in a huge mess underneath the blanket. I thought it wouldn't stop.

When it was all over, I stared up at the ceiling of the bunker. Goddamm the Army. Goddamm this war. God damm.

Early the next morning, Lipscomb and Howard came back from their guard duty.

"You guys get some shit last night?" Frankie asked them.

Lipscomb looked tired, but he was okay. "Yeah, fuckin' Charlie must've been bored. We popped some caps back at 'em and they took their asses back home. No biggie."

I wonder how many *cabrones* in Washington felt the same way about this fuckin' war - no biggie.

CHAPTER SIXTEEN

A month later I was assigned to a crash/rescue team. We had to go out to the jungle and look for pilots who might've been shot down. I'd been lucky so far. I had been there three months and still hadn't seen any dead people, Americans or Vietnamese. Maybe this war was winding down after all. All I had to do there was clean up the mess.

Frankie came in and told us that we were going on a special mission. We had to truck it instead of humping through the jungle on foot. He took out a map and showed us where we had to go. It was pretty far. I noticed on the map that we were crossing a border, going into Cambodia. As far as I knew, the beef we had was here in Vietnam. What the fuck was we going to Cambodia for? Frankie told me not to ask so many questions.

We headed out on two deuce-and-a-halfs. In the back of the truck Velez told me he overheard the meeting with the brass. What happened was that they had secretly sent in some paratroopers from the 101st Airborne into Cambodia. We weren't supposed to go into that country because they weren't involved. "Rules of the War", it was called. I didn't know a war had "rules". Shit, with all the killing goin' on, why didn't they make just one rule - NO KILLING. Made sense to me.

The truth was that the North Vietnamese knew we couldn't go into Cambodia. So whenever they carried out one of their attacks near the border, they'd run to Cambodia afterwards where we couldn't chase 'em. It was like playing "Hot, Peas, and Butter", remember? Cambodia was 'base'.

Well, ol' Nixon was getting tired of that shit. He started ordering some troops to go in there, even though he didn't have the approval of Congress or anything. Nobody was supposed to know we was taking the war to another country. That's why Frankie told me to stop asking so many questions. The paratroopers were on a search and destroy mission. They had to drop in on the sneak, you know, that's why they parachuted at night.

But something had gone wrong. The VC found out they were coming and were layin' for them. As our guys came floating down from the sky, Charlie opened fire on them with machine guns. Poor guys were wide-open targets. They had nothing to protect themselves, no cover, nothing. The best they could do was shoot back as they came down, and hope that Charlie would miss them. Reports came in that there were a lot of casualties. We had to go in and get them.

By the time we got there the next morning, them punk VC troops had booked. Some paratroopers made it down safely and had continued on with their mission, but a squad was left behind with the dead and wounded to wait for us. As soon as we got there, the Captain had Lipscomb take some men out to form a perimeter guard line, while the rest of us helped the paratroopers. We brought some medics with us to take care of the wounded. I was part of the crew that had to bag up the dead guys and throw them in the back of one of the trucks. I wished they had sent me out with Lip'.

Other than at funerals, I had never seen a dead body before. Back home in the Bronx we used to see dead dogs and rats in the empty lots around the neighborhood all the time. Even with them it was scary. We knew they were dead, but we were still afraid to go near them. It's like we expected them to jump up all of a sudden and scare the shit out of us, just like they did in the "Chiller Theater" movies they showed on Sunday mornings. Looking at these dudes was even worse. Some of them still had their eyes open, like they couldn't believe they got shot. After I saw the first one, bro', I couldn't help it. I threw up.

I got my shit together, then started looking around for bodies with this *blanquito* dude named Harper. We found two bodies right away, they were near a tree. While Harper dragged them into bags, I took down their names from the dogtags hanging around their necks. One guy - a blond tough-looking dude - had gotten shot up in the legs and bled to death. His face was still in good shape, he looked like he was sleeping. His name was Smykowski. If it wasn't for the dogtag, there's no way I would have been able to spell "Smykowski". Ain't too many Polish people in the *barrio*, you know what I'm sayin'? The other guy was named Burke, Joseph Burke. I still remember that. After I had the information written down, I helped Harper zip the bags up.

Since they had parachuted down they were scattered all over the place, so it took us about two hours to find everybody. I don't know how far into Cambodia we were, but I couldn't wait to get the hell out of there. We strapped the wounded onto stretchers and loaded them into the trucks. Before we left we made one last sweep to make sure we had everybody.

Me, Harper, and Chito had walked away about fifty yards. Frankie told us to check behind all the bushes, in the trees, everywhere. From the corner of my eye above me I noticed a weird shape. I looked up, and there, hanging from a tree, was one more paratrooper. His chute had gotten tangled up in the trees on his way down. Chito climbed up and cut the dude down. Another blond white dude. I guess the *gringos* are the only stupid ones to sign up to jump out of planes. You don't see too many brothers and Ricans go up there. I took out my notebook and looked for this guy's dogtags. "Smykowski".

The name sounded familiar. As a matter of fact, he looked a lot like that other dude we had bagged up before. I thought we had done this guy already. I wondered about that shit, but it was time to go and we had to get this guy over to the truck. He was the last of them. This shit detail was finally over and we were heading back to camp.

All in all, there were twenty-seven guys killed, another fifteen wounded. We called for choppers to come and pick everybody up. I was still wondering about that blond guy, Smykowski. I was positive he was one of the first bodies we bagged up. I even checked my notebook to make sure, and there it was, Smykowski, one of the first names on my list. How'd this guy get from being on the truck inside a bag, back up into a tree? Later on I found out from one of the medics of the 101st. These guys, the Smykowskis, were twin brothers. They had enlisted in the Army together, and both wanted to be paratroopers just like their old man was in World War Two. The medic said that they were the best, real tough. Weren't scared of shit. They even volunteered for this mission. But they both got wasted, floating down like sitting ducks before they had a chance to do any damage to Charlie. They joined the war together, now they were heading home together in boxes. I thought about their Mom. She was gonna have a tough time dealing with that shit.

We got back to the bunker and flopped down on our racks. Somebody lit up a joint, but not to party. No one was in the mood to have fun. We just needed something to help us get over what we just saw. Pissed off G.I.'s were cursing in low voices. Since we didn't get much action in our camp we weren't used to seeing so much bloodshed, so many guys dead. I thought about Espy, about wanting to be with her so much. I took out some paper to write her a letter, but I couldn't come up with the right thing to say. After a while I gave up and just lay back in my bed.

The Top Sergeant came knocking on the door looking for Frankie.

"What's up, Top?" said Frankie.

"Your orders came through, Garcia. Pack up. You got fifteen minutes to get your shit and get on that chopper with those boys from the 101st. Congratulations, soldier, you're going home."

Frankie just stood there, stunned. Going home? He always said he didn't want to go home. Said he felt better out there in the 'Nam. He was able to put off being shipped out a couple of times when his tour was up before. He argued that they needed all the good trained men they could get, so they always let him stay. But now a new crew of troops was on its way to replace those guys who were due to go home. Frankie had no choice. He had to go.

Chito went nuts. His boy, his teacher, his best friend was leaving him behind. There was nothing either of them could do about it. Without Frankie, Chito would be lost. If he was crazy before, he was gonna be even worse now.

I helped Frankie pack his stuff into a duffel bag. He gave me all the shit he couldn't take with him, like magazines, his radio. Then he handed me some paper that had a bunch of numbers on them.

"What's this?"

"It's my business, Torres. It's all yours."

"What am I gonna do with this?"

"You can take over for me, make yourself some scratch. You already know how it's done, you've gone with me enough times. You know what Mama-san wants, just order it from the PX. Tang, cigarettes, liquor, all that is petty shit."

"I don't know, Frankie."

"Don't sweat it. There's some dudes here that sell entire jeeps and tanks on the Market, piece by piece. Mama-san knows you, I'm sure she trusts you. Shit, you practically adopted her grandson, Le Vien."

I shoulda felt honored, but I knew I was gonna miss Frankie. He taught me a lot out there too. He even saved my life, whether he ever admitted to it or not.

Word came down that the chopper was ready to leave. Frankie had just enough time to run over to the airstrip to catch it. He said his goodbyes to everybody. It's funny how when one of the guys finally got to go home, the other guys being left behind were still happy for him. There was never any jealousy. One more American makin' it home alive. That was enough to make the others feel good for him. The rest of us knew that with the help of God, our day would come too.

Me and Chito ran with Frankie to the airstrip. As tough and crazy as Chito was, he couldn't control the tears in his eyes. He held onto Frankie's arm like he wasn't going to let go. We threw the duffel bag on the bird and gave each other our last daps and hugs. The helicopter blades were blowing dust all over the place, and the noise made it really hard to hear anything. I tried telling Frankie that I would look for him up on Gun Hill Road when I got back to the world, but I don't think he heard me. He forced a smile, waved, then closed the door to the chopper. They took off right away. Me and Chito had to run off to the side to get out of the way.

Frankie was right about so many things over there in Vietnam. He was right about looking out for booby traps. He made the right decisions whenever we were out on patrol so that everybody got back safe. He looked out for me as I was getting to know my way around the camp. The Army was letting a good soldier go.

But the most important thing Frankie was right about was the time he told me about not getting too close to anybody. I realized at that moment how much Frankie meant to me, and that I actually loved the motherfucker. Saying goodbye to him then was as hard for me as it was saying goodbye to Espy and my family back home. But this was different. Me and Frankie had been through hell together. I knew someday I would be home again, be with all my boys again. But as that chopper lifted him up and away, I knew - just as I'm sure Frankie knew - that we would never see each other again. Saying goodbye to that dude was the hardest thing I ever had to do.

I looked over at Chito. He was staring at the helicopter as it flew further and further away. He looked mad. There were no more tears, but I knew he hadn't stopped crying. Whatever pain or loss I was feeling at that moment, Chito was feeling it ten times over.

I had to pull a couple of hours of guard duty that night. I got back to the bunker at about one o'clock in the morning. Whoever was there was asleep. I heard a low noise from the corner, the special corner that used to be Frankie's space. Sitting on the floor, next to a lit candle, was Chito. He was rocking back and forth with his eyes closed. I saw a rubber tube wrapped tightly around the upper part of his arm. A small stream of blood was trickling down his forearm. The blood was coming from his vein, the one where a needle was sticking out of.

I left him alone. I went to my bunk and laid down, pulling the blanket over me like I always did. I could still hear Chito, rocking and humming softly. What a day. Two hundred sixty one more, plus a wakeup. I still had a long way to go.

Soon we had a new shipment of "newbies" come in to replace the guys that had left. There were two Puerto Ricans in the group. One was from New York, Washington Heights in upper Manhattan. His name was Salvador Cardona. We hit it off pretty good right away. He had already been in the Army a year, so technically he wasn't a 'newbie'. He was surprised they sent his ass to Vietnam, but he was a weapons expert. No better place for a weapons expert than in a war.

The other Rican was this real skinny dude named Miguel Santiago. He told us everybody called him "Flaco". Flaco was from some place called Arecibo, in Puerto Rico. Right off the bat I could tell this guy was different than the rest of us. First of all, he was from the island. You would think that a Puerto Rican is a Puerto Rican, no matter if they're from New York or the island. You would think we all hung tight together, right? Nope.

I noticed that in basic training. The Ricans from New York hung out in one group, the dudes from the island hung out in another. Their attitude was different, man. To us they seemed like *jíbaros*, they weren't cool enough to run with us. They laughed at stupid shit. They weren't from the streets like me, and Frankie, Chito, Angel, Ralfy, and now Salvador. They didn't seem too tough. This guy Flaco was like that. To make it worse, he *dug* being in the Army. He said it from the jump-street that he was going to be a lifer, make a career out of this shit. When he got to 'Nam he had only been in the Army for three months. I told him to see me in a year and we'll find out if he still wants to be a lifer.

I got a field promotion right after Frankie left. They made me a Corporal. That's two stripes, one rank lower than a Sergeant. They promoted Lipscomb to Sergeant and gave him Frankie's squad, which included me. We also got a new captain, Captain Bonner. As soon as he showed up he was hanging with us, makin' jokes. The only thing he asked us was that if we were gonna smoke that shit, to not do it in front of him. Also, he said to *please* not get high if we know we're going out on a mission. He wanted us to be sharp in case some shit went down. He said he wanted to make sure everybody got home in one piece, especially him.

The thing with officers in Vietnam was that they only had to stay in-country six months. The rest of us enlisted men and draftees had to be there for a year, sometimes thirteen months. That would piss a lot of guys off when they would see a rich young *pendejo* - right out of West Point - come along and order people around for six months. He wouldn't know shit about jungle warfare. Then we had to watch that same officer hop on a plane and get sent back home, his tour of duty done. Us enlisted men were still there fuckin' with Charlie while the officer was back home, probably getting a hero's blowjob from his blond hair, blue eyed girlfriend. That's why nobody liked officers. Nobody liked special treatment in the 'Nam.

Captain Bonner was cool, though. He didn't go to West Point. He started out as an enlisted man and got his commission in the field out there in 'Nam. He wasn't no *come mierda*, he was one of us. He did everything he could to make our lives easier. He arranged for us to get magazines like "Playboy". We even got to see movies from the world every Friday night. You'd be surprised how a little thing like that could mean so much to us over there.

By then Chito was in his own world. He didn't bother nobody, and nobody bothered him. He still had three months left in his tour, and it looked like he was going to spend the rest of it high on opium, or tripping on smack. Back then there was no place for drug addicts to get help, especially not in the field. So many G.I.'s were getting high or strung out on heroin, and there was nothing the Army could do about it. Moral was low. We was out there doing shit we didn't want to do, in a country whose people didn't want us there. And we knew back home people were bad-mouthing the war, spitting on soldiers coming back. Like this shit was *our* fault. I started getting an attitude myself.

United States Army, big fucking deal. Those cocksuckers in Washington thought that just by sending in the mighty U.S. troops that everybody was gonna run and hide. What they didn't understand was that them Viet Cong was there fighting to protect their land, their homes, and their families. Why were we there? They told us we had to stop the spread of Communism, that if one country went down, they all would. Who the fuck cares. That's their business. Who were we to go over there and tell them how they should live?

Think about it, bro. If somebody comes into your neighborhood startin' some shit, whatchu gonna do? You're gonna do whatever you can to protect it, right? You're fighting for your life, your people. Hell yeah, you're gonna fight harder than the other guy. It don't mean nothing to him, he's just fuckin' around, going through the motions. That was us. We didn't care about nothing over there. We just wanted to do our time, survive, and get back home. Stayin' high so we didn't have to think about the shit they were making us do. To some G.I.'s, the Vietnamese weren't even real people. That's why they did so much crazy shit to them.

That *pendejo* Nixon didn't understand that 'cause he wasn't over there. He didn't see that we was getting our asses kicked because nobody gave a fuck. Maybe in the beginning they did. Troops were still juiced over John Wayne, World War Two and all that patriotic shit. They wanted to do what they thought was right. But by the time I got there, it was like "Why the fuck are we here?" *Sin gana.* No wonder we lost.

The next couple of months were really quiet, except for Charlie's usual attack of the perimeter at night. They were getting to be a real pain in the ass. The funny part was that we'd be shooting back and forth at each other, and nobody would get hurt! It's like they were tired of this war too. They'd fire off some rounds, we'd return it, and that was it. The next day a patrol would go out to see if any of them got hit. They would come back a half-hour later with nothing to report.

But the choppers were still flying all around destroying as much of the countryside as they could. I didn't see the need for that shit. They were supposed to be looking for the VC hiding in the jungles and villages. Instead, they destroyed a beautiful country. I used to see that and get real pissed off. I was getting an "F.T.A." attitude, you know, Fuck The Army. I didn't realize how much I was changing, that the *salsa*-dancing, good kid from the *barrio* was turning into a hard-core, don't-give-a-fuck old veteran. This after being there only six months. I thought I would be able to leave that attitude behind and go back to the world the same way I left. Once I got home everything would be all right. That's what I thought.

What kept me going the most was the letters I got from home. Espy was still writing to me every day. Well, almost. I couldn't believe how she could come up with so much shit to write about all the time. Usually she wrote the same stuff over and over, like what she did that day, what she did in school. She always said she was missing me and couldn't wait 'til I got back home. In one letter she wrote me saying she had joined the cheerleading squad at the high school. She sent me a picture of the whole squad standing with the basketball team. Espy had told me she needed something to keep herself busy after school. I guess being a cheerleader for a bunch of *cocólos* was her idea of keeping busy. I was surprised Dón Ramón allowed her to walk around with that short uniform the cheerleaders had to wear. But there she was, right in the middle of the whole group, smiling that beautiful smile of hers.

I didn't know she even *liked* basketball.

Sal - you know, Salvador - became my partner in the Black Market with Mama-san. We'd go there every two weeks and deliver her shit to her. She used to give me a list, just like Moms used to do when she sent me to Dón Marco's *bodega*. Sal was more of a businessman than me, so when we went to the village he dealt with Mama-san and I played with Le Vien and his little friends. We split whatever money we made. The money was pretty good too, but I didn't have much to spend it on. Bought some herb once in a while whenever it came around. I still wasn't going into Bien Hoa to get laid. I was being good to Espy, just like I promised. Sal found himself

Pedro E. Acevedo

a steady girl in no time. He said he admired me, but he couldn't wait a year to get a piece of ass.

David Velez got transferred to some unit in Saigon about a month after Frankie left. He was short too, so they sent him there to spend the rest of his tour before he got to go home. He had already done his part and some. Flaco Santiago, the lifer from Arecibo, was trying hard to be super-troop, hanging with the Top Sergeant all the time. It wasn't that he was a kiss-ass, actually he was all right. It's just that he took his job seriously and wanted to be involved in everything. He really thought we could've won that war. He wasn't there long enough to know better.

Once in a while I'd give Chito money so he could get his heroin fix. I was the only one he talked to whenever he felt like talking to somebody. I watched him cook the heroin up and suck it up into the syringe, then stick it in his arms. It looked dangerous, but then I would see how easy it was for Chito and how calm he got when he was tripping. I got curious. Still, I wanted to stay away from the shit if I could help it. I was hoping I could get out of that hellhole before something serious happened. I saw how Chito got, and I didn't want to end up like him.

CHAPTER SEVENTEEN

Things really started to get messed up around my eighth month in 'Nam. We got reports that said the Viet Cong were making their way towards us. They were talking about moving us somewhere else. I knew I was too lucky to spend my entire tour in one place. I guess the only lucky thing was the fact that I made it that far without getting hurt.

The Army had this thing they did to try to find the enemy hideouts. If they thought that a village was hiding the Viet Cong, they would move everybody in the village to another area. They would actually make the civilians pack up and leave their homes, then relocate them somewhere miles away. Once the village was empty, choppers and fighterplanes would come along and destroy everything. Rockets, napalm, and bombs, the works. They called that a "Free Fire Zone". They wouldn't leave nothing standing. That way, they'd make sure the VC wouldn't have anything to come back to. The generals saw it as a way to save the civilians from the Communists.

Ain't that some shit. They save the civilians by destroying their homes. What fuckin' sense did that make? Some of these villages had been there for centuries. Their fathers and ancestors lived and died there. Their sacred burial grounds were there. The Vietnamese were pissed off that they had to leave all that behind to go somewhere else. Some of them refused to move. That didn't stop the choppers. If they didn't leave, they got blown away with everything else. Whoever came up with this idea was a *cabrón*.

I'll never forget the day that all hell broke loose in our camp. Chito had come by early in the morning to ask me if I wanted to go out fishing again. This time I told him I couldn't go because Top had ordered me to help Flaco with an ammunition dropoff. Flaco was always volunteering for everything, with his lifer ass. We had to do an inventory of what we had so Sal could call in what we needed. Chito went off fishing by himself.

About noontime the call came down that the village where Le Vien and Mama-san lived was infiltrated by the Viet Cong. I don't know where they got that lowdown from. We went there every week and we didn't see anything different, and nobody tried to pop us. Still, we had to be on standby in case we got the order to go do something about it. I hoped that it was just a false alarm. That village had become like my second home and I was worried for the civilians that had become my friends, especially little Lee.

The order finally came for us to go over there and load everybody up in trucks to move them out. We had to do it quick because they had already called in the choppers to wipe the whole village out. Damn, you'd think they'd give these people time to think about it, right? I knew the Vietnamese civilians weren't gonna just jump into the trucks and leave without pitchin' a bitch. This was their home. Imagine somebody from New Jersey coming to the *barrio* and telling us to move out 'cause they're gonna destroy our buildings. We'd kick his ass all the way across the George Washington Bridge.

But we had to do it. The planes were on their way and we didn't have much time. It took a half hour to get to the village from the camp. Then, by the time we got everybody on the trucks and moving, you figure that would take another couple of hours. Even Captain Bonner came with us to supervise everything. They were going to move the village about thirty klicks to a bigger camp, near this town called Pleiku.

At first these people refused to go anywhere, just like I thought. We had ARVN soldiers there to interpret for us and they were catching hell from the older leaders of the village. I thought Puerto Ricans talked fast, but these dudes were going at it a mile a minute. Everybody was talking at the same time. I felt bad for them, but we were wasting valuable time. We had to get out of there. About an hour went by and these stubborn old farts still wouldn't budge.

From the distance we heard the sound of planes and the "Jolly Green Giants", the bad-ass choppers with the bad-ass rockets. The ARVN interpreters were talking fast and pointing towards the sky, like telling the old men, "We's better get the fuck outta here. Them dudes up there ain't playin'." As soon as the first plane flew by everybody started running around, trying to get as much stuff as they could to take with them. There was only so much room on the trucks, so they couldn't take everything they owned. Women were crying, the old men were cursing us out.

I ran to Mama-san's hooch looking for Lee. She was packing some shit up in a big pillow case, yelling at everybody to hurry up. She stopped to give me a real sad look when she saw me. At that moment, the look in her eyes made me feel ashamed to be a G.I. Why did we have to do this to these people? They weren't hurtin' nobody. The first rocket hit an area about a half mile from the village. I screamed out the door for somebody to get on the radio and tell those motherfuckers up in the planes to hold up, we were still down here. There was so much confusion, with everybody running around. I don't know if it was too late to get them to stop.

The rockets were getting closer and planes were flying real low. It looked like Mama-san and her girls were ready, or about as ready as they were going to be in that shit. I picked Lee up and led everybody out of the hooch and down the main road. There were about ten trucks waiting to drive them out. Some of the G.I.'s had already started setting fires to the empty hooches. Children were crying 'cause they were scared. Women were crying 'cause they were pissed off. People were running in all different directions, everybody was yelling. It was crazy, man.

The first three trucks left. A rocket landed right outside Mama-san's hooch, knocking over a big tree. It crashed down right on top of the hooch, demolishing it. Half the village was already burning.

We were hurrying to get everybody out before the planes started making direct hits on us. The radioman was calling up to the pilots, trying to get them to stop. But they just kept on coming, dropping bombs on anything that looked like it might be hiding VC. I heard some gunfire from a distance. I thought maybe it was true, that Charlie really was in the area and was shooting back at the planes. Another explosion went off about fifty yards from us. I hadn't been that scared since my first firefight.

From the corner of my eye I saw a flash. They were shooting off the napalm now. The whole hillside was on fire. The river where I had gone fishing with Chito was down there. I hoped he hadn't picked the same place to go fishing that day, but I didn't have time to worry about him. Once I got everybody in the truck I had to go out to the perimeter to form a defense line. Lee looked at me with eyes wide open. He wasn't crying, but I could see he was terrified and it looked like he wanted me to make it all better. I wished I could. I tried to tell him not to worry, that everything was gonna be alright. I took off my dogtags and gave them to him. He put them around his neck and gave me one last hug. It was the same kind of hug my little brother Benny had given me before I left for boot camp. Before I could say anything else to him the truck took off. It was one of the last trucks to leave.

The air corps was zeroing in on the village. There was shit exploding all around us. I watched the trucks heading down the hill, the people inside them looking up at the planes, or back at what was happening to the homes they had lived in all their lives. Everything was burning to the ground. We had to get the hell out of there. From a trench, Charlie was firing more shots up to the sky, trying to pick off one of our planes. A squad took off in that direction. We had to take that gun out fast before they could do serious damage.

There were two helicopters flying alongside the truck convoy to give them protection. Charlie must've gotten a beat on them because one chopper was blowing smoke from the side. It had been hit. It looked like the pilot was trying hard to keep control of it, but it was spinning around in the air heading towards the ground. I couldn't believe my eyes when I saw it crash down into the jungle in a loud, orange and yellow explosion. I couldn't see exactly where it went down, but it was close to the road that the trucks were driving on. A big red ball of fire shot up to the sky. There was no way anybody was gonna walk away from that.

It didn't take long for our boys to find that VC machinegun post. Charlie was paying more attention to the sky, so they didn't notice when Flaco snuck up behind them and dropped a hand grenade into the trench. "Fire in the hole!" BOOM! Those motherfuckers were gone. By this time, the whole village was in flames. If anybody was hiding in there, they weren't hiding no more. We got the order to move out and return to camp. On my way back I kept looking behind me at the village, or what was left of it. Why did it have to be like this, I thought. Damn, why did it have to be like this?

About an hour and a half after we got back to camp we received word that some casualties were coming in. Probably the dudes from that chopper that went down, although I couldn't see how anybody could have survived that crash. Since I wasn't a corpsman, I didn't bother finding out who those guys were. I went back to the bunker to get some rest and look for Chito. The bunker was empty, so I figured he hadn't come back yet. Knowing Chito, he would have kept on fishing even with all that shit going down around him. I lay down to read the latest letter that I got from Espy when Sal came into the bunker.

"Bro', man, we got some bad news."

"What's up, Sal?"

"You know those casualties that came in?"

"Yeah. Those them dudes from the chopper that went down, right?"

"No, man. The dudes on the chopper are wasted. They even had a news photographer on board. They're all dead."

"I figured that. That ball of fire was some fucked up shit."

"But that ain't all, Papo."

"What happened?"

"The chopper went down right on the convoy. It exploded right in front of the last two trucks."

I felt a knife sticking right through my heart. "Don't bullshit around like that, Sal. It's not funny. What happened?"

"No lie, bro'. The pilot tried to steer the chopper away from the convoy, but he couldn't do it. It landed right on the road. The explosion caused one of the trucks to go up in flames and explode too. It was like a chain reaction."

"Lee! Where was the truck Lee was in!?"

Sal just looked at me.

"Sal, stop fuckin' around! WHERE IS LEE!?"

"I'm sorry, bro'. The chopper exploded right next to them. The truck Mama-san was in blew up too. The only people that made it was the dude riding shotgun on the last truck and a couple of the civilians. They're the ones they brought in before. Everybody else on those last two trucks are dead - Mama-san, her girls....."

"Le Vien?"

"Le Vien, too. I don't know what else to tell you, man. 'Cept I'm sorry."

It felt like somebody had kicked me in the stomach. I was going to throw up. I pushed Sal out the way and ran towards the medic station. I didn't want to believe him. I thought sure I would get to the tent and see Lee sitting there, playing with my dogtags, getting a band-aid on his knee. I ran in there like a madman. The medics were taking care of the wounded. Most of them were burned up bad. One old lady had a bandage around her whole head. They were moaning. Lee was nowhere in sight.

If I could've gotten ahold of the stupid motherfuckin' commanders of that air team, those *maricones* that kept shooting down on us even though they knew we were still there, I would have fragged them on the spot. I wasn't even mad at the Viet Cong. They wouldn't have fired up at the choppers if we hadn't shown up. Those asshole pilots came in too soon. They didn't give us a chance to clear the area. The trucks should have been long gone by the time the goddamm air strike hit. This shit didn't have to happen.

I stayed in the bunker all night. I must've been a zombie because people said they tried to talk to me and I wasn't paying no mind to nobody. I waited for Chito to come back, maybe he would have something to help me deal with that shit. The way I felt, I would've taken anything he had.

But Chito didn't come back that first night. I stayed holed up in that bunker the whole next day. I wouldn't come out for shit. Sal brought me food from the mess tent, but I didn't eat any of it. The next night came and Chito still hadn't shown up, so I looked in his footlocker and found his stash. Only it wasn't herb. I found his little "kit", the rubber band, the spoon, a couple of needles he stole from the medic, and a little plastic bag. I said fuck it. I seen him do it enough times, how he did it, how he cooked that shit up, how he tied the rubber band around his arm to get to a vein. I didn't know how much heroin was needed for just one hit, but I didn't give a fuck. Chito wasn't there, but I was gonna take his shit anyways. Hell, I probably paid for that batch from the money I lent him. I'll deal with him whenever he got back.

I waited 'til everybody was asleep, then went off into the corner. Frankie's corner. I did everything just like Chito did. I cooked the heroin up, mixed it around in the spoon, then sucked it up into the hypo. It hurt when I tied the rubber band around my arm, but it made about six veins pop up. I ain't never liked needles when I was a kid. It took my moms and a nurse to hold me down when I got my vaccinations for school. But after everything I had seen so far in the 'Nam, a little prick in my arm wasn't gonna bother me. I stuck the needle in the biggest, fattest vein I had.

It was like hot water rushing through my body. I shook when the smack first went in, but in no time at all my whole body was feeling real calm. I closed my eyes saw all kinds of colors in my head. I tried to think about Lee, about Chito. Serves me right. Frankie told me not to get close to anybody out there. I always had to find out the hard way how right he was.

I woke up two days later in a Medavac station in Bien Hoa. Not only did I overdose, but the shit was wack too. It was a little bit of heroin cut with a whole lot of who knows what. The medic told me that I had put too much in the needle, that's what knocked me out for two days. He said that if it had been pure heroin, or even the usual stuff you get around there, I would have been dead. I had no idea who sold that shit to Chito, but he got beat. Whoever it was didn't care if it killed him. That just goes to show you what those Vietnamese thought about us. Not even the drug dealers wanted us around.

I stayed in the hospital for two more days and then they sent me back to my unit. When I got there I was told Top wanted to see me ASAP. The way I felt I didn't want to deal with nothing, and I damn sure didn't want nobody fuckin' with me either. I went straight to the bunker to lie down, and also to look for Chito. I wanted him to tell me if he knew what kind of shit he been sticking into his body the last few weeks.

But Chito still was not back. You know? He never came back. Nobody knows if he got wasted in that air strike, OD'd somewhere in the jungle, or just plain went AWOL for the remainder of the war. They sent a squad to look around for him, but they couldn't find anything, not even his body. It was almost a week since he left to go fishing, and he was never heard from again. I felt like shit because he asked me to go with him. Maybe I could have done something to help him one way or another. Now he was gone, Missing In Action. At least this time I didn't have to say goodbye to another *pana*. By now I didn't give a fuck anyway.

"TORRES!" It was Top. He came bursting into the bunker with a *big* case o' the ass. That means he was pissed off. "Didn't you get my order to report to me as soon as you got back?"

"Yeah, Top, but...."

"Butt-fucker! I don't wanna hear it! Now you get your junkie ass up off that rack and report to the HQ tent. ON THE DOUBLE!"

Junkie? Damn, man, I wasn't in the mood. As he turned around to walk out I said, "Hey, Top. You got a joint you can sell me?" Before I even had time to laugh at my little joke, Top had thrown me against the wall, with his 9mm Glock pistol out of the holster pushing up into my face.

"Corporal Torres, you have one minute to report to my tent, so I suggest you quit your half-steppin' and get there as fast as you can. And if you ever even *think* of talking to me like that again, it's gonna be you, me, and Glocky here taking a walk into that jungle. I guarantee you only two of us are coming back, and one of them won't be you."

I got to the tent before Top did.

When I walked in Captain Bonner was sitting there looking at some reports. He was waiting for me.

"Corporal Torres reporting as ordered, SIR!" I saluted him, but with an attitude.

"At ease, Corporal. Sit down." I sat down just as Top came through the door. "How do you feel?" Captain was always cool with me. The fact that he cared to ask me how I felt helped me calm down.

"Much better, sir, thank you."

"Good. I don't usually like to give lectures about the dangers of drugs. You people are grown men and should know better by now, especially here in this country where these people will sell you battery acid and tell you it's the best heroin in the world. Of course, you'd be dead before you found that out. You were lucky this time."

This time?

"Well, sir, I must tell you that this is the first time I ever tried heroin, and....."

"Yeah, yeah, I know, and you're never going to do it again, right? That's what Private Delgado told me before he disappeared into the woods. You were close friends with him, weren't you?"

He was talking about Chito. I was getting mad again.

"I'm close friends with all my brothers here, Captain. We have to be close so that we can get through this bullshit you're makin' us do."

"At ease, Corporal! Don't forget you're addressing an officer." That was Top. He was still pissed at my little joke.

"That's all right, Sergeant." The Captain held up his hand so Top would step off. "Torres, nobody wants to be here, especially not me. But right now I don't have the time to discuss the morality of this war with you. We are here to perform a job to our utmost capability, for as long as we have to do it, until somebody tells us we can go home. We can't possibly succeed if you're strung out on drugs."

"Like I'm the only one doin' drugs."

"No, you're not the only one. Your friend, er, Chito, was one, and look what happened to him. If you can find him, that is. The thing is that this is becoming a major problem for the Army. There's too much of this going on. We got boys going home in body bags, and we got boys going home with arms and legs missing. It seems like the ones that make it out of here in one piece are addicted to every kind of drug they can find."

"I'd rather get high than kill innocent women and children."

Captain's face got real hard as he stared me down. It looked like he wanted to strangle me right there. He wasn't gonna be cool no more.

"Now that you mention that, about women and children, let me ask you a question. Why were your identification tags found in the wreckage of the helicopter that went down in the Free Fire Zone?"

My dogtags, the ones I had given to Lee when I put him on the truck. Just thinking about him again made me want to scream.

"I had a little friend in that village, sir. He was just a kid, only six years old. Reminded me of my little brother. When they came down with this bright idea of moving the civilians out, I gave him my dogtags as a present. You know, to calm him down."

"To calm him down?"

"Yes, sir. I mean, he was just a kid. He was scared. After what happened to him, I don't blame him for being scared."

"I can understand that, and I'm sorry. But do you know it's against Army regulations to distribute or dispose of your dogtags in an unauthorized manner?"

"With all due respect, *sir*, I stopped giving a fuck about Army regulations a long time ago. I thought everybody here did. So what's the big deal?"

Top got in my face again. "The big deal, motherfucker, is that those tags are your ultimate form of identification. Papers, wallets, even clothes will incinerate to nothing if you get blown up. The last chance of anybody knowing who your charcoaled ass is is with those metal tags, which are always to remain on your person."

"Well, I figured I could always order another set from supply, right?"

"That's not the point, Corporal. Your tags were found in a burned out wreckage of a helicopter and two duece-and-a-half trucks. It was a mess out there. We could hardly tell what were human bodies, much less recognize who they were. If Sergeant Lipscomb hadn't reported you on Sick Call the next day, they would have thought you were dead too, just by the fact that your tags were found on the scene."

"But I'm here, Captain, alive and well. Everything's okay, right?"

"No. Everything's NOT okay!" Top was playin' bad cop to Captain's good cop, just like in *Kojak*. "*We* knew you were here, but the detail in charge of cleaning up that mess and sorting out the bodies didn't. They were ready to report you KIA."

"They would have been wrong. So?"

"So? You ever think about your Momma back home, you little maggot? While you're out here taking your nice little trip chasing different color butterflies, your Momma would've been home crying her eyes out after being informed her darling little soldier boy was killed. You ever think about that?"

I had no wise-ass answer for that one.

After some silence, the Captain spoke up again.

"Corporal Torres, be informed that the United States Army is cracking down on widespread drug use within its ranks. They will do everything possible to help those addicts that want to get help. But they will also excercise appropriate disciplinary action to those who refuse help and continue abusing drugs. Do you understand that?"

"Yes, sir."

"Corporal Torres, please stand at attention."

What now, I thought. I stood up.

"Corporal Eduardo J. Torres, you are being given an Article 15 for improper disposal of an official government-issued piece of equipment, your identification tags. The punishment for that is probation for the remainder of your tour here in the Republic of Vietnam. Our records indicate that you have a little over three months to go. Do you understand the charges and punishment?"

"Yes, sir."

"Very well. We'll continue. Corporal Torres, you are being given a second Article 15 for being found in the posssesion of a controlled substance, and for intentionally abusing said controlled substance in a manner that impaired your ability to perform your duties as a soldier in the United States Army. Your punishment for this charge is demotion of rank to Private First Class. Any repeated offense concerning the abuse of drugs will result in Court Martial proceedings for consideration of your incarceration and possible dismissal from the United States Army under dishonorable conditions. Do you understand the charges and punishment?"

I couldn't believe this shit. I was being busted.

"Do you understand the charges and punishment, Corporal Torres?"

"Yes, sir."

"Very well. Please sign at the bottom of the forms."

I signed the Article 15's, both of them. Top took a copy of them and gave them to me, "for my personal records." He could've shoved those copies up his ass for all I cared.

"You may return to your bunker. And Torres?"

"Yes, sir?"

"Let this be a warning to you. Please be careful. You don't have much time left to go here. Try to make it home all right. Your family is waiting for you."

"Yes, sir. Thank you."

I got back to the bunker ready to smack anybody that came near me. I was pissed off, man. I mean, I only did that shit one time, and I thought I had a good reason to do it. Motherfuckers were shooting up all the time and nobody ever did anything about it. All of a sudden it's ME who gets busted. I didn't give a fuck about being a Private again. I was getting 'short'. I wasn't havin' no more of this Army shit after I got home. But the fact that I had gone this far without any problems, and I had been a good troop most of the time, they should've cut me some slack. Instead, they treated me like some *tecato* fuck-up.

Man, fuck them motherfuckers. I didn't care before, I wasn't gonna care now. All I wanted to do was go home.

CHAPTER EIGHTEEN

Mi querido Papo,

Hola, Papo. How are you? I got your letter the other day, it made me so happy to hear from you. I am glad that everything is alright so far. I am counting the days waiting for you to come home. In case you didn't know, you have fifty-five days left. I am crossing the days off on my calendar.

We are planning a big party for you. We are going to have it in the basement of my building. Your whole family will be here. Wait until you see how big Georgie and Jessica have gotten. Johnny will be coming home from college to be here. Ricky called Louie in Philadelphia to tell him, so he will be here too. I told Chico about it, and he is telling all of your other friends so that they can come too. We are very excited. It will be the best party you ever had, even better than when we won that contest at Tapestry.

Chico has been talking about joining the Army. Everybody says he's crazy, especially with the war still going on. But he says that it will end soon, so he's not worried about it. Chico has been having a lot of problems with his father at home. The man still has not gotten over the death of his wife and he's still drinking a lot. Chico says it is better to be in the Army than to live like that. I still say he is crazy.

The basketball team at school made it to the playoffs, but we lost the first game and got eliminated. They played the game at Fordham University. I got to cheer in front of many people. I was so nervous, I didn't want to mess up. But I did alright. The guys on the team told me so on the busride home.

Well, Papo, I have to go now. Please come home safe, don't get hurt. I can't wait to dance with you in your party again.

Con cariño,
Espy

Like I wasn't gonna know how many days I had left.

I never told Espy that I got busted. I wasn't going to tell her about the drugs either. I knew she didn't go for that shit, not even pot. I was hoping that once I got home I would be able to leave that stuff behind in 'Nam. I thought that it would be easy to give it up. I really did.

Lipscomb got sent home about a month after my overdose. Another brother made it out of there alive. There weren't that many guys left that were there when I got there. I was the senior man in our bunker. If it wasn't for the fact that I got busted, I would have been promoted to Sergeant and been put in charge of the squad. Instead, they transferred this black dude from another unit to take Lipscomb's place. His name was Walter Simmons, from Texas. He was alright, for a country boy.

Everything was fine for a while. I didn't get any more urges to shoot up. I wasn't gonna get hooked after just one trip no ways, no matter how nice it was. I still smoked my herb whenever I got the chance. But besides Sal and Gatewood, there really wasn't anybody left that I could hang out with. By now I wasn't trusting nobody. I got pretty tight with Flaco, but he was still into his "Soldier of the Year" tip, and I couldn't get into that.

Some other newbies came into camp over the last couple of months. Here I thought Nixon was bringing us home. He been sayin' that bullshit for a year. Why the fuck was he still sending motherfuckers over there? It was just one lie after another.

Most of the dudes coming in were *blanquitos*. There was one guy named Hill, Jeff Hill, from Maine. I never met anybody from Maine before. He always talked about the motorcycle he had back home, a Harley Davidson. Then there were a couple of guys from Missouri, Butler and Carlson. They liked to get high too, it's just that they never invited us to party with them. They weren't used to hanging around Puerto Ricans.

Everything had to be done on the sneak now anyways. The "man" thought he could really do something about the drug problem in Vietnam. He didn't have a chance. Motherfuckers were still getting high, still shooting up. They just didn't do it out in the open anymore.

There wasn't much action with the Viet Cong for a while. I started to think that they forgot we were there. That was fine with me. I had seen enough shit to last me a lifetime, and I still didn't have it as bad as some other people. I heard stories about battalions losing hundreds of men trying to take over a hill. Then once they finally captured it, they got orders to leave. Within a week Charlie was back on the same hill, like nothing ever happened. What a fuckin' waste that was.

I heard another story about *putas* putting razor blades in their cunts. That way, when a G.I. stuck his cock up in there, then pulled it out, he'd get his shit sliced up like a *salchichón*. Tell me that's not crazy, bro'. Tell me that we weren't stupid for being there in the first place. That's what everybody was saying about us back home. Look at Chico. People were already calling him crazy for just *thinking* about joining the Army and take the chance of ending up in 'Nam. That means I was an asshole for being there too, like I had a choice. It was *real nice* to know how people back home felt about us while we were over there, giving up our lives over a bunch of bullshit. That was more messed up than being killed or wounded.

The worse thing that could have happened to me over there finally happened. Captain Bonner finished his six months at our camp. He was going home for the last time. Even though he busted me, and even though I jumped stink with him when he was giving me the Article 15's, he still always asked me how I was doing. I knew he didn't have a choice to do what he did. He was under orders like we all were under orders. I'm sure he'd rather have just talked to me to make sure I wasn't getting hooked. But with Top on his ass, he had to show some authority.

After Captain Bonner left he was replaced by a 2nd Lieutenant right out of West Point. Lieutenant Harrison Avery. This dude didn't have a minute of experience in combat, and here he was telling us what to do. It was fucked up that they brought in a 2nd Lewey to take over the command instead of another Captain. I guess we weren't that important anymore. At first I didn't care. I only had forty-two days and a wake-up. I was 'short'! With Charlie's cooperation, I was going to be home doing the mambo with my baby in *no time*!

Right from the start I saw that things were going to be different with that *hijo puta* Lieutenant Avery. He came out there all hard-core, an' shit, like he had to prove something to us. He was making us clean up things that hadn't been touched for years. We were in a fuckin' war, this wasn't Good Housekeeping. He was having three formations a day - morning, noon, and night. Each time he had Top call off a list of shit we had to do. It's like he wanted to turn that camp into a summer resort.

Gatewood was the first one to point out that the Lewey might be a prejudiced bastard. Dwight Gatewood was a black dude from Virginia. He had been there almost as long as me, I think he arrived in-country a month after I did. Gatewood found out that the Lieutenant was from Arkansas, way down deep in Arkansas. Where he came from they still made colored folks drink from different water fountains and ride in the back of the bus. And this was 1971, goddammit!

We noticed that when all the shit work was being handed out, only the Ricans and the brothers were assigned to do it. Our squad, led by Sergeant Simmons, always had to pull guard duty on the perimeter. Sal and Flaco were out there almost every night. Of course, Flaco didn't care. He was eatin' that shit up. Me and Gatewood got stuck cleaning the latrine barrels every day. Those barrels were sitting in holes under the latrine tent. That's where everybody took a shit. We had to drag them out and dump the shit in a big pile so that the Vietnamese could come along and take it away. They spread that *mierda* all over the rice paddies as fertilizer. No wonder the country smelled like shit when I first stepped off the plane. I'd gotten used to the smell by now, but after seeing that they put human shit in the fields to grow rice I swore I would never eat another plate of rice and beans again.

I wasn't complaining about nothing they were making me do 'cause I was 'short'. When a guy got short, everything he said ended with that word. Like, "I'm gonna go get myself something to eat. I need my strength, I'm short." Or "I ain't gonna bother writing home, I'm short." It was the most beautiful word in the English language for a soldier looking forward to going home.

Gatewood, on the other hand, was pitchin' a bitch about everything. He used to call the Lieutenant a "swine". That's what the blacks down South called white people back then. He used to say "That swine is a fragging waiting to happen." I used to goof on him, trying to make jokes so he wouldn't let it get to him and do something stupid. We were both going home soon and all that shit would be over for us forever.

We started going out on more patrols after Lieutenant Avery took over. It looked like he wanted to find every Viet Cong out there and end the war himself, go home a hero. Every day we'd take a hike into the jungle and then come back to camp late in the afternoon. That didn't accomplish nothing except piss people off. It was still hot as hell over there, and who wanted to hump backpacks over some burnt out hillside all day in that heat? Like what we used to say back on the block: Don't look for trouble, won't be no trouble.

It was on one of these patrols when everything changed for me. We were out there like we always were, walking through the jungle like some people taking a stroll in the park. We hadn't had any action in so long people were getting careless. On this particular day, the Lieutenant decided to come with us. I guess he wanted to tell his girlfriend back home that he was out there, engaging the big bad Viet Cong every day. The fool even shined his boots for this little walk.

You're not supposed to have your boots shined on patrol. I told you, he didn't know shit about fighting in the jungle.

There were two squads out there that day. Us, as usual, and Sgt. Harper's squad. You remember him, right? He was the dude who was with me when we had to pick up those dead paratroopers from the 101st. He made it to Sergeant about the same time that Sgt. Simmons came by to take over our squad from Lipscomb. Harper wasn't a lifer, but he didn't do the crazy shit we did, like get high or shit like that. He just wanted to do his time and go home to his father-in-law's construction business. It's funny how everybody in 'Nam had a different story, but we all had one thing in common. We all had a reason to go home. Everybody had something they left behind that they couldn't wait to get back to. And back home they wake up every morning hoping to live a good day. In 'Nam, we woke up every morning hoping not to die that day.

We were walking along an area surrounded by some tall trees. It was a relief because those trees provided a lot of shade and it gave us a chance to cool off in the middle of the afternoon. Lieutenant Avery was hollering out commands to check this and check that. He was making so much noise that if Charlie didn't know we were coming around, they sure were going to find out with this asshole's big mouth.

I was just walking along, minding my own business. Sal was marching a few feet away from me, keeping the proper distance. The ground under our feet felt soft, like fresh dirt in a garden. We were hoping to get a chance to separate ourselves from the rest of the pack to smoke a bowl of some Thai weed that Sal had copped in town. My mind was busy thinking about that, and about the thirty-two days I had left, so I wasn't paying attention to any booby traps they might've put out there. I doubt if anybody had been around that area in years anyway. The trees kept it hidden from everything else until now. I didn't notice the small patch of dead leaves that was right in front of me.

I took one step onto that patch and the leaves gave way below me, causing me to fall into a deep hole. I screamed when I felt the pain of something tearing into the side of my foot. That shit hurt like a bastard. The hole wasn't deep enough for me to hurt myself with the fall, but I looked down and saw one of the oldest booby traps in the world. One that Frankie had warned me about a hundred times. The *punji* sticks.

Punji sticks were bamboo poles that they dug into the ground with the points sticking up. They filed the ends to make them good and sharp. Usually they dug a hole in the ground about six feet deep and buried the punji sticks at the bottom so that the tips stuck out like spears. When some sucker G.I. like me fell into the hole, he would land right on top of the sticks and get stabbed all over his body. If you fell down hard enough these sticks could go right through you. Fuck you up good.

The VC wouldn't just put these punji sticks in holes. Sometimes they hid a set of them behind a tree or something, and tied them to a spring-loaded trip wire. When somebody came along and accidentally pulled the wire with his feet, these sticks would come flying out from behind the tree and chop him up. I heard stories of G.I.'s being found like that, nailed up against a tree with all these punji sticks in them.

It seemed like this trap had been there for a long time because the wood was weak. Most of the sticks broke with my weight. The only one that did any damage was the motherfucker that was sticking right through my boot and into my foot. I yelled out for somebody to help me. The first one there was Sal.

"Whatcha doin' down there, Papo, taking a nap?"

"Kiss my ass, Sal. I'm hurt."

"What happened?"

"What happened . . . .I fell, that's what happened. One of these bamboo poles is stickin' into my foot. Get me outta here."

Sal laid down on his stomach and reached down to grab my hand. Flaco came over to help and between the two of them they pulled me up. The punji stick was still stuck to my foot. I felt the warm blood soaking my socks. My whole leg was throbbing already. I saw stars when Flaco pulled the stick out. He took off my boot and I saw a big gash on the side of my foot, right above the ankle.

Sgt. Simmons came over and joined the group, saying Lieutenant Avery wanted to know what was the holdup. I showed him the wound and he went back to report to Avery. In the meantime, the medic came over and put a bandage around the whole lower part of my leg. All of a sudden, Lieutenant Avery shows up demanding to know how serious my wound was. The medic tried to explain to him that it was a deep gash and needed some attention. All Asshole Avery wanted to know was if I could walk on it. I put my bloody sock back on, then my boot, and got up to try and walk. It hurt like a motherfucker, but I thought I could make it back to camp. Avery had other ideas.

"If you can walk, we'll carry on."

"Whatta you mean carry on? I got to get this thing taken care of. How much further you want to go?"

"At ease, soldier. We still have a few more kilometers to patrol."

The medic said, "But, sir, Private Torres might need stitches on his wound. If he keeps walking it will only get worse. I think he should turn back."

"*I'll* decide when he turns back. If Torres can walk back to camp, he can walk a little more until we have completed our mission. Let's stop wasting time. MOVE OUT!" The Lieutenant headed back towards the point.

We all looked at each other, but there was nothing we could do. I picked up my M-16, put on my helmet, and followed everybody else. With each step I felt a sharp pain, like the punji stick was still in my foot. Sal took my backpack and slung it over his shoulder. The less weight I carried, the easier it might be.

We marched on for about a half an hour and didn't see shit. I was wondering how long it would take the Lieutenant to realize that this was just a big waste of time. Harper's squad was ahead of us by a few yards, checking for mines and other traps. They were making their way around another group of trees, when out of nowhere the rapid fire of a machinegun cut through the jungle. Two of Harper's boys went down. We had walked right into a VC ambush.

Everybody scattered. Fortunately there was a trench a couple feet away and most of us dove into it. We started shooting back, but we weren't sure what we were shooting at because we couldn't see anyhting. All we knew was that it sounded like there were more of them than there were of us. What was left of Harper's squad ran back and jumped into the trench with us. Every time we tried to look up to spot the enemy, another burst of machinegun fire came back at us. We were pinned down. My only thought was that I was short, I didn't need this shit.

Hot shot Lieutenant Avery froze like a punk. This was the first action he'd seen and it finally dawned on him that this was some serious shit. He wasn't in no West Point now. This guy was looking around trying to decide what to do. He had no clue. Looked like he was gonna cry, in fact. He was even stupid enough to stick his head up for a few seconds, I guess looking for a place to run. A few seconds is all a good sniper needs to get a read on a target. If it wasn't for Sgt. Simmons grabbing him by his shirt and pulling him down, Avery woulda had his head blown off.

The shooting finally stopped. We knew Charlie was still out there, so nobody was getting up to move. The radioman was calling for some air support. I wondered how long it would take those *pendejos* to get there this time. For a couple of minutes there was nothing but silence, a spooky silence because we didn't know what was coming next. We weren't going to wait for Avery to tell us what to do because we knew more about this shit than he did. We had no choice but to stay down until the air support came.

From up ahead we heard some groaning. At first we weren't sure what it was. Then Harper said it might be one of his men who had gotten hit. Maybe he was just wounded and was calling out for help. He was moaning and crying like he was really hurt and wanted somebody to come get him.

Frankie had told me that Charlie liked to pull this trick on the Americans all the time. He said that what they do is get one of the VC who could speak pretty good English without too much of an accent. The dude would start making noises like a wounded G.I., begging for his buddies to go out and help him. You'd hear that and really think it's one of your boys out there. A G.I. never wanted to leave anybody behind, whether they's wounded really bad or even dead. So a guy would go out there trying to help his buddy, and BAM! Charlie would open up and take him out too.

This would drive the Americans crazy because you never knew if it was a trap or if there really was somebody out there hurt. It was torture for everybody. It was scary, bro', you never knew what to do.

Of course, Lieutenant Asshole didn't know about this trick. He wanted somebody to go out there and save that man. It was the first order he gave since the shooting started. Now he was screaming at everybody. Nobody moved. We just weren't sure what the deal was so we were staying put. We could hear this guy out there, but there was nothing we could do. Harper was crouched down next to Avery, crying. This was one of his men and there was nothing he could do for him. After a couple of minutes he couldn't take it anymore, so he got up to run out there. I could not believe it when I saw the Lieutenant grab Harper and pull him back down.

"No, Sergeant. I need you here. *Sergeant Simmons!*"

Our squad leader heard his name and crawled over to the Lieutenant. "Yes, sir?"

"Go out and recover that wounded man. Take someone from your squad with you."

"But, sir......."

"No buts, Sergeant. Bring that troop back!"

Simmons just stared at the Lieutenant. He had heard about the prejudism, but he never paid it no mind. He was a black man from Texas, and being from the South I guess he was used to it.

"I'll go on my own." He grabbed the medic's bag that was full of bandages just in case he had time for a quick patchup. He looked at me and gave me the thumbs up, then climbed over the trench and headed out.

We peeked over the trench to get ready to cover Simmons. I think he got as far as twenty yards away when we heard one shot. A sniper. I saw Sarge's body jerk back. He turned around to face us. Blood was gushing out of his neck. One bullet, right to the throat.

He stood long enough to look at us before he dropped to the ground. I heard him choking in his own blood, then he lay still.

The moaning got louder.

"Santiago!" Now the Lieutenant was calling Flaco to do the same thing poor Simmons had to do.

"SIR!" Super-troop was needed.

"Go get that man!"

Without hesitation, Flaco took off his backpack, grabbed his M-16, and with a loud scream, real gung-ho like, ran out like the good troop and stupid motherfucker that he was. He didn't even make it as far as Simmons. Before he could finish his scream, a burst from one of those M-60 machine guns cut him right in half. I saw my boy fall in two pieces right before my eyes.

You think it was a coincidence that the Lieutenant ordered a black dude, then a Puerto Rican to run right into their deaths? *Fuck* no.

Now he yells out my name, "TORRES!" And I go "WHAT?" Fuck that "Yes, sir" bullshit. I say "WHAT?" He tells ME to go out there. I look around and I see all these other guys: Butler from Missouri, Harper, another surfer dude from sunny California that had been there only a month. All white boys. I say, "Lieutenant, man, I'm short, don't make me go out there. Send one of these other crackers."

"Private Torres, you WILL go out and recover that wounded soldier."

"But sir, my foot hurts!"

"MOVE, Torres! That's an ORDER!"

"Fuck you AND your order, I'm goin' home in four weeks, man."

"Don't count on it, soldier." Then he points his little Army-issue revolver at me, like he's gonna shoot me on the spot if I don't obey his order. I look at my odds and I figure either way I'm dead. Then I realize that while he's holding that little pistol at me, I'm holding a loaded M-fuckin'-16 automatic-fire rifle in MY hands. My odds got better all of a sudden. I get up, you know, makin' like I'm gonna go out there. Then in flash I turn around and empty my clip at the Lieutenant.

PLLAAAAATTTTT!! PLLAAAATTT! Pllatt!! Pllaatt...!!! The force of the shots knocked me down.

I didn't kill him, though. I missed. Remember, I never was a good shot. But I'd be lyin' if I said that Lieutenant Asshole Avery didn't drop a load of shit in his pants when he saw me turn on him. His eyes popped wide like he seen a ghost. From far away we heard helicopters coming. It was music to my ears. I didn't want to die out there, not with just a couple of weeks left to finally go home.

It didn't take long for the choppers to pound on the enemy position with everything they had. They wiped out that whole area in minutes. Whoever was moaning out there wasn't moaning no more. After the shooting stopped we policed the area. All we saw were bodies. Our two guys that got hit first, about a dozen Viet Cong, Simmons. And Flaco.

Poor Flaco. He wasn't a bad guy after all. He was a good soldier and he had a lotta heart. Brave like a motherfucker. But he got what he wanted. He wanted to be a lifer, and that is exactly what he ended up being. He stayed in the Army the rest of his life. I'm sure he didn't expect his career to be so short. *Que descanse en paz, mi hermano.*

We made it out of there, believe it or not. And sure enough, once we got back to base camp this motherfuckin' Lieutenant pressed charges on me for attempted murder and insubordination. He called the MP's to come in and arrest me. They took me away in handcuffs and everything. I couldn't believe it. At first I wasn't gonna sweat it. I figured I was going to spend the last thirty-two days locked up. At least I wouldn't be taking the chance of getting blown away out in the jungle.

I got sent to Long Binh Jail, otherwise known as LBJ. Long Binh was a larger city in South Vietnam, bigger than Bien Hoa. The stockade was there, and that's where they put dudes that fucked up, tried to go AWOL, or other shit. A lot of guys were in there for fragging their commanding officers like I tried to do with Avery. But some of those guys did actually kill their superiors. I only made a half-ass attempt to. I figured they would leave me there until it was time to go home, give me another Article 15, and maybe kick me out of the Army with a Dishonorable Discharge. I couldn't care less how I got out, as long as I got to go home.

All my life growing up in the South Bronx I never even came *close* to getting thrown in jail. Pops used to say to me that if I wanted to be like those *títeres* in the streets, I would be on my own. If I got in trouble, he wasn't gonna come down to bail me out. I don't know if he was ever serious, but it was going to be easy for him to be true to his word this time. No damn way was he gonna show up in the 'Nam to help me now.

My cell was small and I had to share it with four other guys who were awaiting trials. There were only four bunks made out of hard plywood. A blanket was the mattress. Since I was the newest guy in the cell, I had to sleep on the floor until one of the other guys got shipped out somewhere else. After almost a year in-country, sleeping on the floor wasn't that big a deal. At least I didn't have to worry about rats the size of alleycats chewing on my face in the middle of the night. There were rats at LBJ, they just weren't the size of alleycats.

I was at LBJ for two weeks before anybody came to see me to discuss my case. A First Lieutenant from JAG stopped by my cell. He asked me for a short explanation of what happened and I tried to tell him that the Lieutenant was a prejudiced fuck. But this dude didn't want to hear that shit. He only wanted the facts. I told him the fact that this pasty-faced punk-ass Lieutenant was prejudiced is why I opened up on him. Those were the facts. I remember this guy exhale in frustration, as if to say, "This wetback is going to be trouble." He closed his file folder, which probably had my whole life in it.

"Your preliminary hearing is scheduled for September 29th. At that time you will be given the opportunity to explain your side of the story to the Adjutant Judge."

"Hold up, SIR. September 29th? I'm supposed to be going home on September 8th. My tour is up, man."

"I wouldn't be making any traveling plans if I were you, young man. You are in serious trouble. This isn't a simple Article 15 for disobeying a direct order. You are being charged with attempted murder of a commissioned officer in the line of combat duty. You are, as they say, in deep shit."

"But it was either that, or let this dude get me killed! Don't you know what happened to those two other guys?"

"Well, under the circumstances of the situation it may be possible that the punishment may not be that severe."

"Punishment? You make it sound like I'm already guilty. Aren't you supposed to try to get me off. I'm innocent!"

"Oh, Private Torres, I am not your attorney. I'm just here gathering statements from you, just like I did with Lieutenant Avery. You know, taking depositions for the case. Your defense lawyer will be appointed to you on September 29th and at that time you can brief him on your, er, *innocence*." The *hijo de la gran puta* got up and looked around the cell. Smiling, he said "I can't predict what's going to happen in that hearing, but rest assured that you will be with us here in the Republic of Vietnam for a little while longer."

He left the cell and the MP guard closed the door behind him. I found my spot at the corner and sat down on the floor. I folded my knees up to my chin and wrapped my arms around my legs. Rocking back and forth, I started thinking. Thinking that things weren't working out like I figured. Thinking that I wasn't going home just yet. I didn't know it then, but I never got to go home. Not the home I once knew.

CHAPTER NINETEEN

It was late at night and I couldn't fall asleep. The pain in my foot was killing me. After we got back from patrol that day the medic cleaned the gash out with water and sewed it back up with ten stitches. He had to do it fast because the MP's were in a hurry to take me away. Lieutenant Avery was still pissed about what happened out on patrol, and I guess he needed to get back some of the respect and authority he lost when I challenged him. But what I did wasn't going to matter to the platoon. After the way the Lieutenant bitched up when we got ambushed, ain't no way the guys in the company were going to follow him into any more battles. The best he could've done was to go on home to mommy, daddy, and fuckin' Peggy Sue.

The light coming in from the MP's post allowed me to look down at my foot. It had gotten real swollen. It'd been three weeks since I fell into that trap and I thought by now it should have healed. But because of the swelling they couldn't remove the stitches, and blood and puss was still oozing out of it. Nobody at LBJ gave a fuck about it anyways, so they weren't going out of their way to examine it.

I didn't talk much to the guys in my cell. What for? I was sure I wasn't going be there that long anyways. Besides, those guys were real problem soldiers. Two were there for going AWOL all the time, but it wasn't because they didn't want to fight. One guy would go into town, pick up a couple of hookers, and spend two weeks smokin' opium and fucking his brains out. He didn't care about getting back to his unit on time, he was enjoying himself. The other dude just disappeared to take walks, a real nature boy. They had him down for desertion, which in wartime is worse than going AWOL.

My two other cellmates were bad news. Both had shot their officers in the field. One of 'em, Clarence, was a black dude from Florida. He shot his CO because he wasn't allowed to play his radio when he wanted to. He couldn't get it through his thick nappy head that playing music at nighttime was not the brightest thing to do, especially with Charlie out in the sticks lookin' for you. The CO tried to take the radio away from him and Clarence put a bullet in his arm.

Then there was the brother from Watts in Los Angeles. His beef was that he just didn't want to be killed. Like, no shit Sherlock. This dude refused every direct order that was given him. They were out on patrol one night when his CO ordered him to walk the point to check out for land mines. Nobody wanted that job. If you fucked up a lotta people would get hurt, starting with you. You'd be heading home in little pieces. Watts, that's what everybody called him, decided if anybody was going home in pieces it would be the CO. Shot 'im right in the chest. Now he was up for murder. "At least I ain't the one dead," he used to say.

It took a while before I got the nerve to write home and tell my folks what was going on. At the time I wasn't sure if the Army had told them. Nobody was telling me shit. It was even harder writing the letter to Espy and try explaining why she would have to cancel that welcome home party she was planning. I knew they were all waiting for me and I felt really bad that I disappointed them. I hadn't written to anybody since that whole shit went down, which had been about four weeks. I was still getting letters from Espy, just not every day like before. I wondered what she was thinking when she didn't hear from me in so long. Maybe she thought I was dead.

September 8th came and went.
I didn't leave my cell the whole day.

Sal was able to stop by the jail to visit me once. He did it by going to Long Binh on an ammo supply detail. He told me that everybody was giving Lieutenant Avery a hard time at camp, even Top. They were pissed off, not only for what he was doing to me, but for letting Simmons and Flaco get wasted too. Flaco was Top's favorite. I'm sure he wanted to take a shot at Avery himself, but he wasn't going to lose eighteen years in the service over it. And that arrogant bastard Lieutenant was being a bigger asshole than ever. It was like he was fighting his own war, and his own troops were the enemy.

The hardest part about being locked up in 'Nam was being cooped up in a hot, cramped cell with the four other guys. Out in the sticks we sometimes went a few days without shaving or taking a shower. But that was because we didn't have time, or there wasn't enough clean water for everybody. As soon as we had the chance we'd all be fighting to get to the front of the line to wash up.

But these dudes in the cell with me obviously didn't give a damn what they looked like or what they smelled like. They were in a prison in South Vietnam. To them it was like who cares. The Vietnam heat didn't help either. Clarence and Watts were funky-assed to begin with. Sweating in that heat made them stink so bad they could've used it against the bad guys. Picture that. We coulda put one of Clarence's nasty drawers on a big stick and charged down the hill with it, right into the Viet Cong camp. Charlie would have *jetted* out of there, sayin', "Go ahead, you want the country, go ahead, take it! TAKE IT! Just get that funky shit out my face." I imagine they would've swam all the way to Korea.

The food was fucked up too. It was just my luck that all they served was rice. All day, every day. That stepped-on, grown-in-the-shit-field-across-the-road rice. I wondered what they did when a civilian got killed in the rice paddies. Did they leave him out there to rot? Is that how we get brown rice? I was thinking all kinds of crazy shit 'cause there was nothing else left to do.

About two days before the hearing, an MP private comes to my cell with my dress greens. They had sent him to my camp to gather up all my personal stuff so they could send it home. If my parents didn't know about me yet, they were going to find out soon. My dress uniform was cleaned and pressed. They must've sent it to the cleaners, 'cause those things had been stuffed in the bottom of my duffel bag underneath my bunk ever since I arrived in Viet Nam. I wondered if they had a Chinese cleaners in Nam. That would be a trip. See, bro'? All kinds of crazy shit was going through my mind.

They brought me my uniform because I was going to need it for the hearing. That was a good idea, I thought. Just like when Pops told me about applying for a job. If I look good and professional, things would go my way. It worked for Mr. Kohler at the discount store. If only Mr. Kohler could be the judge at my hearing.

I tried the uniform on after I took my shower that night. I hadn't worn that thing since graduation at boot camp. That seemed like so long ago. At first I thought they brought me the wrong uniform. This thing was *way* too big. I pulled out the wasteline of the pants and swore I could fit another dude in there with me. The two sides of the jacket overlapped each other. But it was mine. I knew because I checked the inside lining and saw the label with my name on it. We had to sew those labels on in basic training in case our clothes got mixed up. Like little kids in kindergarten.

I couldn't believe how much weight I lost in one year. I was never fat or big in any way. But damn, I never realized it until then how boney I got over there. I was a skeleton. The only fat part of my body was my swollen foot. Even my head must've shrunk because my cap was big too. I couldn't wait to get home and stuff myself with Moms' pork chops, *pasteles*, fried chicken, *platanos, mofongos*.

Anything except rice.

On the morning of the hearing two big MP motherfuckers came to my cell to escort me to the courtroom. I had to be ready to go by eight o'clock. I couldn't sleep at all the night before, hoping that the judge would understand the situation and let me go home. But the way my luck had been over the last year, I really wasn't getting too excited about it. After all, those JAG cocksuckers - the lawyers, the judges, even the clerks - they was all officers. I had attacked an officer, one of their own. I didn't stand a chance right from the start. The cards were stacked against me. The Army is all about discipline and respect for authority. I fucked up on all counts. But I still felt I had a good reason to. I could only pray that the judge would see it my way.

We marched into a big room. Well, the MP's marched, I limped. The room was set up like a courtroom - rows of benches on either side with an aisle going down the middle of it. In front of each set of benches were two tables with a couple of chairs behind them facing the front of the room. That is where the lawyers and us fuck-ups sat. Six chairs were lined up off to one side, three in the front and three in the back. At the head of the room was a long wooden table with folded-out legs. There were four chairs lined up behind that table, facing us. Behind the table were three flags. The United States flag in the middle, the colors of the division stationed there at Long Binh on one side, the flag of the Republic of Vietnam on the other.

When I got to the front of the room the MP pointed to a chair on the right side behind one of the tables. The dudes never talked, they just pointed everything out to you. It was up to you to figure out what the fuck they meant, and do it quick enough so you wouldn't get pushed. I went to take my seat. Waiting for me at the table was another *gringo* captain. From the patch he had on his sleeve I could tell he was a JAG lawyer too. He held out his hand.

"Private Torres. I'm Captain Diehl. I have been assigned to be your legal counsel for this hearing."

"Nice to meet you, Captain. I'm innocent."

He laughed, like this was all some big fuckin' joke. "I'm sure you are, Private Torres." He said that like he was really thinking "Yeah, all you people think you're innocent."

"Private Torres, the purpose of this hearing is to give both parties the opportunity to relate to the court exactly what happened out there. I know it was a tense situation, but fortunately in this instance, all parties are healthy and able to give their account. The fact that Lieutenant Avery is still alive to tell his side might work in your favor."

"You mean I might get out of here today?"

"No, I didn't say that. You are being charged with a serious offense, so it won't be that cut and dry. But all things considered - your past record, the circumstances that led to the altercation, and the fact that your shots missed the Lieutenant, it might not be as bad as you think. All that I ask is that you be honest with me and the court during questioning. Tell the truth and don't leave anything out. And please, respect the court and the officers in it. Your future is in their hands."

I wasn't in the mood to kiss anybody's ass, and I didn't trust this motherfucker either. The only thing I was guilty of was trying to survive and get home safe. All this was bullshit.

I heard some noise behind me. I turned to see the main doors swing open. Walking in, in their sharp, creased khaki summer uniforms, was a couple of lawyer-type officers with Lieutenant Asshole Avery following close behind. They marched to the front of the room and made a quick turn to the left to sit down at the table on the other side. Avery totally 'igged' me, as if I wasn't even there. If I had a weapon I would've popped him again, right there in front of everybody.

We all sat there in silence for a few minutes. Then another big MP called out "All rise!" Why were all them fuckin' MP's so big?

From a side door, four old dudes walked in. More *blanquitos*. They was dressed in greens too, just like me. Their uniforms had a lot more decorations than mine. Each of them had at least three medals pinned to one side of their chests, and a rainbow of ribbons filling out the other side. I looked down at my one and only medal, the marksman medal I had to "earn" for ten bucks in boot camp. It looked like a Cracker Jack prize next to the ones those guys had.

These dudes were the judges, four for the price of one. There was a one-star General, two full-bird Colonels, and a Lieutenant Colonel. These *viejo* farts were going to determine my future. Fuck them too, I thought. They marched in single file to the big table at the front of the room. When they sat down, the rest of us sat down. The flags hovered above them.

The Lieutenant Colonel spoke first.

"We are convened here today for a preliminary hearing on the case of Eduardo J. Torres, Private First Class, United States Army. Private Torres, please stand at attention." Me and my lawyer stood up.

"Private Torres, you are being charged with attempted murder stemming from an attack, in the line of combat duty, against 2nd Lieutenant Harrison Avery, United States Army. Let the record show that said attack occurred on the afternoon of August 7th, 1971. Private Torres, do you understand the charge of attempted murder?"

"Yes, sir." I didn't, but my lawyer made me say I did.

"You are also being charged with insubordination for failing to obey a direct order in the line of combat duty. This offense also occurred on the afternoon of August 7th, 1971. Private Torres, do you understand the charge of failing to obey a direct order?"

Why don't you obey me when I direct you to suck my d---!   "Yes, sir."

"Very well. You may sit down, Private Torres. Counsel for the prosecution, would you begin the questioning."

Avery's lawyer stood up. "Thank you, Colonel. I would like to call 2nd Lieutenant Harrison Avery to the stand." I always hated guys whose first name should be their last name, like Harrison or Montgomery. You never hear a Puerto Rican with a name like 'Rodriquez Rivera', do you?

The asshole walked up to a single chair they had in the middle of the room. An MP came over with the Bible and did all that "do you swear to tell the truth, the whole truth..." bullshit. *Bien* Perry Mason.

"Lieutenant Avery, would you please tell this court your version of what happened on the afternoon of August 7th."

I sat there and heard every lying word this punk-ass could spit out of his mouth. He was making it sound like he was in total control during the ambush. He was making himself out to be some sort of hero, sacrificing himself for the good of the men "trapped in a barrage of gunfire". Each time his lawyer asked him a question, he answered it so perfectly it was like they had rehearsed this over and over. Shit, nobody came to my cell to practice Q and A with me. I hadn't gotten laid in a long time, but I could tell right there that I was about to be fucked.

"I couldn't stand the thought of leaving one of my men out there, especially when there existed the possibility that he may still be alive."

"Lieutenant Avery, what was your reasoning in selecting the men you ordered to move out and recover the fallen soldier?"

"They were the best men I had. Combat-tested. I wanted someone going out there who knew the mission and knew how to carry it out."

"Tell us about them, Lieutenant."

"Sergeant Walter Simmons was a decorated soldier who joined us from the 9th Infantry when we were short-staffed. He had been in Vietnam for sixteen months. His experience was incomparable."

"And what about Corporal Miguel Santiago?"

"Corporal Santiago was one of the finest soldiers I have ever served with. He showed no fear. Although he'd been in Vietnam just a few months, he had already received commendations for valor during a civilian relocation operation deployed in June of this year. He singlehandedly eliminated a Viet Cong position that was attacking our air support during the mission. He was the perfect soldier. I was proud to have him in my command." Avery broke down and cried right there. I couldn't believe this lying sack of shit.

"Thank you, Lieutenant. You may step down and compose yourself. Counsel for the defense?"

Captain Diehl stood up and cleared his throat.

"Private Eduardo Torres, will you take the stand."

I limped over to the "stand", that stupid chair. I got the urge to diddy-bop, but I was cool. The MP came over to do his thing with the Bible, then Captain Diehl started with his questions.

"Private Torres, will you explain to the court your version of what happened."

I went on about how it was a messed up situation, about how we were pinned down and the VC weren't letting us move at all. I told them about the injury to my foot, and that I was scheduled to go home in a few weeks. I told them I was scared, that I didn't want to go home dead, like Santiago and Simmons. I started telling them that Avery was a racist.

One of the full-bird Colonels interrupted the questioning. Damn, I thought, nobody interrupted Avery when he was telling *his* bullshit. The old man had heard enough of my sob story.

"Private Torres, do you know how many young men the United States has lost in the Vietnam conflict?"

"Sir, I don't know how many have been lost in the 'conflict', but if you're talking about this damn war, losing one is one too many." I saw Captain Diehl's eyes go buggy.

The Colonel stared at me so hard I thought I saw smoke coming out of his ears. I didn't have a chance, so what the fuck.

"Let me inform you, Private Torres, that over 40,000 men and women have been killed, over 100,000 have been wounded. What do you think would have happened if all those brave young soldiers refused to carry out their orders because they were *scared*, the way you did?"

This one was easy. "They'd be a lot more real happy families back home. Er, SIR."

"That's enough out of you! You may step down."

I made it back to my seat. Diehl wouldn't even look at me.

Everything was quiet again. The judges were flipping through a bunch of paperwork in my files. Then the General spoke up.

"Private Torres. How long have you had a drug problem?"

That one put me in shock. My heart sank. I looked at Captain Diehl. They wouldn't use that against me, would they?

"General, um..., sir. I don't have a drug problem."

"No? These Article 15's here in your file say that you were demoted in rank for possession and abuse of a controlled substance. Heroin, was it?"

"Well, sir, I wouldn't exactly call it heroin. The medic at..."

"SILENCE! You were also put on probation for unauthorized disposal of official government property. I imagine that if we were to add attempted murder and insubordination to the list, as well as your insolence here in the courtroom, we would have a bit of a problem on our hands here. Wouldn't you agree, Private Torres?"

There was nothing for me to say. I looked over at Diehl. He was no use at all. Some lawyer. He bailed out on me before he even got a chance to help me. That's *IF* he really wanted to help me in the first place.

The General spoke again.

"It has been determined at this hearing that the defendant, Private Eduardo J. Torres, has repeatedly violated the rules and regulations stipulated in the Uniformed Code of Conduct of the United States Armed Forces. This failure to excercise proper discipline and respect to his commanding officer has resulted in a veritable threat to the life and well being of all officers that may be assigned to command him. Private Torres...."

The Captain nudged me to stand up. I couldn't believe this was really happening. I stood at attention. I was so numb I couldn't even feel the pain in my foot.

"Private Torres, this council has unanimously concurred that you are to stand trial for attempted murder on the life of a fellow soldier, and for insubordination of a commanding officer. You will be assigned permanent counsel from the office of the Adjutant General. Trial will begin in this courtroom at 0800 hours, on November 16th, 1971. In the meantime, you will remain incarcerated at the Long Binh Jail. Thank you, gentlemen. This hearing is now concluded."

CHAPTER TWENTY

La, la, la, la, la-la-la
La, la, la, la, la-la-la
To be with you,
One hour of each lonely day;
There would be no end,
I need you so
I want you more than you know.......

Dear Espy,

How are you, muñeca? I guess you are wondering why I haven't written to you in a long time, and why I didn't come home when I was supposed to. Maybe you already know if you talked to my family. Maybe they don't know yet either, I don't know.

The good news is that I am still alive. I got wounded in my foot while out on a patrol about two months ago. I fell in a hole and got stabbed by a big piece of wood. It still hurts me very much and I think pretty soon I will have to see a doctor to find out why it hasn't gotten better.

Although my foot hurts, it's nothing compared to the hurt I am feeling now with the news I am about to tell you. First of all, I still love you very much, that will never change. Just like you, I was counting the days for when we would be together again. I was looking forward to holding you in my arms and kissing you, hearing you laugh at my stupid jokes. But now I must tell you that I don't know when I will be home again.

You see, I got into a little trouble here in Vietnam. I didn't want for it to happen, I didn't go around trying to start anything. I was ordered to do something I didn't want to do. Not because of mala crianza, but because it was dangerous. My Lieutenant ordered me to go out to pick up another soldier who was wounded, but I already saw two other guys get killed trying to do the same thing. I only had about thirty days before I was supposed to go home and I didn't want to get killed too. But the Lieutenant pointed a gun at me and told me he would shoot me right there if I didn't do like he said. I got crazy and shot at him.

Don't worry, I didn't hurt him. But he still had me arrested and now I am in jail. I thought everything would be straightened out right away, but now they are going to put me on trial for attempted murder. I don't know how long that will take. I hope that the judge I get understands how crazy it is here in Vietnam and sometimes things like that happen. We all want to survive and make it home okay, especially me. It would not have been right that I was here for almost a year and nothing happened to me, then at the last minute I get blown away. You understand, right, baby?

It seems like I have had a lot of bad luck since I got drafted. They took me away from you just when things were really going good. I've had to say goodbye to good friends, and I've seen other friends get killed. It'll be something that will stay with me forever. Hopefully when I do get home, whenever that is, I'll be able to forget all the bad things I have seen here. I want to be back there with you, my family, and all my friends. I miss you all so much.

Espy, I am so sorry this happened. I am sorry I missed my party and let everybody down. I tried hard to be a good soldier so that everybody would be proud of me. I didn't plan on staying in the Army longer than I had to. All this is not my fault, I was just doing what the country told me to do. I am not a bad person, I am still the same Papo you met two years ago. But I have seen so many bad things here, and now bad things are happening to me too. I just hope when I get home it will all finally end.

Your letters and cards are what give me hope and keep me going. I sing to myself that song we danced to on the fire escape on my birthday, te acuerdas? I hear those words in my head and think of you. Please keep writing to me. You can send your letters to the address on the envelope. I don't know how long they are going to keep me here, but even if I get sent someplace else, they will take my mail to me.

Tell all the guys that I am okay. Give my love to your parents, but you don't have to tell them everything that happened. I hope you can understand and not give up on me. Remember, I love you.

Papo

I got a letter from my sister Lizzie one day while I was at LBJ. She told me that Moms and Pops were very upset about the problems I was having in Vietnam. The Army had sent them a letter telling them everything I had done, including the drugs. Moms didn't want to believe it. She was blaming everything on the government, saying they never should have sent me over there in the first place. Pops was mad about the drugs, since he always taught me about being a good person and not break the law. He said that if I did the things I did because I was on drugs, then I deserved whatever happened to me.

Lizzie also told me that the company Pops worked for was moving to Pennsylvania. If Pops wanted to keep his job he would have to move there too. That was some weird shit because I could never imagine us living anywhere else but on the block. Even when Lizzie moved to Long Island it didn't seem right. I always thought she would end up back home eventually, twins and all.

The trial lasted about a month. I spent Thanksgiving in jail. They served us something they called turkey, but that was anybody's guess. It was nothing like what I used to eat at home. No *arroz con gandures*, no *batata* with the marshmallows on top, no *pasteles*. Just that make-believe turkey, and the same mashed potatoes I'd been eating since boot camp. Oh yeah, I was *real* thankful.

The trial wasn't much different than the hearing. The dude they appointed to be my lawyer was another *blanquito* asshole who didn't give a shit about me either. I was wondering if there were any black or Puerto Rican officers in the Army, you know, somebody who'd be lookin' out for me, hook me up. This guy came to my cell only a couple of times to ask the same questions over and over. He tried to convince me that if I admitted what I did was wrong, they might go easy on me. I knew I was wrong, but I wanted them to check out Lieutenant Avery too. It wouldn't be fair if he got away with the shit he did to Flaco and Sergeant Simmons.

I don't have to tell you that they found me guilty. They didn't want to hear any shit about Avery. When they announced the verdict, I saw him and his swine lawyers shaking hands and patting themselves on the back. Like, "Good job, we got us another one of them *mi-no-ri-ties*." I was court martialed, busted down to the lowest rank, Buck Private, and sentenced to one year in jail. My lawyer said it could have been worse, but they took into account my good record before I "fell into the evils of drugs". For that piece of good news, I didn't know whether to thank him or bust him the mouth.

I thought I was going to be stuck in Long Binh Jail for the whole year. That meant I would have spent two years of my life in some shit-hole of a country I never even heard of until just a couple of years ago. But a week after the trial ended, close to Christmas, they told me I was going to the states. I was being transferred to the military prison at Fort Leavenworth, Kansas. Clarence was going there too. I don't know what they did with Watts.

It took a while for it to sink in that I was finally leaving Vietnam. Then again, I wasn't expecting to leave as a prisoner. I was supposed to come back to a big welcome-home parade down Randall Avenue. There'd be a marching band, and people waving and cheering me. Women kissing me, kids touching my uniform. I saw in my mind people throwing confetti out the window, like they did on Wall

Street when the Mets won the World Series. I was going home a big war hero, just like Audie Murphy.

Instead, I was going home handcuffed to an MP. There were six of us, including Clarence. Each of us had an MP of our own to be handcuffed to until we got on the plane, then they uncuffed themselves but kept ours on. By having a few MP's standing around with their rifles locked and loaded they made sure nobody was gonna act the fool. They were ready to shoot the first motherfucker who so much as farted without permission.

I had a lot of mixed feelings about leaving Vietnam. It's funny how you wait so long to finally go home, hoping you make it alive. Then when the day comes, it's not as happy as you thought it would be. Of course, in my case it really sucked because I wasn't going home, I was just leaving Vietnam. My hell continued.

As the plane took off at Da Nang airport, I looked out the window the same way I did when I first arrived. I was looking for action - battles, fires, explosions. But just like before, all I saw was a beautiful country with rolling hills and green fields. I was leaving a lot behind, had a lot of memories. Frankie, Chito, Lipscomb, Flaco. Le Vien and Mama-san. Thinking about them made me cry all over again. I'm sure Dwight Gatewood was already home, but my best friend Sal was still down there. I felt guilty leaving him behind. I wanted to go back there to make sure he made it home alive too. I never saw Sal again after he visited me at LBJ. It was just one goodbye after another. I went to Vietnam when I was eighteen years old. I was about thirty-five when I left, fifteen months later.

The trip to Kansas lasted about twenty hours. Twenty hours sitting on a hard bench in a military transport plane, our hands cuffed together the whole time. From Da Nang we flew to Japan. From there we went to Alaska, then to Travis Air Force Base in San Francisco, then on to Kansas. By the time the bus pulled into the post, it was December 23rd. We went from 90 degrees in Vietnam, to 21 degrees in Kansas. Merry Fuckin' Christmas. I had spent one Christmas in Nam, and now I was gonna spend another one in prison. And the Christmas before I got drafted, Chico's mom died. To this day the holidays just bring back bad memories.

If Vietnam was a colorful country, filled with rich jungles and trees, hills and rivers, Kansas was the complete opposite. That state was ugly, man. I got there in the winter of 1971, so there wasn't any green grass or leaves, nothing. Everything was gray. All along the ride all I saw were flat fields as far as the eye could see. There were no mountains or hills. I think I saw two trees, and they was, like, five miles apart. The sky was dark. You could be inside, you know, and look out the window and almost *see* the cold outside, even if there wasn't any snow on the ground. Remember the "Wizard of Oz", when that chick was running around before the tornado hit? Just like that, bro'.

They had two prisons at Leavenworth. There was a federal prison that they called the "Hot House" because of how hot it got in the summertime. I heard that joint had the baddest motherfuckers in the country locked up in there. Those dudes didn't give a fuck about shit. Thems the kind of people that have spent most of their lives in jail. To them, killing people was like me and you stepping on a kitchen cockaroach.

I wasn't sent there, though. Military fuck-ups got sent to the U.S. Army Disciplinary Barracks inside Fort Leavenworth. There's a difference. Didn't matter. They were both prisons, and being in prison, especially in Kansas, was like being in hell. Once summer came around I knew why they called the other place the Hot House. It gets hotter in Kansas than in Vietnam. 'Nam just stinks more.

The first thing we had to do when we got there was get strip-searched. They lined us all up in a room and made us take off our clothes. They checked every part of our body to see if we was hiding weapons or drugs. I wondered when the fuck they thought we had the chance to hide anything when we had MP's up our asses since we left LBJ. And they checked us before we left there too.

The most humiliating thing was when they made all six of us, naked, turn around and bend over. Right there, in front of everybody, this *maricón* doctor shoved his hand up our butts. I don't know about the other guys, but my ass is the *last* place I'd be hiding anything, I don't care how strung out I am. Doc was wasting his time looking up in there. Then again, to have that job he must've liked it, at least a little. I remember thinking to myself that if this dude takes a little longer with my *culito* than he should, I was gonna go "Nam" on his ass. What were they gonna do if I did? Arrest me?

The physical finally gave them a chance to check out my foot, which by now had turned black on one side. The wound still oozed puss. The doctor took one look at it and made an appointment for me to stay in the infirmary after everybody else finished their examinations. I sat in an empty room, surrounded by four plain cement walls. No charts, no posters, not even a diploma from medical school. There was an examination table on one side, and a sink by the wall underneath the only window in the room. I sat on the table, looked out the window, and waited.

I was back in the good ol' United States. I had counted down the days for a whole year to end up in this shit. I couldn't believe I was there, in jail. I thought I had done the right thing, serving my country, fighting Communism, just like I was told. Back in the Bronx nobody gave a damn about all that political shit. The only discussions we had were about who was better, Mickey Mantle or Roberto Clemente. We lived in our own little world, and as long as you respected your parents and neighbors, everything was all right. Yeah, some guys were into stealing hubcaps off of cars, and maybe selling some weed here and there. *Idiotas* like that always gave the rest of us a bad name.

People think about Puerto Ricans and right away they think that we all carry knives and take welfare. Not everybody's like that. Well, *you* know that, bro. I see you here in your nice suit, so I know you done pretty good with yourself. But let me ask you something. Was it that easy getting a job when people found out you were Puerto Rican? Probably not, no matter what college you went to. Sometimes I don't blame them, believe it or not. There's a lot of lowlife motherfuckers out there who rob and steal, getting drunk on rum all the time. There's some Spanish neighborhoods here in the Bronx and other parts of New York that are fuckin' filthy, man. It's like these people don't care that they live like that, like they don't have no pride in themselves.

I should talk, right bro'? You see me like this now, all raggedy an' shit, and you think I'm just like all those other spics, messing it up for people like you. But you know I wasn't always like this. Sometimes shit happens that you don't plan on and it changes your whole life. I don't blame nobody for the way I am. I just had a run of bad luck. That's how I look at it.

The doctor finally came into the room carrying a clipboard and a file. My whole life story was in that file. The doctor was another Captain. He tried to be friendly at first as he flipped through my file, but after what happened to me I wasn't trusting any more officers.

"Says here you have a foot injury." *Chévere.* This guy can read. "How did it happen?"

"I fell into a punji pit and got a piece of bamboo stuck in there. That's not in the file?"

"Oh, yes. Here it is. The old punji stick routine." Now he thought he was that dude from *Get Smart*. "Let's have a look."

I lifted my leg up to the table so he could get a better view. He saw how black it was and whistled. I know he ain't never seen anything *that* nasty before.

"We're going to have to take some blood samples. It's obvious you have some sort of infection." I could've told him that, and I didn't go to medical school.

"Doc, I'm in a lotta pain. This thing been fuckin' with me for months. I can't sleep at night because of it."

"We'll give you something for the pain. Wait right here." This guy talked like there were more people there with him, with his "We" and "Let's". He left the room and a few minutes later a nurse came in with about four needles. Three smaller ones were for the blood samples, the biggest one was the painkiller.

"What's that, nurse?" I asked her, pointing to the big needle.

"It's for the pain."

"Yeah, I know. But what is it?"

"Morphine. It's a sedative, as well as an anesthetic. Roll up your sleeve."

She hit me in the arm with the big needle first. Then she stuck the other three needles in my leg for the blood samples. I just laid back on the table and let her do her thing. After she got everything she wanted, she walked out of the room and left me there, alone once again.

Until then, I ain't never heard of that morphine shit. I always thought that when you were real sick they shot you up with penicillin. Or they gave you aspirin. I didn't know anything about no morphine, but about five minutes after that chick left the room I started feeling *nice*, man. I was relaxed, warm, and for the first time in months my foot wasn't hurting no more. I thought I was cured. I laid back on that cold table and wasn't feeling shit. I don't remember how long I was there - five minutes or five hours - before the doctor came back into the room.

"Private Torres, I have the results of your tests. It doesn't look good."

"I coulda told you that, Doc." That shit had me feeling real mellow.

"You don't understand, Torres. You have a serious septic infection."

"What does that mean?"

"It means that those punji sticks you landed on were covered with human feces. In other words, shit. That's a common Viet Cong tactic. If the stab wounds don't kill you, the contaminated wood will. Once your skin was punctured bacteria entered your blood stream. The fact that you didn't receive immediate proper medical care has made it worse."

"How much worse, Doc. What are you talking about?"

"Well, we are going to try to combat the infection with antibiotics with the hope of saving your leg, but some parts of your foot are beyond help."

"Saving my leg? Beyond help? What the fuck are you saying?"

"We might have to amputate two of your toes. Apparently, that is the area where the infection has festered. By extracting that portion it will keep the infection from spreading throughout your leg. We're going to run some more tests, but either way we'll have to act fast before it really gets too late."

As far as I was concerned, it was already too late. Check it out, bro', I'll show you. They chopped off my big toe and the one next to it. They were able to save the rest of the foot and my leg. It still hurts me, that's why you see me walking with a limp.

I spent three weeks in the infirmary before I finally got assigned to a room. I was walking on crutches the first time any of the other inmates saw me. Maybe because of that nobody ever fucked with me the whole time I was there. I was locked up for fragging an officer in 'Nam. That was considered cool.

They gave me more shots of that morphine right before the operation, and some more while I was recovering in sick bay. I was really getting to like it and I wanted some all the time. It was the only thing that kept my foot from hurting. As soon as the morphine started wearing off, I'd ask for more and they'd give it to me. I didn't know you could get hooked on that shit. I had found myself a new drug.

At first it was easy to get. As long as I was in the infirmary I could ask for it anytime. All I had to do was say my foot hurt and BAM! They hooked me up. But once I got sent to my room they figured I was recovered and shouldn't be feeling that much pain anymore. If the foot hurt, they gave me aspirin. Taking aspirin for that pain was like fuckin' an elephant with a toothpick. It wasn't gonna do shit for me. I had to find a way to get some more morphine. I wished Chito was with me. If anybody could score in the joint, *he* could.

It wasn't long before I got my source. There was this skinny white dude named Maynard. He was another one of those AWOL guys who would go home on leave and never come back. They'd have to send the local MP's after his ass. The funny thing about it was that this stupid *blanquito* would always go to the same place to hide - his sister's house. The MP's always knew where to go to find him. People said it got so comical that Maynard's sister always had some food ready to feed the MP's when they got there. They'd all sit down, have lunch, then cuff Maynard and take him back to the post. I wouldn't been surprised if one of them MP's was getting some of the sister's ass every once in a while. These country-ass *gringos* are some funny people.

Anyways, since Maynard wasn't considered dangerous or anything, he was designated a trustee. He had different jobs, like giving out books from the prison library to inmates. Other times he worked sorting mail in the administration post office. He was able to get into any part of the barracks and nobody asked any questions. Acting like a real doofus made him popular.

But Maynard wasn't the dumb hick everybody thought he was. He took advantage of his position to get things for people - for a price. Some of it was silly shit, like extra food that he would sneak into the cells at night. He got Clarence an old beat-up radio that used to belong to another inmate who had been released. That Clarence. He still fiended for his music, even though it's what got him in trouble in the first place.

Maynard was rackin' up in the joint because everybody trusted him, even the warden. Clarence introduced me to him and that's when I asked him if he could get into the infirmary. No sweat, he said. That was his specialty. Within a week I was getting steady hits of morphine, along with a supply of needles. I paid it with money and cigarettes. The money came from the few bucks they gave us each month for the work we was assigned to do. I worked in the laundry, ironing uniforms. It was the only job they could give me where I could sit down doing it.

I don't know which was worse, being in 'Nam or being at Leavenworth. In either case I was trapped someplace I didn't want to be, a place I never thought I would ever find myself in. The only difference was that in Leavenworth I didn't have to worry about getting blown away by some crazy gook. As long as I minded my own business, didn't snitch on nobody, and didn't try to be no bad-ass, I would be okay. In Leavenworth we were all soldiers once, so it wasn't as cutthroat as other prisons are. We still had to watch our backs, but it was more of us against the guards and the swines running the place. We all stuck together and got high. That was the only way to make it.

Come to think of it, it was just like Vietnam.

CHAPTER TWENTY ONE

I didn't bother to count the days at Leavenworth. In Vietnam, you knew exactly when you were going home, give or take a day. Sometimes dudes got to go home a little earlier for different reasons, like for being wounded. Or dead. But hardly anybody got stuck in-country longer than they should, unless they wanted to, like Frankie. In prison, you never knew what was happening. You could be paroled, or you could be released early for good behavior. You could also get in trouble for any little thing and get more time tacked on. I learned not to get excited about anything because in the last couple of years things had not gone the way I planned it. So, fuck it. Why get your heart set on something that may not happen, you know what I'm sayin'?

I got a little surprise after being in Leavenworth two and a half months. Up until then I had only gotten a few letters from Espy and my sister. I talked to Moms once on the phone, but she was crying the whole time. Pops didn't want to come to the phone at all. By then they had already moved to Pennsylvania, someplace called Allentown. I found out that's where Larry Holmes lived.

Espy wrote about twice a week at first. She was very sad over what happened to me and it seemed like she didn't know what to write about anymore. All her letters were the same. I guessed there wasn't much going on back on the block, so there was never anything new to say. She had graduated from the high school, but still hadn't decided about going to college yet. She told me all she did was stay home all the time.

One Sunday I was sitting in my room with Clarence, playing chess. No one did anything on Sundays, it was our day off. All that meant was that we didn't have to report to our jobs. Everything else was the same. We couldn't go anywhere. Shit, to me a day off meant you can go to town, spend some money, get drunk, get laid. Not in the joint. Sunday meant you might get some extra roast beef with your lunch.

We heard the MP's footsteps coming our way. Nobody in the house liked them motherfuckers, especially me. They were all ass-kissing redneck cocksuckers who thought they were perfect soldiers. Their mission in life was to teach us fuck-ups a lesson, and they loved trying to do it. I never gave them a reason to mess with me, so when I heard them coming near I wondered what was up.

"Let's go, Torres."

"Go where?"

"The Main building. You have a visitor."

A visitor? I wondered who the fuck did I know around there who would come and visit me? I was wondering maybe Pennsylvania is closer to Kansas than I thought. I followed the MP's out to the main building. These *cabrones* were marching fast, they didn't give a damn that I was having a hard time keeping up, limping the whole way. They took me to a room that had a bunch of tables in a row going down the middle, with chairs on both sides. It looked like a cafeteria, without the food. A couple of tables were already being used. There were some women, wives or girlfriends no doubt. I had to stare because it had been a long time since I got a good look at an American chick that close.

They pointed to an empty table and told me to sit down. There were three MP's in the room, all standing at attention ready to kick ass if anybody got stupid. I waited at the table for a few minutes, wondering who the hell wanted to see me. If it was my lawyer they would've let him right to my room. I was feeling the shakes. A door at the end of the room opened up and I saw this dude in a fresh new khaki uniform walk in and head my way. He had a big ol' smile on his face. His shoes were so spit-shined that I could've used them for a mirror to shave. There wasn't a wrinkle on his clothes. He looked familiar at first, but I was still a little out of it from the morph trip I took the night before. Then it hit me. With his new, soldier boy haircut, I didn't recognize him.

"HEY, PAPO! *Qué pasa, panín!*"

"*Me cago en Dies!* CHICO!" It was my boy from back home, Chico. Man, I was never so glad to see this dude as I was that day. Forgetting about my foot, I got up and we ran into each other's arms, hugging tight like brothers who hadn't seen each other in a long time.

"What the fuck are you doing here?!" I didn't want to let go of the guy.

"I came to see you, man."

"Look at you. What's with the uniform?"

"I signed up, Papo."

"No, shit! You always were a *pendejo*, boy. Man, you don't know how good it is to see you." We hugged again, then sat down.

Chico had changed a lot since I last saw him almost two years before. Like I said, the little afro he used to wear was gone, probably shaved off by that same barber that took me for a *pendejo* at Fort Dix. Chico got big too, bro'. He seemed taller and his body was pumped up. He didn't look like the little *mamaíto* we used to goof on back on the block. He was a rock. Looked real good.

"So what's this 'I signed up' bullshit? Ain't nobody tell you the shit I been goin' through in this motherfucker?"

"I know, Papo. But I had to do something with myself, and I didn't wanna go to school anymore. Besides, the war is ending. They say it all the time on the news."

"They been sayin' that for four years. That Nixon be talkin' *mierda* all the time. Where you stationed? How'd you get here?"

"I'm over at Fort Riley. It's about an hour and half from here. I hitched a ride with a buddy who was going to Kansas City to see his old lady."

"'Hitched a ride with a buddy'. You're already sounding like soldier-boy. Fort Riley, eh? That's the First Infantry Division, right?"

"Yeah, how'd you know?"

"Brother, them dudes were in 'Nam big time a few years back. They was all over the place. What's your M.O.S.?"

"Field Artillery. I'm in the First Battallion, Fifth Field Artillery."

"You say that shit like you're proud."

"I am, Papo. For the first time since Moms died I'm feeling good about myself, like I'm worth something."

"You needed the Army to make you feel important?"

"*No joda,* Papo. It's true. Things have been pretty fucked up at home, I don't know if you heard."

"I know your Pops is still messed up. What's up with that?"

"He's really gone, bro'. He doesn't work no more. He's just living off Social Security and welfare. He's always drunk, he don't talk to nobody. The only friend he had was your Pops, and they moved out, you know."

"Man, I'm sorry to hear that, *panín.*"

"Yeah, man, thanks. Well that's why I had to get outta there. The one who's getting the worst of it is Yvette. She's still living there with him. Pops beats her all the time. He comes home drunk and if the food ain't ready, or if he finds any little shit he don't like, he beats the crap outta her."

"What about Yolanda. Where's she?"

"She cut out too, man. She couldn't take it either. Remember that dude, Hector, the guy she was goin' out with when you left?"

"Yeah...Hector. I never liked him."

"Nobody did. Check this out, bro'. Turns out the dude was a junkie. Strung out on heroin and cocaine. That's some fucked up shit, right, bro'?"

Hearing Chico say that made me uncomfortable. I pulled my shirt sleeve down so he wouldn't see my track marks, hoping he hadn't noticed. "Yeah, that's fucked up. I knew there was something wrong with that dude since the first time I saw him."

"That's not all, Papo. Yolanda was suspicious about him. He would get paid from his job and be broke, like, two hours later. Anytime they went out he had to borrow money from Yolanda to pay for everything. And he never paid her back."

"How did it all come out in the open?"

"That's the worst part. Hector came by the house one day looking for Yolanda. The only one there was Yvette, and she was still crying from getting beat up by Pops that morning. I guess Hector laid a rap on her, and when Yolanda came home, she caught him with his hand down Yvette's pants, feeling up her *totin*."

"And Yvette was letting him?!" I couldn't believe what I was hearing. I was balling my fists wanting to kill that guy.

"She didn't know what was happening, she was tripping. He had given her a hit of his shit. The needle was on the couch next to them. Yolanda blew a fit. She called the cops and everything."

"Goddamm lowlife, junkie cocksucker."

"No shit. He cut out before the cops got there. But as he was leaving, he was yelling shit like he was going to come back to get Yolanda. That if he couldn't have her, nobody could. Yolanda had to move out just to get away from that *títere*."

"Where is she now?"

"She got a place in Co-Op City. She's living with a girlfriend who took the apartment over from her parents. Yolie don't come around the way no more. She's scared Hector is going to find her."

"What about Yvette?"

"Pops won't let her leave. She's afraid to do anything. I think she's shot up a few more times since then. She's not the same anymore."

"A lot of things aren't the same anymore. Tell me, Chico. Whatta you know about the other guys?"

"Well, you know Johnny went off to college. He's up in Buffalo somewhere. The State University of New York. I think he's studying business, or something."

"You heard from Louie?"

"*Ese Louie es un* fuckin' *pendejo*. He's still in the Marines, but he got transferred to California. Camp Pendleton. He said he's gonna make a career of it. Last I heard he had met up with some Mexican chick with two kids. They were planning on getting married. I think he knocked her up too."

"Man, I can't picture Louie married with kids."

Chico stared at me long. "Like I could never picture you in prison, Papo."

I looked at him and my first thought was to pop him for the cheap shot. But I knew he was right. Of all people, *me* in jail. We stared each other down until I had to look away.

"Chico, what about Espy? How's she doin'?"

"*Pues*, bro', to be honest with you, I haven't seen much of her. During our senior year in high school she was always running around with that whole basketball team crowd. She was never home. When I went home on leave after basic training, I didn't see her at all. I saw her folks and her sisters, but not Espy."

She wrote to me telling me she was always home. Maybe Chico didn't see her because she stayed up in her room all the time. I had to convince myself to believe that.

"So much has changed in two years, eh, Papo?"

"It seems like I been away forever. But I know once I finally get back home everything is gonna be alright. Maybe I can take Espy to Pennsylvania, try to make it out there."

"Yeah, Papo. Maybe. Hey, man, how *you* doin'?"

"I'm hanging in there, doin' my time, minding my own business. I want to make sure I stay out of trouble so I can get out of here when I'm supposed to. I'm missing two toes."

"Yeah, I heard. Anybody try to make you his bitch yet?"

"Fuck you, Chico. This place ain't like that. We's all soldiers here. Dudes here got the same attitude we had in 'Nam. Do our time, get home safe, and Fuck the Army. We're brothers. The only people we got to worry about is those redneck MP guards. They think they can still turn us into strack G.I.'s. That's a joke."

"Hey, I like the Army."

"That's easy for you to say. You's here in the States, safe and sound. You wouldn't be saying that if you was pulling the graveyard-shift in the jungle, with the night so black you wouldn't even know where the enemy is even if he's standing three feet away from you ready to blow your head off."

"I guess I missed out on all the fun stuff, eh, Papo?"

That comment was so stupid it made me laugh. That was something the old Chico would have said. Believe it or not, it made me feel good, like old times.

"Thanks for coming, Chico. It was really good to see you."

"Hey, I'm just up the road in Junction City. I promise to come by and see you all the time. When you get out, I'll be your personal escort back home. Two Army heroes, *cómo te suena?*"

"Sounds good, *pana*. Hey, how you gettin' back to your post?"

"There's a bus I can take back. One leaves every half hour."

The alarm sounded signalling the end of the visiting period. We both got up and gave each other another strong hug. You don't know how much I wished Chico could take me with him. This was the first taste of back home I had in a long time, when life was simple and made sense. At that point my life made no sense at all.

"Don't forget, Papo. I'll come back to see you in a couple of weeks. I'll come earlier so we can hang out longer."

"*Chévere, hermano.* I'm proud of you, Chico. *Cuídate.*" The MP called for him to leave so he turned to walk away. As the guard held the door open for him, Chico turned back to give me a big smile and the "L" hand sign, the one us Latinos used to flash at each other when we was too far away to dap. Chico learned fast.

That was the one and only time I had a visitor at Fort Leavenworth. *Pero* Chico *me tiró bomba*. He never came back around to visit me, I don't know why. Maybe he didn't like to see me that way, locked up, *cójo*, skinny as a skeleton. Maybe he noticed the track marks before I had a chance to cover them up. Whatever.

I went back to my room and lay down on my bunk. I felt my foot hurting, but this time I had no desire for any morphine. I was thinking about Chico's visit, about all the changes happening around the neighborhood. I was thinking about Espy, wondering what she was doing at that very moment. Damn, I hadn't been gone *that* long, I thought. Then again, maybe I was.

After Chico's visit, I went back to the same routine as always. They woke us up at six o'clock every morning to clean up our rooms and barracks. From there we went to our daily jobs. After dinner at night they let us watch TV for a couple of hours. I didn't bother with that much because dudes were always fighting over what they wanted to watch. They acted like stupid little kids sometimes.

Summer started kicking in and it was getting so hot we slept with nothing on but our underwear, and *still* sweated all night long. Some guys were assigned to do work outdoors, like cleaning up the roadways and shit like that. They'd come back all sunburned from being out there all day. Clarence had to do that. He used to complain that he was black enough, he didn't need no more sun. They made him go out there anyways.

My foot had gotten better, but I still took my shots of morphine whenever I could get it. I was never assigned to do work outside where I would have to stand for a long period of time. That's why they kept me in the laundry room. That place was an oven in the summertime too, so I don't know who had it better or worse, me indoors in the laundry room, or those dudes outside on the clean-up detail. The only time we could cool off was when we took our showers at the end of the day. There was no fuckin' air-conditioning, just a row of fans on the ceiling right outside our rooms. But those shits didn't cool us off, they just moved the hot air around so that everybody could suffer equally.

I started having problems with these two redneck MP's from Oklahoma. I remember their names like it was yesterday: Sergeant Billy Fowler and Sergeant Harlan Gordon. They got off on the fact that they could use their positions to fuck with the blacks and Puerto Ricans any time they wanted to and we couldn't fight back. I tried to avoid them, but sometimes it was hard to turn away. I kept thinking that if we were back on the block and I had Louie and the rest of my boys with me, they wouldn't say jack shit to me. But that wasn't the case, and I had to do my best to ignore them.

One day, about five months into my time, I got a letter from Espy. It went something like this:

Querido Papo,

Cómo estas? I hope you are doing fine and that they are treating you well where you are. I wish there was a way for me to come visit you, but Kansas is too far. Don't they have any Army jails closer to New York? Maybe you can ask for a transfer.

There is some terrible news I have to tell you. Some bad men tried to rob Dón Marco's bodega. They came in one night when Ricky was in the store by himself. Dón Marco had taken the day off because it was his forty-third wedding anniversary. He wanted to take his wife out for a special night. You know Dón Marco never takes a day off, right? Anyway, the men were angry that there wasn't a lot of money in the cash register, so they shot Ricky. He was in the hospital for two days before he died. Ricky's dead, Papo.

Dón Marco was real upset, he blamed the whole thing on himself. He said he never should have taken the night off, that it never would have happened if he was there. I think it wouldn't really matter, it would not have made a difference if he was there or not. Dón Marco could have gotten killed himself. He decided that the neighborhood was getting too bad and he didn't want to take the chance of this happening again. So he closed the bodega and he and his wife moved back to Puerto Rico. The store is all shut down now.

Louie went crazy when he heard what happened to Ricky. He came home on emergency and drove around the neighborhood looking for the guys that did it. He wanted to kill them. After the funeral, Louie convinced his parents to move to California with him and his new family. They left two weeks ago. I didn't even get a chance to get his address.

Papo, so many things have changed around here lately. There's nobody around from the gang I met when I moved here. Louie and his family are in California, Chico is in the Army, Johnny is away at college. Yolanda moved out and Jeanette got married. Your family is gone too, and the most important person of them all — YOU - is far away and I have no idea

*when you'll be back again. I hate New York now and I wish I
was back in Humacao.*

*I'm sorry if this letter has put you in a bad mood. I want
to hear from you more, but I don't get letters from you as much
as I used to. I understand that they may not let you write every
day, so I don't blame you if you can't. But if you can, please
write and tell me when you are coming home.*

Espy

I couldn't believe that Ricky got killed over some penny ante
robbery right there on our block. That shit didn't happen. The
reason there wasn't any cash in the register was because Dón Marco
let everybody buy their food on credit. I had seen enough killing in
Vietnam, now I had to worry about niggas back home too. I couldn't
imagine how Louie felt. I know I would go nuts if somebody did
something to my little brother.

I read the letter over and over in my room. For some reason I felt
guilty over everything happening back home. It's like if I didn't go
into the Army, everything would still be the same as it was before. I
thought if I had gone home when I was supposed to, I could've done
something to prevent everything bad that had happened. It was all
my fault. I felt like shit. I reached into my drawer to see if I had any
cigarettes left. Not that I smoked them.

I just needed to find Maynard.

CHAPTER TWENTY TWO

By now I was catching a serious attitude problem, Jack. I kept thinking about back home, and that's the worst thing anybody in the joint could do. Old-timers will tell you that when you're doing time you can't think about the outside because that's when being locked up gets to you, drives you crazy. But I couldn't help it. I was sick and tired of all the bullshit, one thing after another. No matter how hard I tried to do right, something always happened to knock me down again. I started asking God what the fuck did I do to anybody to deserve this. In Vietnam I served the best way I knew how. In return I saw friends die, then I got shafted over some bullshit. I did everything they asked me to do except for that one time. All I wanted to do was come home alive.

Now I was stuck in a military prison while the world I knew in the South Bronx was slowly disappearing. I kept hoping that it was just temporary, like a dream, that when I got home things would get back to normal. Moms and Pops would be back in our old apartment, the fellas would all be hanging out on the stoop, and Espy would be doing everything to make me happy. I even dreamed that Doña Hilda would still be around. But when I looked out the windows through steel bars, when I put on my socks every day and counted eight toes instead of ten, when it got to the point when the only time I felt good was when I was mainlining that fucking morphine, I knew that those dreams of mine would never come true.

I got put on a special detail one day, cleaning up pots and pans in the prison mess hall. I didn't do anything wrong, it's just that everybody had to take turns doing it and my turn came up. I was with two other white guys, I can't remember their names. Anyways, I'm sitting there, scrubbing those shits 'til you could see your face on 'em. I'm thinking I'm doing a pretty good job, you know? But after about an hour, they decide to replace the guards. With my luck, guess who comes in to take over. Sergeant Fowler and Sergeant Gordon, those two rednecks from Oklahoma that had a bug up their asses for me. Man, I hoped they weren't gonna start no shit now. I oughta had learned by now to stop hoping for things.

"Welllll, Harlan. Lookit what we got 'chere. A greaseball pothead scraping grease off the pots."

"Ain't that appropriate. Hey, Billy, how's he ever gonna finish cleaning them pots? Grease is gonna keep slipping off his body right back into the water."

That was lame, but they both had a good laugh over it. These were the same kind of dudes that got a kick out of knocking over cows when they're asleep at night. I tried to ignore them, but they kept at it. The other two *blanquitos* working with me kept their heads down, trying to mind their own business. They knew the beef wasn't with them.

"Come to think of it, Harlan, I think we owe Inmate Torres here an apology."

"What for, Billy?"

"Well, ain't it those *I*-talians the ones they call greaseballs? *Not* the Porto *Ree*cans!"

"By golly, you're right. Porto *Ree*cans are called 'spics', ain't they, Torres? That's what they are, spics."

I just kept on scrubbing. That shit wasn't worth it.

"How'd they come up with that name, 'spic'? How'd they get that from 'Porto *Ree*can'?"

"I know, Billy. They got that name when they first came to this country off the banana boat."

"Banana boat. That's funny, Harlan."

"I ain't fibbin'. When they first came to this country immigration was askin' for their personal information. Since they didn't know no English, all they knew how to say was *'Me no spica English'*. Then they'd get jobs and the boss would give them work and they couldn't understand. So they'd say *'Me no spica English'*. That way, the lazy fuckers would get out of doing anything. Every time people tried to talk to them, they would say *'Me no spica English, Me no spica English'*. It got so frustrating that people finally said 'You no spica English? You no spica English? YES, you spica English. Yes, you spica. Yes, you SPIC!' And the name stuck."

By now Billy was laughing so hard he was slapping himself on the leg. Even the two *pendejo* white boys were having a hard time trying not to laugh. I was so mad I saw my teardrops falling into the wash water. But what was I gonna do? I didn't want to get in no trouble.

"Hey, Harlan. I got one. How does a spic fuck?"

"How does a spic fuck. Hmmm…. I give up. How DOES a spic fuck?"

"Let's ask Inmate Torres. Maybe he knows this one. Hey, Torres. How does a spic fuck?"

I was scrubbing that pot as hard as I could, trying to ignore them.

"Hey, Torres. I'm talking to you, you motherfuckin' spic. How does a spic fuck?"

"Why don't you ask yo' mama. She came by my cell for a conjugal last night."

It was one of those times when an ass whippin' was worth it. I knew I should've kept quiet, kept my cool. But I couldn't help it no more. Fowler's nightstick smashed across my face before I even had time to duck. I fell back against the wall and could taste the warm blood in my mouth. There was something crunchy rolling around in there, so I spit it out, blood and all, right onto Fowler's uniform. It was my two front teeth. The boy freaked so bad the red on his neck spread all over his face. His partner ran over and held me while Fowler punched me in the stomach like ten times, until I collapsed

223

on the floor. I made like I passed out just so they'd stop beating the shit out of me.

Them hillbillies fucked up though. They had to explain to their commander why my teeth were knocked out without getting themselves in trouble. Otherwise it would be considered brutality. So they reported that I fell in the kitchen and busted my face on a stove. Common sense made me go along with their story, I didn't want no more problems that would add more time to my sentence. So instead of being punished, I spent a day in sick call while the Army dentist pulled out what was left of my front teeth. After that, I got sent back to my room like nothing happened.

Now I was missing two toes and two teeth. I figured at this rate, by the time I'm released all that would be left of me would be a bald head they could roll all the way back to New York like a bowling ball. You think that those MP *hijo putas* would be grateful that I didn't drop a dime on them? Hell no. They did everything possible to make my life even more miserable, doing it *bien disimulado*, so no one could tell. They would pick me for all the shit details without caring about the profile I had because of my foot. Sometimes they made unnecessary noise outside my room in the middle of the night, just to keep me awake. They told their buddies in the mess hall to serve me less food than what everybody else got. *Se jodieron* with that shit because I hated that nasty garbage anyways. They was doing me a favor.

Then Espy's letters started coming in less and less. It went from two a week to one a week. After a while I wasn't getting nothing from her. I was real pissed because I thought it was these assholes who were holding back my mail, just to fuck with me. That's illegal, bro'. I tried to complain to the prison mailroom, but they said that there was nothing they could do for me. They said it wasn't their fault if nobody wanted to write to me no more. They said that shit laughing too. I wrote to Espy all the time, but I wasn't getting nothing back. I'll tell you, man, that's the worst feeling in the world. There I was, locked up in a place with hundreds of people, but I still felt all alone.

I don't remember much about the year I spent in Leavenworth. It seemed like ten years, and I was spaced out on morphine most of the time. My caseworker tried to get me on a program to clean myself up. He kept saying that I didn't need the medication anymore, that the pain I was feeling was all in my head. I said fuck you, it's in my foot. He said that's psychological. It went back and forth like that. I knew he was right, and I tried really hard to quit. But sometimes I got to thinking about Espy, wanting to hear from her, talk to her. I was sure she was writing to me, answering all the letters I was sending her. But they wouldn't give me my mail and I'd end up all depressed. There was nothing else to do in the joint, so me and Clarence played chess, then we'd sneak off to get zooted.

Besides Clarence I didn't have any close friends there. I learned my lesson with that shit from Vietnam. Other than those two asshole MP's I never had a problem with anybody else, especially after the inmates found out what happened with them. I was in the joint for fragging an officer, which made me cool, and I had stood up to two of the most hated guys there without snitching on either one of them. Ratting out somebody is the worst thing you can do in prison, even if it's the guards.

There's a thing called prison justice. That's where you take matters into your own hands when you have a beef. You can't trust the 'Man' to help you when you have a problem. He'll only make it worse. If someone fucks around with you, you find a way to get your payback without getting in trouble. There's dudes in the joint that specialize in getting things done. If you can't take care of a problem, they will - for a price. But no matter what, you don't snitch. If you rat somebody out one time, even though you may be right, you get stuck with that tag and nobody else will trust you again. I didn't snitch on them MP's, I took my lumps and kept quiet about it. For that, I was the man. One way or another my time would come. All I had to do was wait.

Since Clarence had actually wounded his CO, he was doing eight years. He didn't give a fuck about nothing except his radio. With Maynard's help he came up with a payback plan for Sergeants

225

Billy Fowler and Harlan Gordon. I really didn't want to do anything to anybody, I just wanted to get the hell home. But Maynard told us that all they would do is play a trick on those guys. They wouldn't get hurt, not much anyway. He knew that every year, in September, they made all the barracks employees get flu shots. That would keep them from getting sick when the weather got cold again, especially being around all those funky motherfuckers.

So Clarence tells Maynard to see if his contact in the infirmary could make a switch. Like I said, nobody liked those two racist bastards, so it was no problem getting people to go along. The plan was for us to wait for the day when the guards got their shots. They had to go in shifts so there was always some guards on duty watching us while the others went to the infirmary. We knew that these two butt-buddies did everything together, so all we had to do was wait until they took their turn.

It had been a couple of months since I had that fight with them, but I was still worried that if something happened to them they would pin the rap on me. Clarence calmed me down, convincing me that nobody was gonna get hurt, that we was just going to have a little fun with them. When the time came for the shift in guard duty, me and Clarence watched as Harlan and Billy headed towards the infirmary. We were in the prison courtyard at the time, playing basketball.

As usual, brothers can't play ball without getting into arguments. I don't care if they's in jail, or back home in the schoolyard. There always has to be some sort of static about something. A dude calls a foul and everybody on the other team starts yelling "BULLSHIT", even though the guy who got fouled is catching the blood pouring out of his head. They argue about the score all the time, as if they could count, you know what I mean? Yeah, I know, that's cold. I'm just kidding. The point is, there's always something they's fightin' about.

So me and Clarence are playing together, and at a certain point Clarence starts arguing with one of the dudes on the other team, a tall skinny brother named Foots. They called him Foots because he wore a size fifteen shoe. Before you know it, him and Clarence start fighting. They're really goin' at it, pugging it out. Naturally, the siren goes off telling the guards that there's some trouble in the courtyard, so all the guards come running to the yard to squash the shit, including Harlan and Billy.

Back at the infirmary, the nurses giving the flu shots come out to look out the window to see what's going on. They were only gone for a minute. That was enough time for Maynard and his boy to switch the needles. The fight was stopped real quick and everybody went back about their business. When Billy and Harlan returned to get their shots, the nurse, not knowing what the fuck happened, pumps them up with a small dose of.....that's right! My favorite candy - Morphine.

A junkie who knows what he's doing is gonna go look for a nice comfortable spot to take his hit and enjoy the head. He'll nod off and feel real nice. But if somebody DOESN'T know what's inside of him, he don't expect the reactions. Both of those assholes made it back to the courtyard before the shit took effect. Bro, the funniest thing in the world was watching these guys trying to figure out what was happening to them. They was bumping into each other, falling down and trying to get back up. Harlan was even giggling, I don't know why. That shit never made me laugh. Maybe he was laughing at Billy, not realizing he looked just as stupid as his partner.

The inmates in the courtyard were fucking with them, saying shit like "Hey, Sergeant Fowler, can I help you pack for your trip?" Other guys were waving their hands in front of them, trying to bug 'em out. After a while both Billy and Harlan were lying face down on the steps leading back inside the building, their butts sticking up in the air like little babies taking a nap in their cribs. Other MP's had to come and carry them away.

We made it back to our rooms still bustin' out laughing. I hadn't laughed like that in such a long time my side hurt. Maynard came running into the room too. He was holding the two needles that were used on those *pendejos*. He was able to snatch them from the waste basket so they wouldn't find any evidence. A few minutes later, Foots came in holding his right eye.

"Hey, Clarence, man. Didja have to hit me so hard? I thought we was jes' puttin' on a show."

We laughed even harder. "I'm sorry, my brother," said Clarence in between the laughter, "but we had to make it real. C'mon, man, sit down. Rest those big feets of your'n. Hey, Maynard, get Brother Foots here some ice for his face. Yo, 'T', you got those squares?"

"Show your right. Here you go." I handed Foots two packs of cigarettes I had promised to "pay" him for his services.

All in all, that was the best day I ever had in the joint. I got my payback for what those two *cabrones* did to me. They were humiliated in front of all the inmates, and that's the worst thing that could happen to a guard. That alone didn't equal me losing my teeth and being called a spic. But it was enough, and I was glad nobody got seriously hurt, or caught.

Turns out that the doctors never figured out that it was the so-called flu shot that did that to the MP's. Instead, they showed up with traces of unauthorized drugs in their bodies, so from that point on they were under suspicion of using. They were put on probation and transferred to administrative jobs in the Main building. I was out of their reach. I couldn't believe that the whole plan was carried out so easily. No one ever suspected that we had anything to do with it.

Usually, prison justice is evil, even deadly. But for me, this form of prison justice did just fine. It gave us something to talk about for a while. It would make the last three months of my sentence a little easier to deal with. With Billy and Harlan gone, maybe I could finally get my letters from Espy.

Life at the Disciplinary Barracks was what you made of it. You could be a hard-ass and give everybody a hassle for any little thing, or just go about your business quietly. Like the dudes that fought over what to watch on TV. I remember two guys fighting over "All in The Family" and "Room 222". Remember that show? First time I ever saw a white dude with an afro. But that shit was ridiculous, man. Other guys could never do what they were told without giving the guards a hard time. It didn't matter what it was about, they just wanted to be difficult. They wanted the rep. I hated the guards like everybody else, but some of the shit they went through wasn't necessary. Believe it or not, bro', I felt bad for them sometimes. Except for Billy Fowler and Harlan Gordon. Mother-FUCK them.

A lot of times guys wouldn't even bother fighting. If they had a beef to settle they'd do it with a shank. A homemade knife. They'd sneak up behind a nigga and stick 'em, then walk away, like *"yo no fuí"*. They used to make those shanks in the metal shop where some guys worked. They'd make them small so they could be hidden easy, but they'd be sharp as a motherfucker. I saw a guy get sliced in the back and he didn't even realize it until he felt the wet blood on his shirt. He had to ask his buddy to take a look and tell him what was up back there. The dude who did it was so quick that not even the buddy saw it happen, and he was standing right there next to the guy that got cut. It was wild, boy.

Still, most of the inmates there didn't want no trouble. These guys weren't hard criminals, they just fucked up in the Army, that's all. Like me. See, in those days guys who got drafted came from low class places anyways and didn't have a way to get out of it. They weren't no altar boys. Like Frankie, some of them had a choice to go in the Army or go to jail for some petty shit back home. But I figured that if a judge gave them a choice like that, then they must not have been that bad to begin with. A stone cold-blooded killer would be locked up for good in a penitentiary. They wouldn't put him in the Army and hand him a weapon, don'tcha think, bro'?

I'm sure there was some faggatty stuff going on, like Chico wanted to know. Fuckin' guy. I can't believe he asked me that shit. But dudes had to have been fucking each other in the ass and nasty shit like that. There was this one stone *maricón* who was always offering to suck your dick. Leavenworth didn't make him a homo, he *got* there like that. I think that's why he got court-martialed and put away. He'd get drunk and make a move on everybody. So to punish him, the Army *pendejos* locked him up with a bunch of other men. Clarence said that's like locking up a bank robber inside a vault.

I stayed away from that shit. Nobody messed with me about that because I was popular, even though I didn't get tight with nobody except Clarence. And my nigga was no homosexual, that's for shit sure. All Clarence talked about was pussy. He said as soon as he got out he was gonna fuck a stewardess on the flight home. I heard the federal penitentiary at Leavenworth was bad news. People got gang-raped up in there, especially the young, pretty *blanquitos*.

But at the Barracks there was no need for anybody to force theyselves on anybody else. If somebody wanted sex, there were enough punks there to take care of him. And they did it on the 'Q.T.'. Remember, all of us started off as soldiers, real macho men. Usually faggots would have been busted in boot camp and got sent home. Drill Sergeants weren't gonna be sending no *maricones* to Vietnam. To do what? Make a deal with Charlie to promise him a blowjob if he surrenders?

I gotta admit I did a lotta jerkin' off in the beginning. In 'Nam I was able to control myself pretty good 'cause I expected to be back with Espy soon. And even if I got too hard-up, I could always get me one of the hoochie girls Frankie always wanted to throw at me. But by the time I got to the joint, it had been almost three years since I had a taste of booty. I knew I wasn't gonna be able to last forever without bustin' a nut. I had to do something. It was either Mustang Sally, the cocksucking queen, or my own five fingers of death. It was a regular thing. Lights out, and in the dark you could practic'ly see fellas' fists going up and down underneath their blankets. It got to the point where nobody gave a fuck who saw them. It was a natural thing.

But that got boring after a while, so I did more morphine and didn't care about nothing. Got high and nodded out. There was no desire to do anything else.

So that was life in the joint. Days came and went and it was easy to lose track of the time. We went about our business during the day and tried to stay out of trouble and, more importantly, out of people's way. At night, we played chess or cards, usually Spades. Me and Clarence were the best in our block. After the card games we would go back to our rooms. If we had some morph' we'd shoot it up and forget about everything. If not, we stayed in bed staring up at the ceiling, trying to figure out when the nightmare was going to end.

It was November, 1972. I had been away from home since July of 1970. If you figure it out that means I was at Fort Dix for eight weeks, then Vietnam for a year and three months, counting the time I was at Long Binh Jail. Then another eleven months at Fort Leavenworth, Kansas. I ain't never been away from home more than a week when I was a kid. Now I forgot what it was like to be back in the world, back on the block with my boys and my people. I know for sure I wasn't the same person I was when I left. I was hard now, a grown man who been through so much shit that I didn't want nobody fuckin' with me. I didn't care who it was.

I still waited for Espy to write me, but they still weren't giving me her letters. It had been four or five months since the last time I heard from her. We was allowed to use the phone for one call on Sundays and holidays, but I hardly ever tried to call nobody. I didn't want to hear anybody crying, like my Moms did. And I sure as shit didn't want nobody giving me no lectures on being good and all that. Fuck that. People back home had no idea what was happening. This shit was no joke.

After a while I couldn't take it anymore, so I tried calling Espy. I remember my heart pounding when I dialed the number, not knowing what I was gonna say to her, how to act. I wondered if her English had gotten better. Would she ask me if I still did drugs? What if Dón Ramón answered the phone?

All that didn't matter. Her phone didn't ring. All I got was a message saying that the number had been changed. Dón Ramón must've did that when he found out I was in jail, just so I couldn't contact Espy. The new number wasn't listed. Fuck it, I thought. I figured when I get back home, I would go get her and finally take her away from the Bronx, from everything else. I would rescue her just like I dreamed I would a long time ago.

I got called down to the counselor's office in the Main Building one day. My caseworker wanted to talk to me and review my file. I got worried about that because you never knew if there might be something wrong that could cause you problems. I wasn't ready to hear any more bad news.

The MP's took me down to the office where the dude was waiting for me. His name was Fredericks, or something like that. He was a civilian. He studied social work in college. It's like he wanted to change the world with all his psychology crap. I didn't know you had to go to college for four years to learn how to talk to somebody. But I got along with him, though. He seemed cool, not a phony like a lot of other people I met in the joint. When I walked into his office he was looking through my file, just like all the doctors and lawyers always did. I always caught them checkin' out my file when I walked into the room. I guess they needed a head start to deal with me.

"Good morning, Eddie. Take a seat." This was the only person in the whole world who called me 'Eddie'. *Que confianza, verdad?* I never told him he could call me that. I guess 'Eduardo' was too hard for his *blanquito* ass. I sat down across his desk.

"How are you feeling this morning, Eddie? How's your foot coming along?"

"Well, them two toes ain't grown back yet. Other than that, I'm copastetic."

He laughed a little. "That's pretty funny. You want some coffee or something?" I turned him down. I never got into drinking coffee in the Army like most other dudes. If it wasn't *Bustelo*, I wasn't havin' it.

"Eddie, do you realize how long you've been here in the Barracks?"

"Not really. I been having so much fun I kinda lost track of time." I told you, bro'. I had an attitude, even with this guy.

"C'mon, Eddie, relax. I know you've been counting the days. I'm on your side. You don't have to bust my horns."

I just stared back at him, quietly whistling through the gap in my teeth.

"Okay, then. Let's get down to why I called you in. I'm looking through your file here. Let me ask you, did you have some problems with Sergeant Gordon and Sergeant Fowler before they were transferred out?" He was talking about fucking Billy and Harlan. Oh, shit, I thought to myself. I was busted again.

"No, Mr. Fredericks. I mean, we never exchanged Christmas cards or anything, but they didn't hassle me any more than the other guards did." He looked at me knowing I was bullshitting. "Why do you ask?" I didn't even want to hear the answer.

"Oh, nothing. I was just wondering if they had anything to do with you getting your teeth knocked out."

"The report said I fell and hit my face on the stove in the kitchen of the mess hall."

"I can see what the report says right here. I just wanted to hear it from you. Those boys have been written up a few times for giving inmates a hard time, especially the minorities."

Tell me something I don't already know, Freddy Boy.

"Anyway, Eddie. Other than that incident, we've hardly heard a peep out of you for almost a year."

"I shouldn't never been sent here from the get-go."

"Yes, in a way I agree with you. But the verdict came down and we had to deal with the punishment accordingly."

What do you mean "we", cracker.

"Of course, we are well aware of your drug use. We can see it on your arms. Unfortunately, for your sake, you haven't been able to complete the programs aimed at cleaning you up. On the other hand, your drug abuse has not affected your daily behavior, or your performance in your assigned duties. We're still not sure how you have had access to such a steady supply of your, how should I say.... poison? But you haven't been caught either. You've managed to elude us in that respect."

"Mr. Fredericks, can you tell me what your point is? I ain't got all day to be sitting here shootin' the shit with you."

"Of course you don't, Eddie. You're going to be pretty busy the next few days."

"Whatta you mean?"

"Well, Eddie. Let me be the first to tell you. Officially, you have managed to keep your nose clean, so to speak. You have carried out your assigned duties with no incidents. You have cohabitated with the other inmates without confrontations or other problems. You have served your time in an exemplary fashion. In other words, you have been a model inmate. The Review Board has deemed that you are rehabilitated and fully prepared to return to society. The best part is that because of your perfect record here, you are eligible for an early release. You begin out-processing on Monday. You're going home, Eddie."

That boy used a lot of big words there, but the most important thing he said I understood perfectly. I was going home. At first I didn't want to believe him. I thought it was just another trick, somebody else wanting to fuck with me. I sat there and stared at him. Fredericks got up to shake my hand. He had a big *mamao* smile on his face, like this was the part of his job he liked best. I felt my body shaking. It took forever for me to finally get up to take his hand and shake it. All I could say was "Thanks."

"Now remember, Eddie. The processing will take a few days to a week. You'll have to take another physical examination and undergo some more psychological evaluations. Plus, you still have to be debriefed. That's standard military procedure at the time of separation. Your scheduled release date is November 25th. That's almost two weeks. Try to stay clear of trouble during that time. And Eddie, don't shoot at anybody if they order you to do something you don't want to do."

"Don't worry, Mr. Fredericks. I'll probably miss anyway."

CHAPTER TWENTY THREE

The next ten days crawled by. I thought all the clocks were broken. Every time I asked Clarence what time it was he would say "three minutes after you axed me the last time, you short motherfucker. Calm down." I couldn't wait for the twenty-fifth to come, not so much to get home, but just to get the hell out of the Barracks. I was worried that something might happen at the last minute that would fuck it all up for me again. I didn't leave my room unless I really had to. For some reason, the MP's cut me some slack because they hardly came by to put me on any shit details. They left me alone. Maybe Mr. Fredericks talked to them. They couldn't be *that* cool.

I was nervous about going home, if you can believe that shit. After everything I been through I wasn't sure how I would be on the outside. I was worried about how people would look at me, how they would treat me. I got used to dealing with soldiers and inmates, in 'Nam and at Leavenworth. The people back home, the ones I knew all my life, would be strangers to me now.

I started trying to fix myself up, you know, get my shit back together. I hadn't cared what I looked like in such a long time. But now I was going back to my Esperanza, so I had to look good. Papo Salsa was coming home!

The few times I left my room was to go to the gym and work out, lift some weights to pump myself up. All this time I never bothered with that shit, not like some of these other dudes who spent every free minute of their day in the weight room. Now I was gonna try to build up thirty pounds of muscle in ten days.

You know, that's another thing I could never understand about prison. You get guys in there who got locked up for robbery, assault, murder, you know, real bad-ass *hijo putas*. So what do they give them to keep them busy? A gym so they can bulk up and be bigger and stronger and meaner than they were before. That didn't make no sense. They come out of the joint more dangerous than they were before they went in. Leave it up to me and I would pump these motherfuckers up with morphine and every other kind of drug, just so that when they come out they'd be so weak and stupid they wouldn't know if they was coming or going.

I tried to get in touch with Chico over at Fort Riley to see if he was going to come through with his promise to go home with me. But they told me his unit was in Germany, in something called REFORGER. That's when they pack up the entire 1st Infantry Division and ship them to Germany to train in a make-believe war. More stupid shit. Didn't they get enough practice in Vietnam? Or better still, why didn't they learn their lesson yet and practice how NOT to have a war?

Since my folks were living in Pennsylvania, the only person I could call in New York to tell them I was coming home was my sister Elizabeth. She sounded happy, but not as excited as I thought she would be. I guess, like me, she didn't know what to expect.

The day finally came for me to say my good-byes. If ever I needed some crank it was that day. I was nervous and scared, like I felt more comfortable staying in the joint. I was afraid I was going to feel lost being on the outside. But I fought the urge to shoot up. I wanted to show up back on the block clean, let people know I was alright. The fact that I was court-martialed meant I lost the right to wear my uniform. They took that shit away from me when I got to Kansas. For my release they bought me some civilian clothes from town. It was a white shirt, a pair of brown chinos, and some shoes from the Salvation Army. I got a cheesy wool coat for the cold weather. I looked like a real country boy.

I went over to Clarence's room. He always said the right things to make me feel good, make me laugh. But on that day I found him laying on his bunk looking bummed out. He had his hands behind his head, looking up at the ceiling with his eyes half closed. He probably just finished having his "lunch". That's what we used to say when we would sneak off to shoot up instead of going to the mess hall to eat.

"Ey, Clarence. My man. Hey! It's me, 'T'. YO!"

"Uh?"

"Clarence, man, wake up, you black son of a bitch. It's me, Papo." We were tight, we could talk to each other like that.

"Uh. Oh, hey, 'T'. What's happening."

"I'm leaving, man. Today's the day."

"I know what today is, man. You ain't got to remind me. Shee-it, you been talkin' all that shit for two weeks now." He sat up and swung his legs over the side of the bed. His short, nappy afro was flat on one side and full of lint like always. He rubbed his face to wipe the funk off. I thought I heard a fart.

"I come by to say good-bye."

"Uh-huh. Good-bye."

"C'mon, Clarence. That's all you gonna say?"

"Nah, man. I'm just fuckin' witcha. Yo, man. I hates to see you go, but I'm happy fo' you." He held out his hand for me to shake it, straight up, man to man. Sometimes a dap ain't the right thing to do.

"Thanks, 'C'. I'm gonna miss you, man."

"That's bullshit. You ain't gonna miss nuthin' about this motherfucker. As soon as you walk out them doors you gonna forget all about us. That's what I'm gonna do." He reached over to turn his radio on, a coat hanger acting as an antennae. Then he lit up a cigarette.

"You may be right. But still, it was nice knowin' you. I wouldn't have gotten through this without you."

"Whatcha gonna do, kiss me now?"

"Ey, if I ain't wanted to kiss your black ass all this time, I sure ain't gonna start now."

"You ain't left yet, you rice-and-beans-eatin' homo. It ain't too late to get it on." We both laughed and threw some soft punches at each other.

"You gonna be alright here, Clarence?"

"Do I got a choice? Don't worry 'bout me, man. I'll be cool."

"You'll be going home soon too, just you wait."

"Nah, I ain't gonna sweat that. If they let me out, they let me out. Otherwise, I'm just gonna stay here and take one day at a time. At least this place is better than Vietnam."

"Show your right. Listen, I gotta go. I wanna cut outta here before they change their minds. Hey, man. Thanks again. Thanks for everything."

"Yeah, man, you take care."

"Yo, Clarence, if you're ever in New York....."

"I know, I know. Look you up, right? Take it easy, Papo. Be good wit' yo'self. I don't want to see your Puerto Rican ass around here again, you hear?"

"Yeah, I hear ya. Later, my brother."

I went back to my room and collected all my personal stuff I had already packed up in a small suitcase. The MP's came by to get me. I had to sign all the final paperwork and be escorted outside. That was the only time I was happy to see them guards come by my room.

Mr. Fredericks and the Barracks warden were waiting for me in the Processing room. For Mr. Fredericks, when a guy finally finishes his time and gets out, it's a happy day. He feels proud of himself, like it was all because of him and his psychology rap that an inmate changed his life around. But for the warden - who don't trust nobody, especially an inmate - he just looks at you like he expects to see you again.

I signed whatever I had to sign. They handed me two bus tickets. One was to take me from Leavenworth to Kansas City. The other one was for the busride from Kansas City to New York. These cheap bastards couldn't even pay for a plane to take me home. They also handed me an envelope. Inside was over two thousand dollars in cash. Some of it was the salary I earned in prison working in the laundry. But most of the money was what I had saved up while I was in Vietnam. Since I didn't need money there, I arranged to have most of my pay deposited in a bank account. This was the balance I had left before I got arrested.

They finally led me outside the walls of the camp. I looked around at the rest of the compound. Fort Leavenworth looked like any other Army base I had been to in the states. But it was nothing like Bien Hoa. I wasn't gonna feel free until I was completely clear from all that military bullshit. A car was waiting for me there. Another MP was gonna drive me to the bus station in town. Once we drove past the main entrance to the fort I had this funny feeling. It was the feeling of being back in the world. Not my world in the Bronx, but still. A world where I could come and go as I wanted to for the first time in over two years. I was getting nervous again.

The ride to Kansas City lasted about an hour. When I got to the bus depot in KC I found out that I had an hour to wait before the next Greyhound was to leave for New York. I looked around for something to do. The first thing I did was go to the nearest Mickey D's. I hadn't had a Big Mac in years. I ate two of those suckers. Then I walked around and found a store that sold all kinds of household shit. I went in and picked out a nice AM-FM clock radio. There was a small post office right next to the bus station. I went over and had them wrap up the radio and send it back to Leavenworth. It was my good-bye present for Clarence, to thank him for helping me get those two MPs off my ass. I also bought a couple of stuff toys for my niece and nephew. Couldn't wait to see them. Then I got me a nice cold beer, and sat in the waiting area until my bus was ready to leave.

The trip home took thirty fuckin' hours, man. I never knew this country was so big. We made a few stops along the way, like in St. Louis, Indianapolis, and Columbus, Ohio. I remember each one because I noticed all those places looked dead, like there wasn't shit happenin' there. It was nothing like here in the Bronx. What surprised me was that when the bus passed through Pennsylvania, I saw signs for Allentown. That's where Moms, Pops, and Benny were at. I thought about getting off there and calling them up, but then

I said fuck it. Let me get back to the home I knew, the Bronx. I'd have plenty of time to see them some other time.

I spent most of that trip sleeping. I started off looking out the window, thinking about all the shit that happened the last two and half years. The faces of all the people I met flashed through my mind and I was wondering if I would ever see those guys again. I never did, you know that? It was all over. For some reason, even though I was happy to be heading home, I couldn't force myself to show it. I couldn't let go of the attitude I had. It was like I was still mad over everything I had to go through. I looked around the bus, and outside at every town we passed through. I saw dudes, man, young dudes. It was pissing me off that I had to live through all that Vietnam bullshit, then got fucked and sent to prison. Yet these *pendejos* were walking around with their long hippie hair like nothing was going on anywhere else outside their own little world. It wasn't fair. Why me and not them?

On Sunday night, November 26th, we finally pulled into the Port Authority in Manhattan. I thought we'd never get there. My brother-in-law, Alberto, was supposed to be there to pick me up. I didn't see him in the terminal, so I went looking for the exit to see if he was somewhere outside. Even though it was late Sunday night, there was still about a million people running around there. Everybody was moving so fast, like they was in a hurry to get somewhere. A few times I had to jump out the way so I wouldn't get knocked over by somebody flying by. I had to get used to this pace all over again. Shit, it was not that long ago that I was there with Johnny, saying good-bye to Louie when he left for Philadelphia. Now I was like a foreigner, in the big city for the first time.

Outside was crazier than it was inside. I wondered what all these people were doing out so late on a Sunday. Most of them were beggars and hookers. I saw a dude on 42nd Street playing the three-card monte game, with a whole bunch of people around him, thinking they were sharp enough to actually win. These people were suckers. Even *I* knew that much. I leaned up against the building and looked around at all the bright lights and sex shops. This is what

I went to Vietnam to fight for. We couldn't let the Commies take over our pornography, our *bellaqueras.*

"PAPO! PAPO! Over here!" I turned towards Eighth Avenue, and there was Alberto standing by his car, half-way in, half-way out. He musta just got there. I picked up my bag and walked towards him. I can't remember if I smiled to let him know I was happy to see him. Maybe it was my *complejo* because of my teeth.

"Hi, 'Berto. How you doin'?" He opened the trunk and I threw my bag inside. The dude looked like he put on a little weight since the last time I saw him. I figured Lizzie must've learned how to cook in the last two years.

"Hey, Papo. How've you been?"

How've I been? I been fucked, that's how I've been, you stupid pendejo. "I'm doin' alright, 'Berto. How about you?"

"Good. Real good. Your sister and the twins been keeping me busy. You ought to see them. They're getting bigger every day. And the job is going good. I just got promoted to Assistant Manager in my office. I'm working for an investment company now. You know, stocks, bonds, Treasury Notes. We're looking to get into commodities in the........."

After 'Berto had said "Good, real good", I stopped listening. I didn't give a fuck about all that other old shit. I just stared out the window as he headed towards the East Side to get the Midtown Tunnel to Queens. Again I was surprised at how many people were still walking the streets this late at night. I was used to the Army life where nine o'clock meant lights out. Now it looked like these people were just on their way out. I noticed how everybody's hair was longer too, even 'Berto's. I couldn't wait for my shit to grow back.

After a while 'Berto must've realized he was the only one talking because he stopped. I wasn't in the mood. I just wanted to look out the window and take it all in - the city, the people, the lights. The freedom. I wished he could've taken me straight to the Bronx to see Espy. But then again, I'd just been riding on buses for a day and a half. I was a rumpled mess. I wanted to look my best when I saw her.

A half-hour later we was pulling up into his driveway. All the lights inside the house were shut off, except for the kitchen. From the window I saw my sister get up and look outside to make sure it was us. She opened the front door and stood inside the hallway while we got out of the car. She looked a little chunkier herself. I handed my suitcase to Alberto and walked over to her. I thought I caught her lookin' down at my feet. She must've noticed my limp.

"Hey, Papo. It's good to see you." We gave each other a long hug. I never hugged my sister so tight as I did that night. Seeing 'Berto was okay, but Lizzie was family, my blood. Being home was finally starting to sink in for me.

"Hi, Lizzie. It's good to see you too. You don't know how glad I am to be back." I didn't know either.

"Damn, Papo. *Esta flaco.* Didn't they feed you over there?"

"They wanted to. But they said some bitch in New York was eating up all the food. There wasn't enough left for the soldiers."

She slapped my arm. "*Véte al carajo*, Papo. What are you trying to say, I got fat?"

"I ain't sayin' nothin'. It's these *chichones* you got here on your hips that's doing all the talkin'."

"What can I say. I GOT my man. He likes me the way I am. I don't need to look good for anybody else. Come in, come in. You hungry? I saved some food from dinner for you. Your favorite. Rice and beans, and *chuletins.*"

Rice. Damn. I *was* hungry, but rice? Damn.

"Thanks, Lizzie. But just make me a pork chop sandwhich. I had something to eat before we pulled into New York."

While the pork chops were being warmed up, Lizzie took me into the kid's bedroom where I saw Georgie and Jessica sleeping. Man, they got big. They weren't babies no more. We had to be real quiet so they wouldn't wake up. I put the stuffed toys next to them in their beds. They'd be surprised in the morning.

Alberto had to work the next day, so he said goodnight and went to bed. Me and Lizzie stayed in the kitchen and talked while I ate my sandwhich. She wanted to know more about how I got in trouble. I tried to answer all her questions, but the truth was I didn't really want to think about it anymore. I kept trying to change the subject.

"Lizzie, how's Moms and Pops? They happy over there where they're at?"

"They're okay, I guess. They got a nice house that Papi's company is helping him pay for. It's practically in the country. Benny loves it there. He's already got lots of friends. You know how easy it is for kids to make friends, no matter where they are. He's playing baseball in the Little League too."

"That's cool. I'm glad he's got the chance to grow up in a better place than the South Bronx. But how's Moms?"

"Ah, you know Mami. She never really talks about how she feels about things. I guess she's happy. But since you left she hasn't been the same. Like she's no fun anymore."

"Me getting thrown in jail didn't help much either, eh?"

"Yeah. She took that pretty hard. The whole time you were in Vietnam she always worried about you being killed. She never thought in a million years you'd end up the way you did."

Somehow, the way Lizzie said that didn't sound right. I decided to ignore it.

"How about Pops?"

"He's a different story, Papo. I'll be honest with you. He was real mad about you getting into drugs. He thought he raised us better than that."

"How'd he find out?"

"Oh, they sent him a letter. The Army was good for that. They wrote down everything you had been charged with and all the other problems you had. The attempted murder, the drug abuse. Papi thought he was reading about somebody else, not his son."

"He don't know what I went through over there. If he don't understand, then fuck him." I surprised Lizzie when I talked about Pops like that. The attitude wouldn't go away.

"*Calma, nene.* Don't take it out on Papi. He was worried about you just like everybody else. As soon as you get the chance to go to Pennsylvania, I'm sure you can explain everything to him and show him you're clean and over it now. You are clean now, right, Papo?"

"Um, yeah, sure, Lizzie. That shit's a thing of the past."

"*Bien*. I'm glad to hear it. *Bueno*, it's getting late. I put some blankets and pillows on the living room sofa. I don't know what your plans are, but you're welcome to stay here as long as you want to."

"You sure it's okay with 'Berto?"

"Excuse me? He may be the man of the house, but as long as he wants a piece of *this*, he's gonna do what *I* say. It's alright, don't worry."

"Thanks, Lizzie. Oh, here." I took out a couple hundred dollars and offered them to her.

"What's that for?"

"Take it. It's for my rent and food."

"Get the fuck outta here. You're my brother, I ain't charging you for anything. Besides, Alberto is doing pretty good now. We don't need any money. We're alright."

"C'mon, take it. Buy something for the twins. You can call it two years worth of birthday and Christmas presents from their Tio Papo."

"Well, if you put it like that, okay. But you worry about you, you hear me? Get yourself some clothes. You look like 'Jethro' in them things."

"Thanks, Granny. I picked these out myself."

"I know that's bullshit, Papo. You always knew how to dress better than anybody else on the block."

"Yeah, you're right. Give me time, I'll be back in the swing of things in no time."

"You gonna go dancing anytime soon?"

"I don't know, Lizzie. With this foot I don't know if I can do it anymore."

"*Pobresito*. I'm sorry I asked. Well, listen. Let me go to bed. The twins will be up at six. I need my rest to keep up with them. Make yourself at home. If you watch TV, keep the volume down, okay? See you tomorrow." Lizzie gave me a kiss on the forehead. It felt real good.

I went to the living room to make myself comfortable on the sofa. I wasn't that sleepy, but there was nothing else to do. The house was too quiet. I tossed and turned on the sofa for about an hour before I finally laid down on the floor. That was much better. I slept like a baby after that.

By the time I woke up the next morning Alberto had already left for work. I didn't hear him. What woke me up was the sound of footsteps running all up and down the hallway. I also heard a TV blasting in one of the bedrooms. Cartoons. I tried to roll over and go back to sleep, putting the pillow over my head to block out the noise. I was just drifting off again when I heard the footsteps, about a hundred of 'em, come running into the living room and stop. Then I didn't hear nothing else. I waited. Nothing. Even though I kept my eyes shut, I was wide awake. That ever happen to you? You want to go to sleep, but something is fuckin' with you so that you can't?

Anyways, I waited for the footsteps. Still nothing. I lifted the pillow up off my head a little and opened one eye. Sitting on the floor, just three feet away from me, were the cutest little kids I'd ever seen. There was two of them. Both looked just like their mom. I said "Hi", and they got up and ran back to their room.

It was time to get up and begin my first day back in the world. I wasn't used to making my own plans. First thing I wanted to do was shop for some clothes. Lizzie told me about this place near her house on Hempstead Turnpike, called TSS. She said I could get a lot of stuff there real cheap. She took me there after breakfast and I bought a couple pairs of dress pants, some shoes, underwear, and sweaters.

The twins were real shy with me at first. They'd run up to the kitchen door, look at me and giggle, then run back down the hallway. But by the time I got dressed up to go out, they were giving me good-bye kisses. Lizzie told them it was me who gave them the new toys.

I headed back to Hempstead Turnpike to catch the bus that would take me to the subway on Hillside Avenue in Jamaica. From there I would make my way to the Bronx. It was the same trip I had taken a few times with Moms when Lizzie first moved out there. I had to refresh my memory a couple of times.

There seemed to be a lot more people on the subway than what I remembered. I swore they were all looking at me everytime I got on. I kept checking my clothes to see if everything was alright. Maybe they were goofin' on my limp, as if they could see through my new shoes and tell I had something missing. I wasn't gonna open my no-teeth mouth, fuck that. Maybe it was my short hair. I sat in the furthest seat at the end of the train, as far from everybody else as I could.

When I got to the block it seemed everything had changed, everything looked smaller. I still kept hoping my boys would be on the stoop like before, playing bid-wiz, listening to music. But there was nobody around. It was a Monday morning, and it was cold out, but in the old days there was always *somebody* hanging out. I saw Dón Marco's bodega on the corner. It was closed up. It looked like it hadn't been opened in a long time. The metal gate was pulled down and it was filled with all kinds of grafitti. We never would had done that to Dón Marco's store when we was kids.

There were more cars parked in the street. I wondered how many people had moved to New York since I been gone. I kept feeling so crowded all the time. I walked up to my old building. It looked the same. As usual, there was noise coming from all the apartments, but they were voices I didn't recognize. A couple of new families had moved in. But up on the fifth floor, where I lived, it looked empty. It didn't look like anybody lived in our old apartment because there was a dresser and bedframe stacked up against the front door. The hallways were sometimes used as storage rooms, even when I was growing up.

There was some low music coming from the end of the hall. That was where Chico's apartment was. I walked over carefully, just in case Chico's dad was in there drunk. The door was open a little, so I peeked in.

That apartment was a mess, man. It was all fucked up. Dirty. Holes punched out of the walls. There was a sink full of nasty dishes that looked like they'd been there for days, maybe weeks. I saw a couple of dead roaches on the floor with their legs sticking straight up in the air. Blasted by a shot of Raid, no doubt. Instead of curtains, torn sheets hung from all the windows to keep the sunlight out and make the place look uglier than it already was. This wasn't the same place Doña Hilda kept. She'd roll over in her grave if she saw this shit.

"Hello? Dón Guillermo?" I walked in slowly. "Hello?"

"Who's there?" I heard a girl's voice from one of the bedrooms. "Yvette?"

"Who's there?" The voice was walking up the hall.

The person who walked into the living room was someone Chico's little sister might've looked like in twenty years.

"Papo?"

"Hi, Yvette." I thought I was looking at a ghost in a bathrobe. Yvette was, what? Fourteen or fifteen when I left? That means she was only about seventeen now. She ran up to me to give me a kiss and a hug. She used to be so cute. I noticed her wipe her runny nose.

"When did you get back (sniff)?"

"Just last night. I stayed at Lizzie's house in Long Island. Damn, Yvette. How you doin'?" I didn't want her to catch me looking around.

"Can't you tell? I'm doin' great. Sit down. Want some coffee?"

"No, thanks. I'm going across the street to see Espy. I just stopped by to look at the old place."

"You thinkin' of moving back? Your apartment's empty. The super put that furniture there to keep the junkies out. Don't matter. They still hang out in the halls anyway. And up on the roof."

"I don't know what I'm going to do yet. All depends on Espy. How's your father?"

"Who the fuck cares (sniff). Sometimes he comes around, sometimes I don't see him for a month. I think he's fuckin' some *Dominicana* up on the Concourse."

"Oh. Listen, Yvette, I gotta go. I'll see you around, okay?"

"C'mon, Papo. Don't go. I ain't seen you in a long time. Stick around, let's talk, have some fun."

I didn't know what the fuck she was getting at, but she got up close to me as she said it.

"Sorry, Yvette, I gotta go."

"Oh, damn (sniff). Well, listen, Papo. You got a couple of dollars you can lend me? I'll pay you back when the welfare check comes in." She put her hand on my leg, real close to my johnson. I took a long look in her eyes and felt sorry for her. At least I wasn't the only one who had it bad the last few years. I took forty dollars out of my pocket and gave them to her.

"Here, Yvette. Buy yourself some food, okay? Me and Espy will come by later and help you clean up this place."

"Yeah, sure, Papo." She turned around and went quickly back to the room. I guess I had to show myself out.

I walked across the street to Espy's building. I knew she'd be happy to see me. Johnny was away in college so I didn't bother stopping by his apartment to say hello. Instead, I ran up to Espy's apartment. When I got there I knocked on the door without noticing that the "Malavé" nameplate wasn't on it anymore. I waited a minute and knocked again. I didn't hear nothing from the inside. Then the fifteen locks that I knew so well started opening up down the hallway. Doña Josefa was still on duty. We should've had her pulling guard duty with us in 'Nam. Charlie would never've gotten *near* us.

"*Hola, Doña Josefa. Soy yo*, Papo."

"Eh, *muchacho. Cómo estas?*"

"*Muy bien, gracias.* I'm just here to see Esperanza."

"*Oh, lo siento, pero no están.* Didn't anybody tell jou? They moved. They do not live there anymore."

CHAPTER TWENTY FOUR

I found out from Doña Josefa that since I was gone for so long Esperanza couldn't wait no more. She started hangin' out with the *cocólos* from Tremont, those dudes on the basketball team at school. Things happened. The more Doña Josefa talked, the more my heart pounded against my chest. Espy fuckin' got pregnant from some nigga named Alvin and moved to Hunts Point. Dón Ramón and her family was so ashamed that they packed up and moved back to Puerto Rico. Imagine that (sniff), I never touched her all this time, waiting for that special moment. Didn't play her dirty, not once in three years. And along comes this afro-pickin' motherff....

And now she was gone. My Esperanza. My Hope. Everything, gone. I walked outside the building spaced out. I don't remember how I got back to Lizzie's, but by the time I got there I had drunk about three 40 ounce Colt 45's. If I knew where to cop something, even if it was just a joint, I sure would have. I didn't know what to do with myself, especially since I didn't have my own private room where I could just hide. I sat quietly on the living room sofa, looking at the TV without really seeing anything.

I decided the next day that I was going to look for her. I had no idea where to go or who to ask, but I was gonna do it anyway. I made the trip back to the Bronx, and then flagged down a gypsy cab to ride around the old neighborhood. I told him to keep driving, that I had enough money to pay him. I was hoping I'd find Espy walking around, maybe spending the day visiting her old friends, like Jeanette. We wasted a half hour doing that.

Then I had the guy drive me to Tremont Avenue. I didn't have an address, number, or nothing. Still, I was positive I would find her walking around in the street, that I could track her down with the signals I was sending with my heart. We drove up and down the avenue. Every time I saw a black guy, I would stare at him, wondering if that was Alvin. He had to be a tall dude, he was on the fuckin' basketball team. A couple of times I saw a girl going into a store and I swore it was Espy. But when I'd get out of the car and follow her, it would be somebody else. I was going nuts. Every girl looked like her.

From there we went to Hunts Point. I didn't know much about that area, except that there was a block by the warehouses where a lot of hookers hung out. I guess it was too early for them because when we drove by there was nobody around. Nobody at all. I had taken up about three hours of this gypsy cab's time, practic'ly going all over the Bronx looking for that chick. The final fare came to be like fifty dollars, or something like that. I didn't want to give up, but the driver needed to go home. He dropped me off at the nearest subway station and I made my way back to Elmont.

About a week after that I decided to make my first trip to a club. I hadn't left the house that whole week, stayin' inside watching TV and drinking beer all day long. Lizzie didn't say nothing, but I could tell with her mood that she didn't like what she was seeing. Even the twins started getting on my nerves with all their screaming and running around. I yelled at them a couple of times and made them cry. My sister didn't like that either.

A few nights later I got dressed up to go to Tapestry. I didn't even know if that place was still open, but I wanted to go somewhere I had been to before and felt comfortable in. Maybe I would run into some people from back in the day. Maybe I could find a place to crash so that I wouldn't have to make that long subway trip back to Long Island late at night. Maybe I'd find Espy at the club.

When I finally got there I saw that the usual crowds were hanging around outside waiting for the right time to go in. I was glad the place was still open. I wouldn't have known where else to go. I looked at people's faces and didn't see anybody I recognized. The crowd looked much younger, or maybe I felt much older. It cost fifteen dollars to get in.

Once inside, bro', I heard the beat of the *clave* and the *guiro*. My Salsa music was the sweetest thing to hit my ears in a long time. I felt the deep bass pounding in my chest. By instinct, I started moving my feet a little with the music, you know, a step to the side, a step to the other side. I didn't have my timing, felt a little rusty. And I felt a pain in my foot. I thought I did.

I can't remember when I first got into Salsa music, that's how long it's been. My Moms said I was dancing when I was a year and a half old. She said I used to move around to the beat when company came over and Pops played his records. He had everything - *Machito, Tite Curé Alonzo, Tito Rodriguez*. As I got older I spent a lot of time listening to them all. My favorite was the *Sonora Mantancera*, especially when Celia Cruz sang with them. Sometimes I preferred to stay inside playing records and singing along instead of going outside with the fellas.

By the time I was six my Pops was making me dance with my cousins so they could take pictures. That got me used to being the center of attention and I liked it. I liked showing off. I'd watch the grown-ups doing their thing and try to copy them if I saw them do a cool move. I was good at that. It's like the music was in me and I would let it out through my feet. All I wanted to do was practice, practice, practice. Most of the time it was with Yolanda, sometimes Lizzie. Back then it was hard to find a girl my age willing and able to dance with me. That's why I got used to dancing with older girls. I felt more comfortable with them, they were a lot more fun. Those were the best days of my life. When I walked into Tapestry that night, those days felt like a hundred years ago.

I still wasn't comfortable being around so many people. Like everything else, that place seemed more crowded than before. I

251

looked around and didn't see anybody I knew, so I stood by the bar and drank me some Michelobes. A wanted to dance, but I didn't have the nerve to ask anybody. Dig that. *Me.* Papo Salsa, and I was scared to ask a *mami* out. It should've been like a bicycle, right? You never forget. I saw one fine girl walk by and my body automatically jumped like I was gonna go for it. But instead, I turned around and ordered another Michelob as she walked right on by. My foot hurt anyway. It did.

I was there about an hour when I saw Big Ray Rodriguez making his way through the crowd. Why was I so sure that *that* motherfucker would be there? Some things never change, right? He walked past me to get to the bar without even looking my way. I reached out to grab him and turn him around. He wasn't expecting to see me there so he didn't recognize me right off. Then it hit him.

"Oh-h-h-h, SSHIIT! *Chiquitín!* When the fuck you get back?!"

"I been here a couple of weeks. How you been, Ray?"

"Ah, you know, same-O, same-O. Still coming here, messin' with these young honeys. They can't get enough of me. How 'bout you, how were things in the Army. You were in Vietnam, weren't you?"

"Yeah, I did my tour."

"Man, that's messed up. You ain't gonna catch my skinny ass over there. Doña Rodriguez didn't raise no fool."

I guess Doña Torres did.

"Hey, Papo, c'mere. You still cool, right? 'Cause if you are, I got something real nice. You gonna like it."

"Whatta we talking about, hot watches?"

"Nah, man. I got some pure Peruvian blow, crystals and all. I could cut it with flour and it'd still kick ass. Wanna hit?"

"Where we gonna go? You got a car?"

"We'll go right here in the men's room. It's cool. Here, you go first." He handed me a folded up ten dollar bill with a book of matches that had a corner already bent into a "V".

I made my way into the bathroom. There were a couple of club guys hanging around in there shooting the breeze in the bathroom. Ray said it was cool, so I walked over to one of the stalls and closed the door. I faced the wall, you know, to make like I was taking a leak, and opened up the bill. The white powder shined up against the light. I could even smell it, it was so strong. I dipped the matchbook into the small pile, scooped up a nice *cantaso*, and sucked it up one nostril. That first hit made my body shake a little bit. I went back to scrape up another hit when I heard a banging sound in the stall next to me. I wondered what the fuck was that, but I kept my head down to keep making believe I was peeing.

Then the biggest, blackest hand I had ever seen in my life appeared in front of me. I followed the thick arm hanging down from the top of the stall's wall and looked up at a black giant with a Smokey-The-Bear hat staring down at me. I had a flashback of my Drill Sergeant in basic training. He said, "GIVE IT TO ME!" He sounded like God, echo and all. Why didn't those other *pendejos* hanging out in the bathroom warn me he was coming?

Smokey led me to the club's security office. What had become of the club scene? Back in the day there wasn't no security office there. Remember No-neck and G.I. Joe, with his black beret? Those *cabrones* were the security force back then. Now there were about five other officers standing around, they looked like they were each gonna take turns smacking me around. A couple of them were checking out the ten dollar bill. I heard one of them say that it was the shiniest cocaine he'd ever seen. They put me in handcuffs and led me outside where there was a squad car already waiting for me. My only thought was that I was on my way to the joint again. I didn't even last two weeks on the outside.

Down at the precinct they was having a busy night. A couple of dudes were there for fighting. One of them was stabbed and he was bleeding all over the floor while he waited for an ambulance. I saw some other plain-clothes getting ready to go out on their shift. There must've been too much going on because when they got to me they decided that I didn't have enough blow in the bill to make their time and paperwork worth it. They didn't even check my record. I wished I had these lazy dudes in Vietnam. Coulda saved me a lotta time.

But they said I was forbidden to go back to the club, management didn't want me there again. And I had to have somebody come and sign for me. I had no choice. I had to call Lizzie.

Alberto didn't say shit to me on the way home. Once he pulled into the driveway he got out the car and went straight inside and up the stairs to his room. Elizabeth was waiting for me in the kitchen.

"Lizzie, I can explain...."

"C'mon, Papo. I don't wanna hear it. You said you were clean."

"I am, Lizzie. That was the first time I touched anything since I been back. I swear."

"I don't care, Papo. It's obvious you got a problem. You ain't the same person you were before. You've changed."

"I've changed? FUCK yeah, I've changed! If you seen the shit I seen, you'd change too. You don't know, so don't say shit!"

"You can't blame everything on what you been through. Everybody's got problems, you're no different."

"Oh, yeah? Has *everybody* seen little kids blown up right before their very eyes? And guess who strapped the bombs on 'em. Their parents, that's who. Has *everybody* seen that? HUH? Has *everybody* been locked up like animals while people laugh at them from the other side of steel bars!? HAS *EVERYBODY* SEEN THEIR WHOLE WORLD DISAPPEAR ON THEM WHILE THEY'RE STUCK THOUSANDS OF MILES AWAY AND CAN'T DO SHIT ABOUT IT!? HAVE THEY? HUH?! *FUCK EVERYBODY!*"

I was pissed off. Lizzie tried to calm me down.

"Listen, Papo. I've got kids too. I got to look out for them. That's why we came out here, to get away from all that shit. Alberto's not happy about this either. He feels he has too much to lose if you start bringing your drug problems around here."

"What are you saying, sister dear?"

"Papo, I love you. You can stay the night. But in the morning, Alberto and I would like for you to look for another place to stay."

"Oh, really? *Pues*, you know what? Let's not wait 'til the morning. I'll cut out right now."

"C'mon, Papo, don't be an asshole. It's three in the morning, where you gonna go?"

"What, you gonna start worryin' about me now? Well, don't worry. I'll be alright."

"Papo, wait until tomorrow. We'll look for a place together."

"No, Lizzie. You're right. I gotta get out of here, the sooner the better. Listen, thanks for everything. Give the kids a kiss for me. Tell them Tio Papo loves them."

"Papo...."

I didn't wait to hear no more. I packed all my stuff and was outta there.

It took me about two and half hours to make it back to the Bronx. I was beat. I had no idea where I was gonna go. I could have gone to Johnny's house, ask Mr. DeJesus to let me crash there. But I didn't want to bother him at that hour. I thought about breaking into our old apartment, even sleep in my old room. Picture that. I climbed up to the fifth floor. It was past five-thirty in the morning, but it was still dark outside.

I heard that music down the hall again. I went over there real careful. This time, when I looked inside, I saw Yvette laying on a mattress by the wall, a bottle of wine sitting next to her. There were some lit candles all around the living room. She was having herself a nice little party, even though she was alone. Her and her needle. When her sleepy eyes looked up and saw me, she smiled and held out her hand. I don't know if it was because of the light of the candles, or that I was tired. But Yvette looked pretty good to me that night. After thinking about it for a long moment, I walked in and quietly closed the door behind me.

You know anything about drugs, bro'? I ain't talkin' about herb, man. That's kid's stuff. I'm talking heroin, LSD, crack. That shit's like an evil woman you meet in a dark corner in the back of an empty bar. In the dim light she looks beautiful to you, and she's willing to spend some time with you. She becomes your friend and you're not used to that. At first you think you're just gonna fool around with her, have a good time. It ain't gonna hurt nobody, right? You think that in the morning you can get up and walk away, take care of business and lead a responsible life.

But all day long you can't stop thinking about her, about how good she made you feel. Remember, you're not used to that. So you say to yourself that maybe you'll call on her again that night, see what she's doin'. Of course she's waiting for you. She's always waiting for you. Just one more time, you say. I'll call her just one more time. Pretty soon this evil lady is calling *you* every day. She is no longer your lover, you are hers. She's the one telling *you* what to do. She tells you not to go home tonight, to stay with her. Your family will understand. Fuck 'em if they don't.

Then she starts telling you to take that paycheck you have in your pocket and spend it on her. The rent can wait, she says. They won't dare evict you. Just one more time, it ain't gonna hurt. I promise, tomorrow will be different. I won't see you tomorrow, you tell her. But tomorrow never comes. It's always today. When you're with this evil lady it's always today. Tomorrow never comes, and you can't remember yesterday and you really don't give a damn. But you promised, didn't you? You said you weren't gonna see this bitch no more. But without her you ain't shit. She pulls you back into her bosom and you can't believe you actually thought about leaving her. I'm sorry, you say, I'm really sorry. Make me feel good again. I need you, girl, I need you. You're the only one who understands me.......

I stayed with Yvette for about a year (sniff). I paid the rent for a month or two, but pretty soon we had spent all the money I came home with on heroin. I kept sayin' "this is the last time, I gotta stop this." But we couldn't. We was both hooked real bad. I was broke in no time. She was getting money from welfare, and I got unemployment from being in the Army. But after a while we needed more money than that, so we had to start begging. I even think Yvette got pregnant a couple of times, but I was never sure (sniff). She wouldn't tell me. She lost them anyway. Yvette only had one thing on her mind by then, you know? When we copped, I got the feeling she was taking extra hits while I was nodding (sniff).

One time after a binge I opened my eyes in a haze and looked over to the living room. I coulda swore I saw this dude sitting on the sofa with his pants down by his ankles. Yvette was kneeling on the floor in front of him and her head was bobbing up and down. I didn't recognize the dude and I passed out again before I could say anything. It might've been a dream, but later that night me and Yvette were shooting up a new batch of smack she had copped. I'll give you one guess where she got the money to buy it. The sad thing was that I didn't care. But I had to cut her loose after she kept stealing from me. I don't know what the fuck ever happened to her, or Chico.

That was twenty five years ago, man. I tried going to Pennsylvania once to see my parents. But that didn't work out either (sniff). Pops gave me a hard time at first and I didn't wanna hear it. I popped off on him and Moms had to calm us down. Fuckin' Benny kept askin' me if I killed anybody while I was in Vietnam. That got on my nerves. These people didn't know, they just didn't know, man. Benny fucked with me once too many and I almost smacked him. That was it. Pops kicked me out and I had to come back to New York. I've only seen them a couple of times since then (sniff).

That Dishonorable Discharge made it impossible for me to find a job, you know what I'm sayin'? Nobody wants to hire a crazy veteran with a bad discharge who did time like me. Would YOU? Hell no, don't give me that shit (sniff). But that's alright, I been getting by. I stay at the shelter not too far from here. I quit drugs a few times over the years, but then I'd fall right back. The lady didn't want to let me go. I got to hanging out with the wrong crowd too. But now I'm on a methodone program they offered at the shelter (sniff), been at it about a year. We'll see what happens (sniff).

I don't blame Vietnam for how I am, never did. I wish it never happened, but I made my own mistakes. I just happened to be in Vietnam when I made them.

Now I spend all my days here in the streets, lookin' to do little odd jobs for people here and there. I make a couple of bucks. I don't steal from nobody, I just hustle. I do alright, 'cause I'm Papo Salsa, right? The Fred Astairs of Soundview. Hey, didn't he die, man? (sniff) Damn, it's cold... Like I said, man, that's a nice coat. Hey, whatcha doin'? You really gonna let me try on the coat?! Say what!? I can have it?! Man, you alright. You look familiar, too. Do I know you? Wow, check this out. Oh, this is nice - hey, wait a minute, you ain't one of those *maricón* kind a guys, are you? (Sniff) 'Cause I ain't lookin' for no sugar daddy right now, you know what I'm saying? I ain't wif' that, no sir. Not even for a pint o'Bacardi. I just listen to my music and try to get by.........Papo Salsa, yes indeed......

HEY, man! You got a quarter, man (sniff)? All I need is a quarter. I know you got it, look at you, man........

* * * * * * * * * * * * *

As I watched Papo Salsa walk off with my coat, I couldn't help wondering what would have become of him if he never had gotten drafted into the Army. I remembered a kid who came from a nice home, had decent parents. That was nothing like the guy I just finished listening to for the last two hours. Most of the stuff he talked about the Bronx and the neighborhood I already knew. It was obvious he had been needing somebody to talk to for a long time. I didn't mind being the one to listen. This guy was my idol once.

Actually, meeting Papo Salsa again, and seeing what became of him, opened my eyes to a lot of things I never bothered to think about before. First of all, you see homeless people in the streets all the time. There are beggars who look like they haven't showered in years and you don't care. You don't even look at them as human beings. All you think is that they fucked up and put themselves in that situation. But then you hear the whole story, like I just did with Papo, and you realize that these are real people. Each one of them has a different story, a different reason for being the way they are. Sometimes it's not their fault. Nobody cares to find out.

A lot of people think that all Vietnam vets are crazy. They all went to war, killed women and children, and came back so strung out they started shooting people from rooftops. I went to the library and did a little research. The truth is that over two million American men and women served in the Vietnam Conflict. Of those, only about ten percent actually saw steady heavy combat. Some G.I.'s never even fired a weapon the whole time they were there. It's a damn shame that 58,000 Americans were killed. It's a shame when just one person gets killed. But not every Vietnam vet can say his life is messed up because of the war. A lot of them talk a lot of shit.

Who knows, maybe Papo's story is a bunch of lies. But he remembered too many specific things that were too wild to make up. He was right about everything he said about the clubs and the Bronx. I lived it too. Vietnam was a bad experience for a lot of people. But there has to be a point where a guy has to let it go and move on. If he can't do it on his own, maybe somebody could help him. Papo looked like he was trying. He just turned out to be a dumb fuck, that's all. But I know he wasn't always like that.

There's also a lesson to be learned about the perception of Latino families, not just here in the Bronx, but all over. Too many ignorant people don't give us the credit we're due for the contributions we make to society and to our country. I'm not jumping on a racist tip, not at all. It's just that we've always been looked at with little regard towards family values and morals. Groups that don't know us think we're all a bunch of lazy, welfare-taking, rum-drinking, cockaroach stompers. Nobody knows who their real mommy and daddy are, right? Well, I come from a wonderful family. I wouldn't trade in my parents, brothers and sisters for the world. And Papo Salsa came from a good family, so did Louie and Rickey Jimenez, Papo DJ, Johnny DeJesus, and a lot of my friends that came after those guys.

There are many exceptions, like Chico's father, Yvette, even Papo himself. But for a long time life was good for all those people. We have a right to mess up like any other group, right? Yet there's a lot of good in our culture as well. The pride of Puerto Ricans knows no boundaries.

Papo Salsa was halfway down the block when I saw him turn around. He was heading back my way, taking something out of his pocket. Oh-oh, I thought. Wasn't the coat enough?

"Listen, um, by the way (sniff), what's your name again?"

"José. My friends call me Joey."

"Well, yeah, Joey. Listen (sniff). My father always taught me never to take anything *cachetea'o*, you know, without working for it or giving something in return. Now you know I can't always do that, look at me. I got to get by somehow, so I gotta beg for money out here any way I can get it (sniff)."

"Don't worry about it, Papo."

"No, really, *escúchame*. This is a nice coat and I appreciate it, God bless you. I don't have much to give you, but I want you to have this. It's not much, but it's the most valuable thing I own. *Gracias*, man, for the coat. And thanks for listening."

Papo handed me an old dirty plastic bag and walked away, still limping. It looked like this might be his stash of drugs. I was going to call out to him but he was already boppin' down the street. I unraveled the bags, there were about two others inside the first one.

I reached in a bag and pulled out an old wrinkled-up card. I read the faded words. It was from the Tapestry Nightclub, on Westchester Avenue. It was a free pass, the free pass that Esperanza had won in that dance contest on Papo's eighteenth birthday. He still had it after all this time. I looked to see what else was in the bag. A found a ceramic figurine, broken in two pieces. One piece, the smaller one, looked like it was supposed to be a leaf. The other piece was a little green frog. It was a *coquí*, the gift Esperanza had given to him on his seventeenth birthday. She had made Papo promise to hold onto this *coquí* as his little piece of Puerto Rico until they got to go there together. He kept his promise as long as he could.

Papo Salsa had been around the world and back, had fought battles in Vietnam, as well as at home. He had been beaten up, shot at, locked up, thrown out, cut up, and laughed at. He lived most of his forty-five years in the streets. But through all that he never gave up hope that he would be with Esperanza again. He always hoped that he could use that free pass to dance with her one more time. He never stopped hoping that someday she would show him the beautiful island of Puerto Rico. Until now.

I looked for Papo down the street. There he was, shaking his shoulders and moving his feet. By some unsurprising coincidence, salsa music started blaring out of the second story window of the building he was walking by. I could see the moves. I could see he still had it, that he was going to be okay. He never hurt anybody, he just had to learn not to hurt himself. Because you see, even if Papo gave up his hopes for Esperanza, he never gave up his hope for life.

That's just the way he was.

EPILOGUE

I went home and couldn't get Papo Salsa out of my mind. I told my wife about my encounter and she said that I should stop worrying about it. After all, I gave him my coat on a cold day, right off my back. How many people in this city would do that, she asked. She was right on that one, but I still felt I had to do more.

I work for a bank in downtown Manhattan, near Wall Street. I've been there a few years, and even though I don't have much juice there, I do know some people in important places. I asked around and spoke to the Human Resources department.

I was able to convince them to give this guy a chance, even if it was just temporary. They didn't want to at first. After all, we were talking about a homeless ex-junkie, a little old to be starting off in banking. But there had to be *somewhere* they could put him. And as a Vietnam Veteran he was covered under the Vietnam Era Veteran's Readjustment Assistance Act of 1974. The bank would need a real good reason not to hire him once he applied. About the only place he could work was the mailroom delivering interoffice memos and stuff like that. If his foot could hold up, they said, he could do that.

Once I got the go-ahead, I had to find Papo Salsa. That wasn't too hard because he was still working the same block where I had found him before. When I gave him the news he hesitated a bit. He still didn't trust anybody, and he wasn't sure if he could do it, or wanted to. But I told him to just try it. If it doesn't work out, *que se joda*, we tried.

I took Papo to get some new clothes, and my wife and I cleaned him up. He worked his charms on her right away and they got along real well. He seemed genuinely grateful for all the attention. I even had him get checked up for AIDS before he went in for the mandatory physical at the job. I wanted to avoid him the embarrassment in case he was sick. To our relief, he was clean as a whistle. That was pretty amazing considering all the needles he shared over the years.

I also began petitioning the Veteran's Administration to issue Papo the Purple Heart I felt he was entitled to. After all, he was injured in combat and he deserved the award no matter what happened to him afterwards. There were also some medical issues that had to be addressed, maybe even a lawsuit against the government for not treating his foot properly. I decided to call a lawyer friend of mine about that.

Out of curiosity, I made an attempt to look up Papo's friends from the old days. What I uncovered proved to be very interesting:

Louie Jimenez and his family made California their permanent home. They only came back to New York to exhume Ricky's remains and transport them to a cemetery closer to them near Los Angeles. Louie eventually was forced out of the Marines on a medical discharge, but had a successful career working as a cameraman in various Hollywood studios. He and his Mexican wife had four children of their own in addition to the two she had when they met.

Chico Montañez is still in the Army to this day, even made it to the rank of Sergeant Major. He earned citations for his actions in the Gulf War a few years ago. It was during a tour in South Korea in the late seventies that he met and married a young Korean girl and together they have two kids.

Johnny DeJesus did in fact follow his father's footsteps in the building management field like Papo had said, but not as a "super". Along with a business partner he met at college in Buffalo, Johnny bought his old building, along with five others throughout the Bronx.

Today he is a very wealthy man, having married his childhood sweetheart, Brenda, and living comfortably in New Rochelle, New York.

Yolanda Montañez, Chico's older sister, is still living in Co-Op City in the Bronx with Sheila, the roommate who opened her doors for her when she escaped her alcoholic father and that drug addict, Hector. As a matter of fact, in Sheila Yolanda found the comfort and love that she had missed ever since her mother died. They've been "married" for ten years now.

Little sister Yvette wasn't as fortunate. She was arrested several times for solicitation, prostitution, and possession of drugs. Sadly, police reports show that the body of one Yvette Montañez was found in a crack house in 1988.

I couldn't find out anything about Dón Guilliermo. He disappeared and nobody ever heard from him again, not even his son, Chico.

Papo DJ and Big Ray Rodriguez went into business promoting dances and parties in various clubs around the city. They're heavily involved in the annual Salsa Festival at Madison Square Garden, which brings in all the latest, most popular acts in Latin music from around the world.

As for Papo Salsa's buddies from Vietnam, I wasn't able to find anything on Frankie Garcia, Harold Jenkins, or Michael Lipscomb. I found Salvador Cardona working as a security guard for the United States Post Office on 34th Street in Manhattan, a job he's held since he completed his time in the Army. It was one of the many benefits he took advantage of from the G.I. Bill. He was surprised to hear about Papo, but he wasn't really anxious to have any kind of reunion with him. Like many others, Sal left that part of his life behind him and moved on.

Elizabeth and Alberto now live in Glen Cove, Long Island. After almost losing everything he had on Black Monday, that Wall Street Crash of 1989, 'Berto is currently a Senior Vice President in an investment firm specializing in 401K Plans. Little Georgie and Jessica are both married now and have families of their own, so Lizzie spends her days doting on her three grandchildren while Jessica works as a Real Estate agent. They too were a little apprehensive about seeing Papo again. They found it hard to believe he was finally getting his act together.

Papo's mother lives down in Tampa, Florida with Benny and his wife. They have three children as well. Sadly, Papo's father died of cancer five years ago. They said it might have been something that he was exposed to in the factory where he worked in Allentown, Pennsylvania. How ironic that he left the South Bronx to follow his job and provide a better life for his family, and in the end it's what might have killed him. Papo never got to see him alive again.

As for Esperanza Malavé, she might as well have vanished into thin air. I could not find one trace of her. What made the search harder, aside from the twenty years since the last time anybody saw her, was the skepticism I met when going around the different neighborhoods. People don't trust anybody snooping around asking questions, especially if you're like me and have the word "COP" written all over your face. I tried to reassure them and swear that I wasn't a policeman, but they didn't believe me. If there was one person I really wanted to find it was Espy, but unfortunately, it just wasn't meant to be.

I never told Papo I tracked all these people down, and I'm not so sure he cares to know about any of them either, with the exception of Espy. With time he'll learn about the death of his father and maybe make amends with the rest of his family. But for now, he needs to concentrate on getting his own life back together and see what the future has in store for him.

Papo Salsa started working for the bank in October delivering mail around the office. By November he was given the keys to the supply room so that if anybody needed anything - paper, pens, notebooks - they would ask him. Everybody liked "Eddie" because he was cool. He didn't act stupid and he looked serious about doing a good job. Like he always said, all he needed was a chance.

One person caught his eye, though. Her name is Alicia Tirado. She's one of the most beautiful women in the bank, with long auburn hair always combed real nice, and a body that could stop traffic. All the guys want to go out with her, even the married ones. But although she's a fun person to be around, she's very private with her personal life and she doesn't mess around with anybody, especially anybody at the job. That's her policy.

Alicia is a divorced Latina with a son about ten years old. She lives in Brooklyn and loves to party, loves to dance and hang out. Anytime the co-workers get together for drinks after work, she's right there with us. But she always goes home early to pick up her son at the babysitter's, and she always goes home alone. She's considered classy by everyone and is very popular.

It didn't take long for Papo to get friendly with Alicia. He playfully flirted with her, but always spoke to her with respect. The first thing Papo did when he was eligible for the bank's medical plan was see a dentist to get his teeth fixed. In a couple of weeks he was wearing two brand new false teeth. That alone made him feel ten times better than before.

We had our annual office Christmas party not too long ago. There was food and drinks. As always, the bank paid for everything. Since there are people from all ethnic backgrounds working there, the deejay had a full collection of all kinds of music. We hire the same guy every year.

For most of the night Papo sat down and talked to different people, whomever came by his table. I only saw him drinking one beer the whole night. He was behaving himself real well, and he seemed to be having a great time. It was a lot easier for him to smile since he got a full set of teeth.

I went to the deejay with a request. I was a little drunk, I didn't care. I asked him to play a nice Salsa record, but one that's not too fast. He picked out one of my favorites, *Devórame*, by Lalo Rodriquez. When it came on I ran to Papo Salsa to get him to get up and dance, to show me the moves he still had. He laughed and told me no fucking way. He wasn't going to dance. He hadn't danced Salsa in a long time. I begged him, but no dice.

Then, making her way through the crowd, Alicia shows up and asks Papo to dance. How could he say no to her? Flashing his new teeth, Papo got up and took Alicia's hand. They walked to the middle of the dance floor, he put his arms around her and gracefully began doing his thing. It looked like they had been dancing together for a long time. With Papo Salsa, it always looked like he and his partner had been dancing together a long time.

Even after all these years I could still see the talent that man had for dancing. He didn't move as much as he used to. In fact, he pretty much stayed in one spot and made Alicia do all the work, turning her this way and that. But it was beautiful, almost artistic. I knew Alicia was a good dancer, but not *this* good. People stepped aside to give them more room. Both of them looked like they were having the time of their lives. I felt very happy for Papo. When the song ended everybody gave them a big ovation. Even the non-Hispanics in the crowd appreciated it. Papo was one of us now, he was back in society.

They stopped the music and began the traditional raffle. The bank always gave away a lot of gifts at these Christmas parties. One of the big Vice Presidents dressed up like Santa Claus and called off the numbers on the tickets they gave us when we arrived. The first few gifts were simple, inexpensive ones, but thoughtful just the same. But as the raffle went on, the prizes got more valuable. Nobody wanted their name called just yet, everybody was hoping for the big prize. This year, the grand prize was an all expense paid trip for two to Puerto Rico. *Se botaron* with that one.

When it was time for the final number to be called out, everybody got real quiet. I noticed that Papo wasn't paying much attention to the raffle, he was busy rapping to Alicia.

As I write this story for you, I am sitting on my bed, tapping away at my laptop. The snow is falling outside. My wife is lying next to me reading one of her *Cosmo* magazines. We're enjoying a nice bottle of Hennesey together, with some mellow music on the stereo. Everything is real warm and cozy.

Somewhere, a thousand miles away, on a hot, sun-drenched beach in Puerto Rico, Eduardo Torres and Alicia Tirado are enjoying a fabulous, fun-filled vacation. All expenses paid. That's right. The winning raffle ticket for the grand prize was held by Papo Salsa. He had won, the bastard. Everybody cheered him on when he limped up to the stage to pick up the prize. He was finally going to see the island for the first time.

Papo immediately asked Alicia to go with him. Of course she said no. They were just friends and co-workers, she said. But he kept insisting and everybody kept telling her to go. Papo promised that he would arrange for separate rooms. If it cost extra for that, he'd pay it. Check him out, Mr. Moneybags. Finally she agreed to go, as friends, of course.

So who knows what's going on down there right now. I'm sure Papo and Alicia are having a great time. I'm very happy for both of them. Even though they are two entirely different people, they've both been alone for too long. They found each other under strange circumstances when they least expected it. A wise man once said: "Love is like a butterfly. No matter how much you chase it and try catching it, you never will. But if you leave it alone and don't think about it, someday when you least expect it, it will land gently on your shoulder."

Puerto Rico is a romantic place. It's easy to fall in love down there. There are lots of butterflies. I can't wait for them to get back, I want to see what I started. I hope it's something good.

And you can never give up hope.

269

GLOSSARY OF SPANISH WORDS, PHRASES, AND OTHER SLANG TERMS

(Spanish words and phrases are in italics, English are in regular print)

Abogado – Lawyer, Attorney
Abuelos – Grandparents
Adelante – Come in, enter
Aguacate – Avocado
Alcaguete – Lacky, gofer
Amigo, mi amigo – My friend
Amor, "Mi amor…" – Love, "My love…"
Anoche – Last night
Arroz con gandures – Rice and peas
Article 15 – Official military document outlining regulation violations and appropriate punishment
"Aqui tienes" – "Here you have it", or "Here you go"
ASAP – As Soon As Possible
Avanza – Hurry
Averiguá – Nosy, curious

Bacalao – Cod fish
Baile, bailar – Dance, to dance
Barrio – Spanish neighborhood, usually in the ghetto
Batata – Sweet yams
Bellaco, bellaqueras – Horny one (horniness)
Bejuco – Vine, like what Tarzan swung on
Bendición – Blessing
Bendito séa – God bless
Bibí – Baby's bottle
Biddies – Young girls
Bien – Good; very; or very well
Bien disimulado – Very discreet
Blanquito (blanco) – White; a caucasian person
Bobo – Sucker
Bodega – Neighborhood grocery store
Bolero – Slow Spanish love song, or ballad
Bolitas – Small balls; also used for illegal numbers gambling
Bon-bones – Bon-Bons, balls of hard candy
Booked – Street slang meaning "left in a hurry"
Borracho, borrachón – Drunk, drunkard
Beaucoup – A lot of......, pronounced "boo-coo"
"Buenas tardes" – "Good afternoon"
Bueno – Good, or "Well…"
"Bueno que te pase" – "Good for you" or "Serves you right"

Caballero – Gentleman
Cabrón, cabrones – Cuckhold, one who's wife is cheating on him
Ca-ca – Slang for human waste, also bullshit; same as *mierda*
Cachetea'o – Taking a handout or freebie
"Cagándote en la madre" – "Shitting on the mother", a typical Spanish insult
Caliente – Hot
Calma – Calm down
Cantaso – In drug vernacular it means a good hit, or dose
Cantínflas – Legendary Mexican comedian and actor
Cara-chocha – Pussy-face

Chévere, bien chévere – Good, very nice

Chicas – Chicks, or girls

Chichones – Love handles, extra fat around the waist

Chilla – Mistress, same as *corteja*

China – Orange, like the fruit, pronounced "Chee-na"

Chiquito, chiquitín – Small, the little one

Chota – Rat fink, squealer

Chuletas fritas (chuletins) – Fried pork chops

"Cierra la boca" – "Close your mouth"

Clave – The rhythmic beat to a song

Cobalde – Coward

Cochino – Dirty pig

Cocólo – Slang reference to a black person

Cójo – To walk with a limp

Cojones – Balls, as in testicles; to be brave

"Cómo esta tu mamá?" – "How is your mother?"

"Como pasa el tiempo" – "How time goes by"

"Cómo se llama?" – "What is his/her name?"

"Cómo te suena?" – How does that sound to you?"

Complejo – Complex (inferiority)

Comprendes – Understand

Compy – Short for *Compadre*, what two men call each other when one is the godfather of the other's child; a good friend

Conga – Spanish drum, played with bare hands

Conjugal – Conjugal visit by a prisoner's wife, usually for sex

Coño – Exclamation word, similar to "Shit!" or "Damn!"

Coquí – Small frog indigenous to Puerto Rico

Corazón – Heart

Correaso – Beating with a belt

Corteja – Mistress, same as *chilla*

Crank - Slang word for heroin

Crib – Slang for home

"Cual es tu nombre?" – "What is your name?"

Cualquiera – Literal: "Any one you wish", term used to describe a girl who'll go with anyone

Cúlo – Anus
Cupones – Food stamps
Curva – Curve

Dap – Elaborate handshake
"Darte prisa" – "Hurry up", to make haste
'Dear John' – Letter from a girl informing her soldier boyfriend
    that she's breaking up with him
Descarga – Solo, or ad libbed musical portion of a salsa song
Deseo – Desire
Desgraciado – Disgraceful person
Devórame – Devour me
Dón, Doña – Respectful title of an older man and woman

"El cartero ya llegó" – "The mailman has already arrived"
Embusteras – Women who don't tell the truth
Encanto, "Me encantaría" – Delight, "That would be delightful"
    or "I'd love to"
"Escúchame" – "Listen to me"
"Ese Louie es un pendejo" – "That Louie is a fool"
Espera – Wait
Esperanza – Hope; also used as a girl's name
"Espero que si" – "I hope so"
Estricto – Strict

Fiended, fiending – Craved, desire
Fiera – Wild woman
Fiesta – Party
Fondillo – Rump, ass, behind

Gasta'o – Slang for wasted, tired, used up
Gracias – Thank you
Gringo – American, or non-Hispanic white person
Guapo – Tough; Also means handsome
Guayabera – Elegantly tailored dress shirt, commonly worn by
    elderly men

Guille – Slang for attitude
Guillaíto – On the sneak, sneaky
Guiro – Musical instrument made out of a hollow piece of wood
    and scraped with a metal comb
Gusto – Joy, gusto

Hermano(a), hermanito(a) – Brother (Sister), little brother (little
    sister)
Hijo puta – Son of a bitch or whore
Hijo(s) – Son(s)
Hola – Hello
Homies – Friends from the same neighborhood or city
Huele-peo – Fart smeller
Humacao – City on the eastern coast of Puerto Rico

"Ida y vuelta" – "Going and coming"
Idiotas – Idiots
"Igged" – Slang for ignore
Infeliz – Miserable person

Jack – Slang for nothing; term also used to strike or attack
Jayuya – Small town in the central mountains of Puerto Rico
Jíbaro – Hick, country bumpkin
'Jody' – Name given to the guy back home who has taken away
    a soldier's girlfriend
"Jones" – Hang-up, obsession, addiction
Judios – Jews
Jump stink – To talk back disrespectfully

Klicks – Short for kilometers

La tipa, el tipo – Not too complimentary term for a girl or guy
Loco – Crazy
Luto – In mourning

Maduro – Ripe, like a fruit (see *"mas duro"*)

Mala crianza – Spoiled, trouble maker
Malagradecidos – Ingrates, those who don't appreciate
Mama'o – Dummy
Mambo – Form of music and dance, the predecesor of Salsa
Mami(s) – Good looking girl(s)
'Mano – Short for *hermano*, meaning brother or good friend
Maravilloso – Marvelous
Maricón – Faggot, homosexual
"Mas duro.." – Harder; When spoken quickly, sounds like *maduro*
"Mas duro que el mio no!" – "Not harder than mine!" Hence, the play on words is the joke here.
Mayor – Older, elder
"Me cago en dies!" – Literal: "I shit on ten", a variation of a more vulgar exclamation of excitement, substituting 'ten' for God (*Dios*)
"Me jodí" – "I'm fucked"
"Me tiró bomba" – Slang expression meaning to be stood up, or let down
Merengue – Style of music and dance, originating from the Dominican Republic
"Mi nombre es…" – "My name is…"
Mientras tanto – In the meantime
Mierda – Human waste, shit
Minyon – Jewish prayer meeting
Mira – Look
Mis padres – My parents
Mocoso – Snot-nosed kid
Moño – Hair bun
M.O.S. – Military Occupational Status. The specific job a soldier is trained in
Muchacho – Young boy
Muchas gracias – Thank you very much
Mulatta – Girl from mixed parents, half black, half white
Muñeca – Doll, affectionate reference to a woman
Muy, "Muy bien" – Very, "Very good"

Nena – Affectionate term for a young girl

"No hablas Ingles?" – "You don't speak English?"

"No joda" – "Don't mess around"

"No me atrevo" – "I don't dare"

"No sé" – "I don't know"

"No vengan tarde" – "Don't come home late"

Novela – TV Soap Opera

"Olvídate de eso" – "Forget about that"

Orgullosa – Proud lady

Otravez – Again

Otro, "Otro pendejo" – Another, "Another idiot"

"Pa' la casa de Papo DJ!" – "To Papo DJ's house!"

"Pa' qué fue eso!" – "What was THAT for!" (rhetorical)

Pana, panín – Slang for close friend

Pasteles – Meat pies made from mashed plantains

Pava – Traditional straw hat used for protection from the sun

Pendejos – Literal: Pubic hair. Also defines an idiot, dummy, or fool

Perdón – Pardon

Permiso, "Con su permiso" – Permission, "With your permission"

Pernil – Roast Pork, traditionally served on special occasions

"Pero esta bien..." – "But's it's alright..."

Pescado – Fish that has already been caught

Pinga – Slang for penis

Pive – Small boys, same as *muchacho*, but younger

Platano – Plantain, a large fruit from the banana family; can be fried, baked, or boiled

"Pobresito niños" – "Poor children"

Ponce – City on the southern coast of Puerto Rico, named after Ponce De León

Poquito – A little bit

Por favor – Please

'Pound' – The act of slapping hands with someone else, like "gimme skin"

Por supuesto – Of course

Profile – Military document outlining work restrictions due to medical problems

Pueblo – Town

Pues... - Well...

Pugging – Slang for fighting, or boxing

Puñeta – Literal: An orgasm through masturbation; Also an exclamation similar to "dammit!"

Puta madre – Whore mother

P.R. – Abbreviation for Puerto Rico

'Q.T.' – On the sneak, discreet

"Qué?" – "What?"

"Que come mierda" – "What a shit-eater", as in stuck up

"Que confianza" – "What confidence"

"Que descanse en paz" – "May he rest in peace"

"Qué deseas?" – "What do you want?"

"Qué pasa?" – "What's happening", or "What's wrong?"

Que se joda – Fuck it

Ramas – Bouquets of flowers

Relajo, "eso es relajo" – Joking, "I was only joking"

Rosario – Prayer sessions to pray for the soul of the recently deceased

Rubio, el rubio – The blond one, slang for the sun

Salchichón – Hard salami

Salsa – Style of music and dance, originating in N.Y. and P.R.

Salseros – Devoted fans of salsa music and dancing

Sancocho – Thick Spanish stew

Scratch – Slang for money

Se botaron con eso – They went all out with that one

Señor, Señora – Sir, Ma'am (lady)

Short – Term used by servicemen and prisoners when they
    approach the day to be released
"Show your right" – Declaration of affirmation or agreement
Si – Yes
Siéntese – Sit down
Sin gana – Without desire
Sobre todo – Above all
Sofrito – Condiment, a mixture of various tropical seasonings
Soy – I am
Square – Slang for cigarette
Square business – Slang for the truth
Suegros – In-laws (mother and father)
Super – Superintendent of a building, custodian

Tecato – Drug addict
"Te tengo una sorpresa" – "I have a surprise for you"
"Tengan cuidado" – "Be careful"
Tia(s) – Aunt(s)
Timbales – Drum instrument inherent in Latin bands
"Tipo es loco" – "That dude is crazy"
Titere – Common, street-wise man
Titi(s) – A more informal term for aunt(s)
Tostones – Slices of plantain, mashed flat and fried in oil
Tótin – Innocent slang word for vagina or pussy
Trigueña – Dark-skinned woman
Tumba'o – Beat, as in the beat of music

Vámonos – Let's go
Vamos a bailar – Let's dance
Vaya! – Exclamatory slang for something good, similar to
    "Alright!"
Vecina – Neighbor
Vén, "Vén a comer" – Come, "Come and eat"

"Véte al carajo" – "Go to hell"
Viejo(a) – Old, or old man (woman)
Visco, El – person with crossed-eyes

Wack – No good, weak

"Yo no fui" – "It wasn't me"

Zangano – Dimwit, dummy; also a type of bee
Zooted – To get high on drugs